The ABCs of
America Online

The ABCs of

America Online®

David Krassner

SYBEX®

San Francisco · Paris · Düsseldorf · Soest

Associate Publisher: Carrie Lavine
Acquisitions Manager: Kristine Plachy
Developmental Editor: Dan Brodnitz
Editor: Julie Powell
Project Editor: Linda Good
Technical Editor: Michele Petrovsky
Book Design Director: Cătălin Dulfu
Book Designer: Design Site
Electronic Publishing Specialist: Dina F Quan
Production Coordinator: Kimberley Askew-Qasem
Indexer: Ted Laux
Cover Designer: Design Site
Cover Illustrator/Photographer: Harami Kubo

Library of Congress Card Number: 96-69284
ISBN: 0-7821-1958-1

Manufactured in the United States of America

10 9 8 7 6 5 4 3 2

Software Support

The software on this disk and any offers associated with it are supported by America Online. America Online can be reached by calling 1-800-827-6364.

Should the manufacturer cease to offer support or decline to honor the offer, Sybex bears no responsibility.

Warranty

Sybex warrants the enclosed disk to be free of physical defects for a period of ninety (90) days after purchase. If you discover a defect in the disk during this warranty period, you can obtain a replacement disk at no charge by sending the defective disk, postage pre-paid, with proof of purchase to:

Sybex Inc.
Customer Service Department
1151 Marina Village Parkway
Alameda, CA 94501
(800) 227-2346
Fax: (510) 523-2373

After the 90-day period, you can obtain a replacement disk by sending us the defective disk, proof of purchase, and a check or money order for $10, payable to Sybex.

Disclaimer

Sybex makes no warranty or representation, either express or implied, with respect to this medium or its contents, its quality, performance, merchantability, or fitness for a particular purpose. In no event will Sybex, its distributors, or dealers be liable for direct, indirect, special, incidental, or consequential damages arising out of the use of or inability to use the medium or its contents even if advised of the possibility of such damage.

The exclusion of implied warranties is not permitted by some states. Therefore, the above exclusion may not apply to you. This warranty provides you with specific legal rights; there may be other rights that you may have that vary from state to state.

Copy Protection

None of the files on the CD is copy-protected. However, in all cases, reselling or redistributing these files, except as specifically provided for by the copyright owners, is prohibited.

*To Hugh, who loves
computers,
and to Kamiar, who
doesn't*

Acknowledgments

The book you hold before you is the result of a concentrated effort by many individuals. I would like to thank Dan Brodnitz for giving me the opportunity to write this book (as well as for allowing me to feed Bill's Stratocaster to the cat). In addition, I would like to thank the following individuals, each one *sine qua non:* Julie Powell, editor; Linda Good, project editor; Michele Petrovsky, technical editor; Dina "Gromit" Quan, typesetter; Kimberley Askew-Qasem, production coordinator; Molly Sharp, technical coordinator, and last but not least, Ted Laux, who compiled the wonderful index.

On the home front, I'd like to thank my family for their continued support, as well as Christian Crumlish, Guy Hart-Davis, Bob Thomas, and John Steiner for their invaluable insights into computers, online access, and fruitbats. Thanks also to the gang at Hydra Devices for building me the perfect beast instantly, and to my colleagues at the UCI Pathology Department for their good humor and support when I was cranky from lack of sleep. Thanks also to Douglas Orr, whose expertise about home pages I shamelessly stole. And, of course, I extend my appreciation along with a juicy bone to Sunrise, our golden retriever, who wrote all of the best parts.

Finally, my heartfelt gratitude to Judy d'Albert, Will Baker, Max Byrd, David Harvey, Dean Lane-Smith, and Miriam Thompson, who collectively taught me how to articulate my thoughts in writing.

Thank you all!

Contents at a Glance

Table of Contents

Chapter 3: Customizing Your AOL Account 55

PART 2: COMMUNICATING ONLINE 79

Chapter 4: Learning to Use E-Mail 81

Chapter 6: Automating E-Mail with FlashSessions 147

Introduction

America Online (AOL) for Windows is the best-selling Internet access software in the world. The new version of AOL for Windows builds upon the success of earlier versions, adding a number of new features such as advanced chatting (including sound bouncing), enhanced Internet features, new multimedia features, and some terrific right-click features, including the ability to add hypertext links to an e-mail messages.

What Will You Learn from This Book?

This book aims to tell you everything you need to know about AOL to use it productively, either at home or in the office. AOL has many features that you'll not only probably never use but that you'll never need to know about. This book discusses only those features that you're likely to use most. If you need to learn about an esoteric feature of AOL, the logical approach presented in this book will prepare you for puzzling out what each feature or command does or for searching the Help file.

How Much Do You Need to Know Already?

In order to be concise, this book assumes that you know a few things about Windows 95, including the following:

- How to use Windows 95 and navigate its interface well enough to start up AOL, either with the keyboard or with the mouse.

NOTE   In this book, "mouse" is a generic term that refers to any mouse, trackball, touchpad, or other pointing device that you use.

- How to use Windows programs—starting them and quitting them; using menus and dialog boxes to make choices; and getting help when you need it by pressing the F1 key or clicking on a Help button.

NOTE If you are running Windows 3.x, never fear. Most features of AOL work the same irrespective of what version of Windows you have. See Appendix B for tips on installing and using AOL with Windows 3.x.

- How to click on icons to engage commands.
- How to navigate Windows 95's windows and dialog boxes, double-clicking items (such as folders) to open new windows, and clicking on the Up One Level button (or pressing Backspace) to move back through them.
- How to manage files within Windows 95's common dialog boxes by using the commands on the context menu.
- That you *select* a checkbox for an item by clicking in it to place a checkmark there, and that you *clear* a checkbox by clicking to remove the checkmark.
- That you normally click the left (or primary) mouse button to choose an item or perform an action, and that, in Windows 95, you click the right (or secondary) mouse button to produce a shortcut menu (or *context* menu) of commands suited to that item.
- That Windows 95 applications let you open many windows (messages, Internet sites, menus, chat areas, etc.) and that you can switch among them using the taskbar.

Windows 95 frequently offers many ways to accomplish the same task. One of the easiest ways to get around in Windows 95 is to use the Windows Explorer. Throughout this book, I'll use Windows Explorer whenever I need to perform Windows file-management tasks such as creating an alias. If you're an experienced Windows 95 user, feel free to use whatever file-management approach you prefer. While I'll be covering many Windows 95 features along the way, if you're looking for more comprehensive instruction, please see Sharon Crawford's excellent introduction to Windows 95, *The ABCs of Windows 95,* also published by Sybex.

How This Book Is Organized

This book is organized so that you can go straight to the topic you want and instantly learn what you need to know to get the current task done. The parts divide the book by general subject, while the chapters divide those subjects into more specific topics; each chapter is then sliced into easily digestible sections.

Part 1 teaches you how to set up both the AOL software and your AOL account. You'll also get a look at the AOL interface and how to navigate through it, both online and offline. The chapters break down as follows:

Chapter 1 shows you how to install the AOL software and set up your account.

Chapter 2 explains how to navigate AOL while you're online.

Chapter 3 tells you how to customize your account to fit the way you'll use it.

Part 2 ushers in e-mail. Since e-mail is one of the most popular reasons for using an online service, four chapters are devoted to basic and advanced e-mail, FlashSessions, meeting other AOL members online, and chatting. The chapters break down as follows:

Chapter 4 introduces the rudiments of e-mail.

Chapter 5 shows you how to become an e-mail power user.

Chapter 6 demonstrates how you can automate your e-mailing with FlashSessions.

Chapter 7 shows you how to meet other AOL members and get involved in chatting.

Part 3 introduces you to the many areas on AOL where you can find information of all kinds, whether for business or pleasure. You will also learn where the good company areas are. The chapters break down as follows:

Chapter 8 shows you how to find stuff in AOL's own areas—from sports scores to stock updates, software libraries to computer games, and much, much more.

Chapter 9 introduces a few of the numerous company areas on AOL, including how to find out what they're selling and how to order products.

Part 4 takes you out onto the Internet, where you'll be drawn into the World Wide Web, burrow with Gopher, and learn about a lot of cool sites. You'll also learn about the all-important *search engines,* your ticket to finding what you're looking for on the Internet. The chapters break down as follows:

Chapter 10 teaches you how to get around in the World Wide Web, a major part of the Internet.

Chapter 11 tells you how to find mailing lists, newsgroups, Gopher sites, and other Internet treasures.

Finally, **Appendix A** outlines how to get help when you need it; **Appendix B** offers guidelines for using AOL with Windows 3.*x*; and the **Glossary** lists many AOL and Internet buzzwords, some common and some not so common, so that you can look up terms you don't know without having to search through the book.

NOTE Notes, Tips, and Warnings, each identified clearly with this shading and a keyword, give you extra guidance on specific topics.

Conventions Used in This Book

This book uses a number of conventions to convey information accurately and unambiguously. They include the following:

- ➤ designates choosing a command from a menu. For example, choose Mail ➤ Compose Mail means that you should pull down the Mail menu and choose the Compose Mail command from it.
- + signs indicate key combinations. For example, *press Alt+Tab* means that you should hold down the Alt key and then press and release the Tab key. Some of these key combinations can be visually confusing. For example, *Ctrl++* means hold down Ctrl and press the + key—which actually involves holding down the Ctrl key *and* the Shift key and then pressing the = key.

WARNING   If you hold down a key other than Ctrl, Alt, or Shift, you run the risk of performing a desired task repeatedly, rather than once. For instance, if you want to switch from one application in Windows 95 to another, and you hold down both the Alt *and* Tab keys, you will cycle repeatedly through your applications. It's okay to hold down the Alt key, but you don't want to press the Tab key more than once while doing so.

- **Boldface** indicates items that you should type in, letter for letter, as they appear in the book.
- *Italics* indicate either new terms being introduced or variable information (such as a drive letter) that will depend on the situation and that you'll need to establish on your own, using your common sense.

Author's Note

Do you like to think that your money is going to where it will make a difference? I do, and that's why I am donating 10 percent of all royalties I earn from this book to charities, nonprofit organizations, and other worthy causes. Which causes, you ask? How about a day-care center for homeless children? Or public radio? How about a rape-prevention hotline? And grass-roots democracy groups? Whatever your interests and social concerns, you can be sure that a portion of the money you spent on this book is going somewhere it is needed.

I truly hope you enjoy this book and find it useful. Should you have any questions, comments, or suggestions, please don't hesitate to e-mail me at dkrassner@aol.com or dkrassner@medinfo.rochester.edu; or write me, in care of Sybex, at the following address: Editorial Department, 1151 Marina Village Parkway, Alameda, CA 94501.

David Krassner
Rochester, New York

Part 1

The Nuts and Bolts of AOL

Chapter 1

INSTALLING AOL AND KICKING THE TIRES

FEATURING

- **Yes, you need a modem**
- **Installing the AOL software**
- **Starting the AOL program**
- **Setting Up your AOL account**
- **Recognizing the parts of the AOL window**
- **Exiting AOL**
- **Getting help**

In the first three chapters of this book, you'll find all the basic information you need to know about working with America Online (AOL). You'll learn how to navigate AOL both online and offline, and how to customize your AOL account to make using the service even easier and more fun. This chapter covers installing America Online and setting up your account, and it gives you the chance to "kick the tires" of AOL by looking at the menus and other features of the software.

You might be used to other software packages where all you have to do is install the program and away you go. Not so with America Online. The difference between its installation and that of other applications is that, while some of the

AOL software resides on your local hard disk, much more of the service exists on big computers somewhere out in cyberspace. Indeed, this distinction is one critical feature of an online service. By having much of the service on network computers that are accessible to all its members, AOL can constantly update, revise, and expand features, as well as add new ones, without requiring every user to purchase and install new software.

If you're an old hand at Windows 95 and you've installed lots of programs, you can probably get away with skimming this chapter, although you might want to pay closer attention to the sections on setting up your AOL account. If you've never installed *any* software and even the thought of turning on your computer makes you nervous, never fear. This chapter will walk you through each step of the installation and setup.

WARNING Users who already have AOL accounts cannot make use of the free trial period included on the CD that comes with this book. This offer is good only for new subscribers, so there's no point in installing the CD software unless you're upgrading to 3.0.

Yes, You Need a Modem

While you must install the AOL software on your computer, most of the features of the service are *not* stored there. Rather, you must access them, and to do this, you need a modem.

Simply put, a modem is a telephone for a computer that allows it to talk to another computer. The word *modem* is an acronym of sorts. It stands for *modulator/demodulator*. (This is very useful to know if you want to impress people at cocktail parties.) A modem "modulates," or alters, the electronic signals that a computer produces so that those signals can travel across phone lines.

If you bought your computer fairly recently, chances are it came with a modem. While the scope of this book prevents me from discussing modems at length, it is important that you know what they are, as your modem is your key to reaching both AOL and the Internet. Whether you are shopping for modems, or trying to figure out how they work, there are a few terms you should know.

Most important is the speed of the modem, called the *baud rate*. The baud rate determines the amount of information the modem can transmit in a given amount of time, measured in *bits per second*, or *bps*. Knowing what this measurement means is not as important as having a sense of what a fast modem is versus a slow one. A 28,800 bps modem is fast compared to a 2400 bps modem. You will want to get at least a 14,400 bps modem; anything slower, and you'll grow old waiting for data to go to and from your computer.

> **NOTE**
> There are faster ways to connect to AOL than with a modem, by going through mysterious and wonderful things called direct connections. (These include TCP/IP, PPP, and SLIP connections). Chances are, you will have access to such a connection only if you work for a company or other institution that has had the foresight to install one. Generally, individuals do not have access to direct connections from their homes.

You also have a choice between a modem that resides inside your computer's casing (*internal*) or one that sits atop the computer in a casing of its own (*external*). There are many good, inexpensive modems out there. Regardless of which you choose—and you might take cost, convenience, and aesthetics into account when making your choice—your modem must then be hooked up to a telephone line. The phone line is your lifeline to AOL and to the Internet. You must *connect* to AOL to make use of its array of features.

Once you've got your modem ready, you can install AOL.

Installing the AOL Software

Before you can use AOL, you must install the AOL software on your computer's hard disk. We've included this software, complete with a free trial period for new users, on the CD that comes with this book. Installing this software is perfectly straightforward and is covered here in detail. Before installing the software, though, it is worthwhile to check whether AOL is *already* installed on your machine. Follow these steps:

1. Choose Find ➤ Files or Folders from the Start menu.
2. Type **AOL*.*** in the Named: box.

3. Make sure that the Look in: box shows the name of your hard drive. Also be sure that the Include subfolders checkbox is checked.

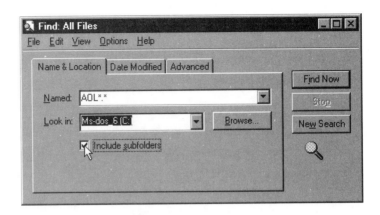

4. Click on Find Now. If there is a copy of AOL on your hard disk, this search will locate it, and you can skip ahead to the section titled "Setting Up Your AOL Account." If not, you must install it, as described next.

NOTE If you do have an older version of AOL already running, don't worry. The installation program allows you to use your old Address Book, Personal Filing Cabinet, etc.

Running the Setup Program

The CD that comes with this book contains a special program called Setup that automates the installation of the AOL software on your hard disk. To run the Setup program, remove the CD that comes with this book from the envelope, and then follow these steps:

1. Place the disc in your floppy drive.
2. Move the mouse pointer down to the lower-left corner of the screen; the taskbar should appear. (If you've configured your machine differently,

the taskbar might appear on the right or in some other location.) Click on the Start button, and then click on Run.

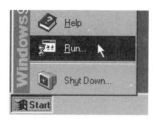

3.   The Run dialog box will appear, probably with the words **a:\setup** (or **b:\setup**, depending upon which drive the CD is in). Click on OK. If something different appears in the Open box, type in the name of your disk drive and then the word **setup**.

4.   The America Online for Windows Setup window will appear, as shown in Figure 1.1. Click on Install to get the ball rolling.

5.   Setup will install the files you need to run AOL, apprising you of its progress as it does so. When the setup program has run its course, you will see a congratulatory menu. Click on OK.

TIP

You can sign on to the AOL service using any version of the AOL software. Older versions will give you access to fewer AOL features, though, so it's always a good idea to use the most up-to-date version. Upgrades are free, and you can get them online as soon as they are released.

Notice that several things have happened. There will now be a window called America Online open on your desktop, as shown in Figure 1.2. Inside this window are several files. It's a good idea to drag the one called Double-Click to Start to the desktop. This way, you will always be able to double-click on the icon from the desktop to start up AOL, even if the AOL window somehow gets closed down.

NOTE

If you already had a version of AOL on your hard disk, perhaps an earlier version, you will get a message saying that your settings have been transferred to the new version.

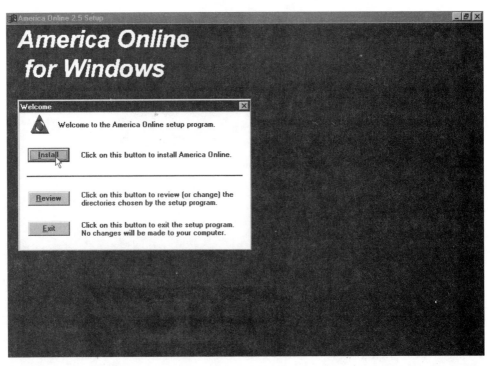

FIGURE 1.1: Click on the Install button in the America Online for Windows Setup window to install the software.

FIGURE 1.2: When Setup has finished installing AOL on your computer, you will see a window like this one.

If you are ready to start up America Online, just follow the instructions on the icon that says "Double-Click to Start," and turn ahead to the section titled "Recognizing the Parts of the AOL Window."

Starting the AOL Program

Before you can set up your account, you need to connect to America Online. The term *connect* in the context of online services can be understood in the context of other phone calls you make. If you want to reach your friends, you call them up. Calling an online service is quite similar. Just as you need your friends' phone numbers to call them, you need AOL's phone number to call it.

Of course, if you have a friend who lives in another city, state, or country, then you're stuck with long-distance charges for the call. Not so with AOL. One of the nice things about AOL is that almost anywhere you go in the United States, you can find a *local access number*. A local access number is simply a local phone number that connects you to America Online. You'll identify several local access numbers when you set up your account, which we'll do in a moment (see Chapter 3 for more information about local access numbers). But first, let's start the AOL program.

Starting a program is just like starting up a chainsaw, only quieter. You must start your chainsaw before you can cut anything with it; similarly, you must start AOL before you can use it. There are three ways to start AOL:

- Double-click the AOL icon (or a shortcut), either on the desktop or in Windows Explorer.
- Choose AOL from the Windows 95 Start menu.
- Add AOL to your StartUp folder.

These methods all accomplish the same thing, so how you choose to start AOL depends upon which one you find most convenient. All are straightforward, even for a beginner.

Starting AOL by Double-Clicking Its Icon

You can start any program by double-clicking its icon. If you have just installed the software and followed the instructions given earlier in this chapter, you should see an icon called Double-Click to Start either on the desktop or in a window. To run the AOL software, all you have to do is double-click on this icon.

Double-clicking an icon (or a shortcut file) on the desktop takes even fewer steps than starting a program from the Start menu. (See the next section, "Creating a Shortcut File for AOL.") The disadvantage of starting AOL this way is that if there is no icon on the desktop, you have to search for it.

To start AOL by double-clicking its icon, locate the icon on the desktop (or in Windows Explorer) and simply double-click on it, as shown below.

TIP If you do have to search for the AOL icon, AOL and its files are most likely installed on your hard disk in a folder called Aol30.

Creating a Shortcut File for AOL

A shortcut file is essentially a small file that points to another, larger file. The larger file can be a program, a document, or a folder. The icon you moved to the desktop back in the section "Running the Setup Program" was a shortcut created by AOL. The advantage of shortcuts is that you can have several copies, move them around, delete them, and generally abuse them without endangering the actual file they point to. For example, it is usually a bad idea to move a program somewhere away from its support files, yet it is often inconvenient to access a program if it's buried on your hard disk.

The solution is to create a shortcut file, and move it instead of the original file. You can create more than one shortcut and keep them in different locations to make it really easy to open programs that you use often. To create a shortcut, follow these steps:

1. Locate the file for which you wish to make a shortcut.

2. Right-click on the file's icon. Notice that a pop-up menu appears.

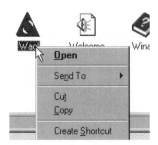

3. Choose Create Shortcut from the menu, and a shortcut will appear, as shown below.

It's easy to recognize a shortcut file, because it has that tiny curved arrow on the lower-left corner of its icon. Now you can just move the shortcut wherever you like. The desktop is often a good place to put your most important shortcuts, because then they are easy to find—provided you don't put so many shortcuts on the desktop that it becomes hopelessly cluttered. To move the shortcut you just made, click and drag it to the Desktop icon in Explorer, as shown below.

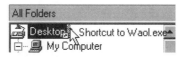

TIP   You can rename shortcuts, or any files for that matter, and it won't affect their functionality. Just click once on the name, and either type the name that you want, or click with the I-beam to place the cursor where you want to begin editing the name.

Starting AOL from the Start Menu

The principal advantage of starting AOL from the Start menu is that the AOL icon will always be in the same place. So if you're on a foreign machine where you don't know your way around, this is a good way to go. The disadvantage of using this method is that it is not automatic; you have to actually lift a finger. It's not much effort, though. Just follow these steps:

1. Using your mouse, move the pointer to the lower-left corner of the screen.

The taskbar should appear, as shown below, unless you've configured your machine to display the taskbar in some other location.

2. Click on the Start button to bring up the Start menu.

3. Slide the pointer up to Programs, and the Programs submenu will appear.

4. Next, slide the pointer up to America Online; another submenu should appear. (If it doesn't, refer back to the section "Creating a Shortcut File for AOL.") Click on AOL in the submenu, as shown in Figure 1.3, and AOL will start up.

Arranging for AOL to Start Up Automatically

The easiest way to start AOL is to have it start automatically when you start Windows. You can accomplish this by placing a shortcut in the StartUp folder. The advantage, of course, is that you don't have to lift a finger to start AOL. The disadvantage is that this means AOL starts *every* time you start Windows. This might be a problem if you just want to go into Windows, do something quickly, and get out.

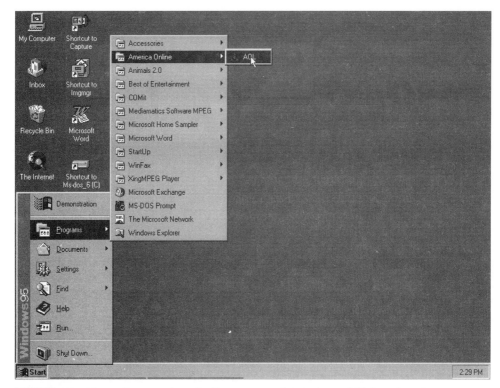

FIGURE 1.3: Choose Programs from the Start menu, and then choose AOL from the submenu.

To add AOL to your StartUp menu, follow these steps:

1. In Explorer, scroll down to the Aol30 folder and click on it once. Your AOL files will appear in the window on the right-hand side, as shown in Figure 1.4.

2. In the left-hand side of the window, scroll down to the Windows folder, and click once on the little plus sign, *not* on the folder. If you accidentally click on the folder, go back to step 1 and try again. Notice that when you click on the little plus sign, another level of folders appears, and the plus changes into a minus.

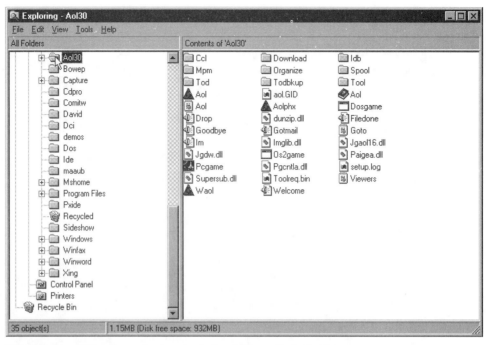

FIGURE 1.4: Click once on the America Online folder to display its files.

3. Next, click on the little plus sign next to the Start menu; if Programs is showing, click on its plus sign instead. Now the StartUp folder should be visible in the left-hand window, and the AOL files in the right-hand window.
4. Right-click on the AOL icon and create a shortcut, as you learned to do in the section "Creating a Shortcut File for AOL."
5. Finally, click on the shortcut you just created, and drag it to the StartUp folder in the left-hand window. When you notice the StartUp folder change color, release the mouse button to drop the shortcut into the StartUp folder. The next time you start up Windows, AOL will start as well.

Setting Up Your AOL Account

Now that you've got AOL installed, you're ready to set up your AOL account. In this section, we will go step-by-step through the setup procedure. Before you start, make sure your computer has a working modem that is plugged into a phone jack. In addition, you should have ready the following:

- Your credit card or checking account number. AOL charges are usually billed to a credit card. You can have your AOL account fees billed to a checking account, but there is a surcharge. If you decide before the end of one month that you don't wish to keep the service, be sure to cancel it (see Appendix A); otherwise, you will be billed for future months automatically.
- Your registration number and initial password (you need this to get into the system). You can find these with the free disk.
- A screen name. It's a good idea to try to think up a screen name before you actually start setting up the account. For tips on screen names, consult the following section, "Choosing a Screen Name."
- A password. It's also a good idea to devise a password before you get started. For help making up a password, see the section titled "Seven Pointers on Passwords" later in this chapter.

Choosing a Screen Name

Your screen name is what you give to people whom you wish to contact you at your AOL address. Nothing terribly interesting or complicated about that, right? But take a moment to think about it.

Whenever you move, which most people do periodically, you change your address, of course, and often your phone number. If you change jobs as well, that address and phone number go out the window. If you have a P.O. box, you can keep that, but what if you move to another city? In each case, you've got to go through the laborious process of notifying *everyone* you know (or at least those with whom you wish to stay in touch) of your new address, phone number, etc.

Now, what if you could have an address that never changed, irrespective of your physical location? Wouldn't that be great! Well, your AOL screen name is just that: a non-site-specific address that never changes as long as you have your AOL account. With that in mind, it is wise to give some consideration to your screen name, because the value of a screen name is its constancy. If you choose a frivolous screen name, such as *bubblekins*, you'll probably end up changing it, and that defeats its purpose.

Once you're ready to set up your account, follow these steps:

1. Start up AOL. The first thing you'll see is the window shown in Figure 1.5, which asks you a few questions based on some determinations that the software has made about your computer.

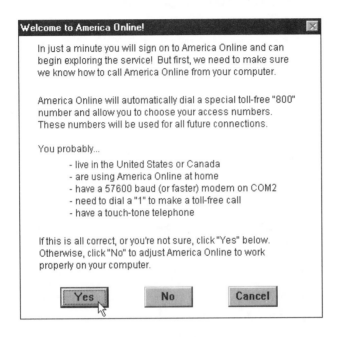

Welcome to America Online!

In just a minute you will sign on to America Online and can begin exploring the service! But first, we need to make sure we know how to call America Online from your computer.

America Online will automatically dial a special toll-free "800" number and allow you to choose your access numbers. These numbers will be used for all future connections.

You probably...

- live in the United States or Canada
- are using America Online at home
- have a 57600 baud (or faster) modem on COM2
- need to dial a "1" to make a toll-free call
- have a touch-tone telephone

If this is all correct, or you're not sure, click "Yes" below. Otherwise, click "No" to adjust America Online to work properly on your computer.

[Yes]   [No]   [Cancel]

FIGURE 1.5:
You'll probably be able to click on Yes in this dialog box.

2. Click on Yes, and another dialog box will appear, reminding you of what information to have at your fingertips. Click on OK to dismiss this dialog box. AOL will then dial up a toll-free number to get the ball rolling.

Dialing 800 Number

[Cancel]

3. If all goes well, next you'll see a welcome screen asking you to enter your local area code.

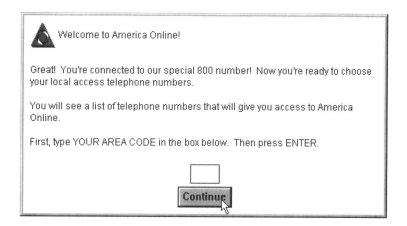

4. Type in your local area code and click on OK. This will bring up a dialog box with a list of local phone numbers, as shown in Figure 1.6. Click on a number in a city that's close to you, and then click on Select Phone Number. You will be asked to select a second local number in the same way.

5. Another dialog box will appear, asking you to confirm your choice of numbers. Click on OK.

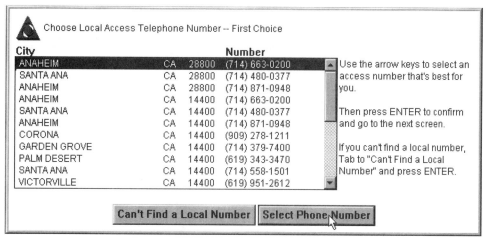

FIGURE 1.6: You select your local access numbers from this list.

6. Finally, you will see the dialog box shown in Figure 1.7, in which you input your registration number and temporary password. You will assign a permanent password in a few moments. When you have entered the information, click on Continue.

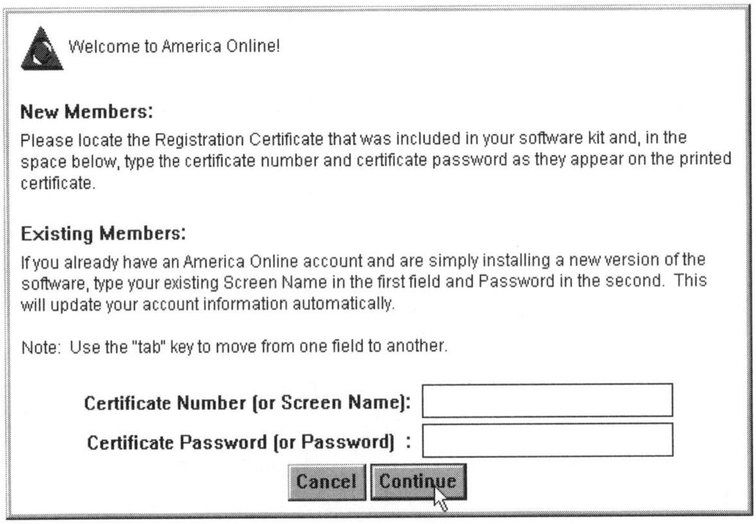

Welcome to America Online!

New Members:
Please locate the Registration Certificate that was included in your software kit and, in the space below, type the certificate number and certificate password as they appear on the printed certificate.

Existing Members:
If you already have an America Online account and are simply installing a new version of the software, type your existing Screen Name in the first field and Password in the second. This will update your account information automatically.

Note: Use the "tab" key to move from one field to another.

Certificate Number (or Screen Name):

Certificate Password (or Password) :

Cancel   Continue

FIGURE 1.7:
Type your registration number and temporary password in this dialog box.

7. From here, just follow the prompts. You will be asked for your name, address, phone number, and credit card (or checking account) number.

WARNING
It's okay to give your credit card number here, but don't be too free with it in other areas of AOL or on the Internet. No AOL representative will ever ask you for your credit card number; in fact, be very suspicious of *anyone* who asks you for a credit card number.

8. At this time, you are given the chance to set up your account in such a way that AOL disables call waiting while you are online. This is an excellent idea, since call waiting will cut your online connection and might cause you to lose valuable information or interrupt a great search.

Seven Pointers on Passwords

1. Choose a password you can remember. If you think up something esoteric like *T1k8F92h*, you'll probably forget it.

2. Make sure your password is not something that others who don't know you could easily guess. For example, if your name is Robyn, don't assign *Robyn* as your password.

3. Make sure your password is not something that others who *do* know you could easily guess. For instance, if you are a hockey fan, don't use the word *puck*.

4. *Do* write your password down somewhere. That way, if you forget it, all is not lost.

5. *Don't*, however, write down your password anywhere obvious. Someone once hacked into the Stanford University mainframe by using binoculars to look through dormitory windows to read passwords off people's bulletin boards. Better to jot it down in an address book or some such place where there is no reference to AOL.

6. Try to *randomize* your choice of password. One way to do this is to take the day and month of your birthdate and run them together; then open your favorite book to the page that matches that number, and choose the first unusual word you see as a password. For example, if your birthday is March 30 and your favorite book is *The Magic Mountain*, you might look on page 330 of that novel and see the word *pomade*. Notice that the steps you've taken to arrive at this password are simple in and of themselves, yet it is unlikely that someone could retrace the steps you used. There are many similar methods you could use to arrive at very hard-to-guess passwords.

7. Change your password regularly. Online services and server managers at businesses and universities always advise users to do this, but it's rarely done. People think, "I don't care if someone reads my mail, so why should I care if they get my password?" Well, while you might not care whether someone reads your mail, if hackers gets your password, they can then access the online service or server and do a lot of damage. So, change your password regularly.

9. Now you are asked to choose a screen name. Read the information here carefully. There are a number of criteria for inventing a screen name:
    - Your screen name must start with a letter.
    - Your screen name may be no longer than 11 characters.
    - You must limit yourself to letters and numbers.
    - Your screen name must be unique.

    Try to think up an unusual but catchy screen name that will be easy to remember. For example, my online name is *dkrassner* (from David Krassner). So if your name were, say, Adenoid Hinkle, you might choose *ahinkle* as a screen name. Don't worry too much about whether your screen name is unique. AOL will let you know if it's not. If you are having trouble coming up with an original name, see the section called "What to Do if the Screen Name You Choose is Taken" in Chapter 3.

> **TIP**
>
> Your screen name might be the *only* address you have that won't change in the next ten years, so choose wisely!

10. Finally, you are asked to choose a password. Choosing a password is slightly different from choosing a screen name. You want a screen name to be simple, whereas the opposite is true for passwords. Don't worry too much if the password you devise is less than scintillating. You can easily change your password, and you should do so periodically, as described in Chapter 3.

11. When you have chosen and entered your password, you will be asked to retype it. Do so, and click on OK. If all goes well, you'll be signed off and whisked back to the AOL window, where you can begin exploring the offline aspects of the service.

Recognizing the Parts of the AOL Window

Once you've set up your AOL account, if all goes according to plan, you should now see the AOL window, as illustrated in Figure 1.8. Since it's a good idea to get comfortable with AOL before you go online, we'll be taking a tour of some of the AOL features you can use offline. Why? Well, you pay for online time, and the faster you can get

Title bar   Menu bar   Flashbar   Window

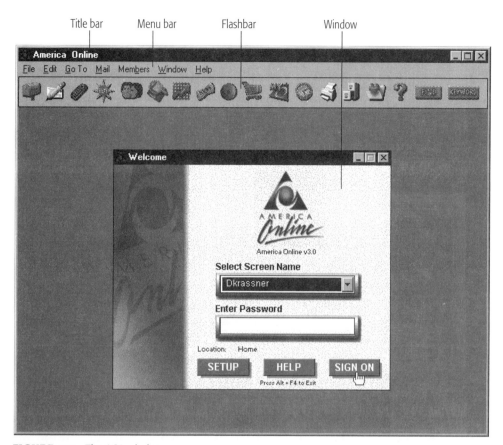

FIGURE 1.8: The AOL window.

around, the better you'll be able to use your online time. (See Chapter 2 for an in-depth discussion on saving money online.)

Just so you know where you are, most windows have a *title bar* that tells you the name of the window. This is always right at the top of the window. As with most Windows programs, there are several ways to access and use the features of AOL. For starters, there's the *menu bar*, which is the area at the top of the AOL window with the words *File*, *Edit*, *Go To*, *Mail*, and so on. The *flashbar* is the area just below the menu bar with the little pictures; you can also perform tasks from the flashbar. The *Welcome screen* (the smaller box in the middle of the AOL window) is a window, as is the AOL screen itself. There are no dialog boxes showing in Figure 1.8, because when you start up AOL, this is what you'll always see. Let's look at each of these screen elements in a little more detail.

The Menu Bar

The menu bar, which runs along the top of the AOL window, will be your primary access point for many of AOL's features. While you can perform many tasks from the flashbar (discussed next), *all* of AOL's features are found somewhere in the menu structure, and some are found nowhere else. The menus at the top of the AOL screen are called *drop-down menus,* because they drop down (a bit like a window shade) when you click on them with the mouse.

> **TIP** You can also access menus from your keyboard. Notice that one of the letters in a menu is always underlined (such as the *F* in *File*). If you hold down the Alt key and press the indicated letter on your keyboard, the menu will drop.

The words you see on the menus are generally called *commands,* since, as with most Windows programs, they tell AOL to do some task or other. As you look through the menus, you'll notice several things.

First, some of the commands are "dimmed"; that is, they are not blacked-in like the other commands are. This is AOL's (and Windows') way of telling you that that particular command is not accessible or functional. Often the reason for this will be self-evident. Just as a simple example, the Copy and Cut commands on the Edit menu will be dimmed if no text is selected, because you can't cut or copy nothing! If you try to choose a dimmed command, nothing will happen.

Also, some of the commands will have a notation next to them such as *Ctrl+S*. This indicates that you could have accessed that command by pressing the Ctrl key and the S key simultaneously from the keyboard.

Such notations are called *keyboard shortcuts*. They are handy to know, and as you use AOL, you will become acquainted with many of the common keyboard shortcuts, simply because they can speed up your navigation around AOL and your execution of tasks.

Finally, menu commands can do many different things. Some commands actually execute a task (such as saving a file), while others simply lead to dialog boxes, where you can give other commands.

The best way to understand the menus is to explore a little. Let's do that now. Say you want to write a message to a friend. Follow these steps:

1. Click once on the Mail menu. The entire menu will drop down, revealing it and all its commands, as shown in Figure 1.9.

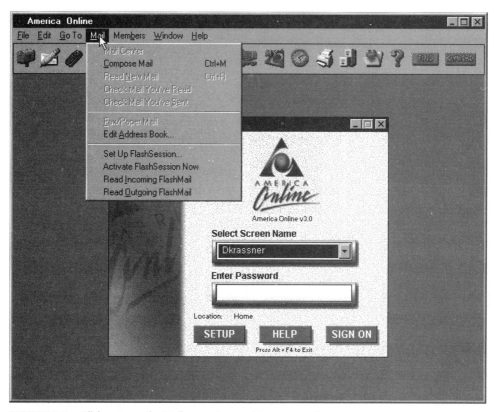

FIGURE 1.9: Click once on the Mail menu to reveal its commands.

2. Move the highlight down to Compose Mail, and click again. Notice that this command has a keyboard shortcut, Ctrl+M. If you had simply held down the

Ctrl key and pressed the M key on your keyboard, you would have executed the command just as we are doing now.

3. Finally, click once on Compose Mail to bring up the Compose Mail window. If you really were intending to send a message, you could fill in the various boxes and scoot it on its way. For now, though, click the close box in the upper-right corner to get rid of the Compose Mail window.

You've now learned two ways to access commands in AOL: choosing commands from the menus and using keyboard shortcuts. Let's look at a third way by exploring the buttons on the flashbar.

The Flashbar

The *flashbar* is the area just underneath the menu bar. The buttons you see are called *icons*. You can think of an icon as being essentially the mouse equivalent of a keyboard shortcut. You can click the mouse on an icon to instruct AOL to perform a certain task, just as you can use a keyboard shortcut. Often you will find that the same task can be performed by clicking an icon, choosing a command from a menu, or using the keyboard shortcut. The advantage of this flexibility is that you can execute commands easily no matter what you're doing. If you are mousing around, an icon-click might be the best way; however, if you are typing, the keyboard shortcut might be faster. (Choosing commands from menus is usually reserved for commands that can't be accessed any other way or for commands you use less frequently, when you can't recall the quick routes.)

Notice that, like the menu bar, the flashbar often has items that are dimmed. This indicates that those icons are not functional. When you are not actually signed on to AOL, many of the icons will be dimmed, as most of them are shortcuts to features you access in AOL while online. Another nice feature of icons is that, like real buttons, they depress when you click on them to indicate your choice.

Let's try using an icon to perform a task. Say you still want to write that letter that I didn't let you write in the previous section. It's easy with the flashbar. Just click once on the Compose Mail icon, as shown below.

As you were moving to click on the Compose Mail icon, you might have seen some words flash below the icon. Try moving the mouse until the pointer hovers just over the icon and the words *Compose Mail* appear, along with a short explanation. This is called a *Tooltip,* and it's very handy, since it means you don't necessarily have to know exactly what an icon does to use it. If you're not sure, just position the pointer over the icon and AOL will tell you what function the icon performs. Sometimes, you'll know what a button does just by looking at the little picture on it. If you want to get an idea of what all the buttons do, just tiptoe through the Tooltips! By the way, Tooltips do take a few seconds to show up, so be patient. Also, for dimmed items, Tooltips won't show up at all.

Don't close the Compose Mail window just yet, because windows are what we're going to explore next.

Windows

Explanations of windows always seem self-referential (a *window* is, uh, well, like a window…). Perhaps a good way to think of a window is to see it as a container. This analogy holds well, because when you start up a program, as you started up AOL, the program was contained within its application window. If you clicked outside the AOL application window, you probably found you were not able to access AOL commands until you clicked the window once again. If you click on the window of another application, it springs to the fore, and you can work in that application instead.

Nearly all Windows programs let you have multiple windows open at the same time. In a word processor, you might use this feature to keep several documents open at once. In AOL, windows hold everything from chat rooms to company areas to the Internet. As you explore AOL, you'll often find that you have several of these windows open simultaneously.

Similarly, within an application window, there can be all sorts of other windows. To see an example of this, click on the Window menu in AOL. It should look something like Figure 1.10.

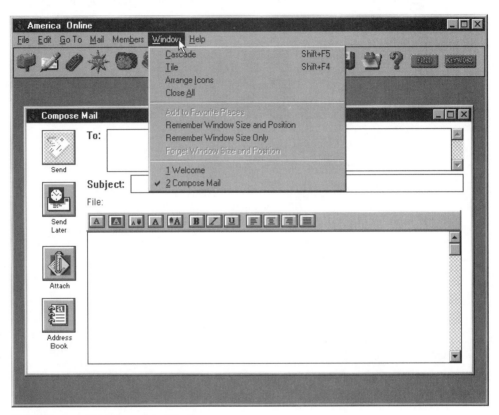

FIGURE 1.10: Click to reveal the Window menu.

At the bottom of the menu are two (or more) items. These are names that refer to open windows within AOL. If you were to highlight the name of a window (or press the number corresponding to its name), that window would jump to the front of all other windows. A very important concept to remember in AOL, or any other Windows application, is that you can work only in the window that's in front, also called the *active* window.

TIP   One way to tell which window is the active window is to look at the title bar. The title bar of the active window always looks a bit different from that of the other windows. If you haven't changed your Windows settings from the default, the active title bar will be blue, while others will be gray.

Choose Compose Mail from the Window menu so that we can look at the parts of a window. The Compose Mail window is shown in Figure 1.11, with the important parts labeled.

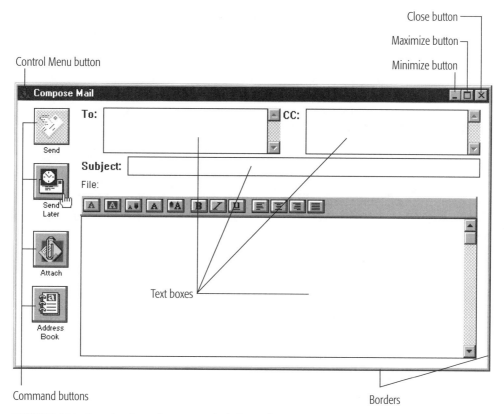

FIGURE 1.11: Knowing the various parts of windows allows you to get around quickly.

Control menu button—You can close the window by double-clicking the control menu button. If you click it once, you reveal a menu of commands that allow you to move, size, minimize, maximize, close, or restore the window to its normal size. If there is more than one window open, the Next command will also be available.

Minimize button—Click on this button to quickly minimize the window down to an icon.

Maximize button—Click on this button to quickly maximize the window to fill your screen.

Close button—Click on this button to close the window.

Text boxes—You type information into these boxes.

Command buttons—You can click on these buttons to perform the indicated commands.

Borders—These indicate the confines of the window.

> **TIP**
>
> **If you are in a window with text boxes and command buttons, you can move from box to box to button by pressing the Tab key. This will cycle you from one box to the next and then from one button to the next. To choose a highlighted button, press Enter. Pressing Shift+Tab cycles in the reverse direction.**

You can move a window with the mouse by clicking in the title bar and holding down the mouse button. Then, as you move the mouse, the window will move with it. Similarly, you can resize the window by moving the mouse until the pointer hovers just above one of the borders of the window; then click and drag to resize the window.

Dialog Boxes

The distinction between a dialog box and a window is an artificial one, because in Windows, all dialog boxes are set into windows. Conversely, many windows are also dialog boxes. A key difference is that a dialog box is usually a window that you bring up to execute a specific task and then get rid of. The way to tell if you are dealing with a dialog box is to look at the title bar. The title bar of a dialog box is different from that of a normal window in three respects:

- It will not have a control menu.
- It will not have minimize and maximize buttons.
- It will have a help button.

For example, if you choose File ➤ Open, you will see the Open a file dialog box, as shown in Figure 1.12.

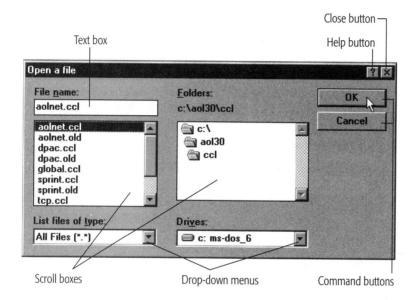

FIGURE 1.12:
The Open a file dialog box.

It's important to know what the various elements of a dialog box are, so here is a handy list of them:

Help button—Click on this button, and then click on the element you want to know more about. A small window will appear to enlighten you. Click outside of it to dismiss it.

Text boxes—You type information into text boxes. In this case, you would type the name of the file you wanted to open.

Scroll boxes—You can click on the up and down arrows to scroll the lists in these boxes, sort of the way the credits roll at the end of a movie. In this case, you would scroll to find the file you wanted to open.

Drop-down menus—Just like the drop-down menus at the top of a window, these offer you options that will probably simplify whatever task you happen to be doing. Here you can choose the type of file you want to look for, thereby reducing the number of files displayed in the scroll box.

Command buttons—Most dialog boxes have OK and Cancel buttons. Click on OK to execute a command or to save your settings and close the dialog box; click on Cancel to abort a command or to close the dialog box without saving your settings. In our example, if you were to choose a file and click on OK, AOL would open it and try to read it for you.

Close button—Click on this to close the window without saving any settings you have specified.

Exiting AOL

When you are finished using AOL for the night (or day), it's a good idea to exit the program. You also need to exit the program when you are ready to turn off your computer. Exiting a program is essentially like shutting off your chainsaw before you put it back in the storage shed. There are three easy ways to exit AOL:

- Double-click the control menu icon at the top-left corner of the AOL window.
- Choose File ➤ Exit.
- Click on the close box at the top-right corner of the AOL window.

That's really all there is to it.

> **NOTE** Don't confuse exiting the AOL program on your disk with signing off from your AOL online connection. You're not charged for just having the program running on your computer; you are, however, charged for your connect time if you exceed your allotted free time. See Chapter 2 for more advice about online charges.

Getting Help If Things Go Wrong

If something goes wrong when you are trying to set up your account, you will likely see an error message explaining (perhaps cryptically) what the problem is. The first thing to do is, *don't panic*. The next thing to do is to choose Help ➤ Search for Help

On… and click on Error Messages, Troubleshooting. Click on the Display button and you will see a list of error messages, one of which probably matches the one you saw.

Common problems include the modem not accessing ("handshaking" with) the access number, the host number being busy, or the modem settings being at odds with the access line you've chosen. Also, it's a good idea to check all your telephone wire connections, and to make sure your modem is turned on if you have an external one. If you're really desperate, you can call AOL toll-free at (800) 827-3338.

> **TIP**
>
> If you cannot resolve your problem using the built-in help, there are other resources upon you which you can draw. See Appendix A for details.

Chapter 2

NAVIGATING IN AOL WHILE ONLINE

FEATURING

- **Optimizing your online time**
- **Downloading art**
- **Avoiding viruses**
- **Signing on to AOL**
- **The Welcome window**
- **Checking out Channels**
- **Searching with Keyword and Go To**
- **Visiting your Favorite Places**
- **Signing off from AOL**

With online services, you're charged for your access time, so it's very important to be able to get around quickly. This chapter will familiarize you with the quickest ways to navigate through AOL's many features. You'll also get a firsthand look at AOL online, which will give you a better sense of the breadth of the service. To make sure you're equipped to protect yourself, we'll also discuss computer viruses and how to avoid them. You'll draw upon the principles outlined in this chapter throughout the book, so it's a good idea to read through this chapter in its entirety.

Online and Offline Time

For most programs you use on your computer, you can learn your way around in a leisurely manner. You can take a coffee break, make a phone call, chat with friends, even leave the program running all day long, and it won't make any difference. When you are connected to America Online, however, the meter is running most of the time (we'll discuss those occasions when it's not shortly), so time is at a premium. In general, if you plan on using AOL a lot, the faster you can find what you're looking for and sign off, the better.

As I mentioned in Chapter 1, being *connected* to AOL is different from simply having the software running. Being connected, or *online,* means that you have signed on to the service. Think of it in terms of a long-distance call; you are not charged for simply picking up the phone and having it off the receiver, but you are charged once you connect to a person, and you continue to accrue charges for the duration of the conversation. AOL works in much the same way. A key difference is that you have a certain amount of free time to use each month—much like a local phone call that's free as long as you pay the monthly service charge.

(At this time) the standard AOL account allows five hours of access time per month, for a flat rate of about $10. There is a fee for each hour thereafter (about $3). Other pricing schemes are available (such as 20 hours for $20), but the five hours is a pretty good benchmark.

WARNING	Beware of any online service that offers you "free" access. You will be charged in some way, because it's impossible to operate an online service (at a profit, anyway) without charging a fee.

One advantage of AOL is that its features are set up in such a way that, once you know your way around, it's very easy to get where you want to go in a hurry. Initially, it may take some time getting familiar with the service (that's where the free trial period comes in handy), but once you do, you'll be amazed at how much you can accomplish in AOL without exceeding the five-hour time limit. All it takes is some intelligent planning of your online sessions and the help of a few tools. Features such as *FlashSessions, Favorite Places, Go To, Keyword, Download Manager,* and the *AOL Browser* all serve to automate the more time-consuming activities in AOL.

In fact, after you have had a chance to really explore the program and get it set up just right, you will probably find yourself spending more of your AOL time *offline* than online. Once you've mastered AOL, if you still find yourself surfing the Net for more than an hour a day, I have just one thing to say to you: Get out of the house! Go to a movie! Get some exercise! Moderation in all things.

Optimizing Your Online Time

There are many ways you can optimize your online time. Generally speaking, the more you do offline, the better. Following are a few pointers for getting the most out of your online sessions. Throughout the book, we'll reexamine some of these points in more detail as we take a closer look at each AOL feature.

- The most important point is to *plan* your online sessions. You don't have to write down everything you want to do (although this isn't a bad idea if you have a long list), but just going over it mentally before you start can save you a lot of dead time when you're connected. For instance, you might think to yourself, "Once my FlashSession is finished, I'm going to check the baseball scores, find out how market finished up today, update my home page, and visit the Monty Python site on the Web to see if there is anything new there." (Don't worry, we'll cover all these things and more, as well as ways to simplify each of these tasks.)

- Get a fast modem and connect at a fast baud rate. As discussed in Chapter 1, the baud rate is the speed at which your computer sends and receives information to and from AOL. The faster your modem, the faster you will be able to move around in AOL and send and receive files. Also be sure that you are connected to a *high-speed access line* (check the setting in the Setup dialog box). It does no good to have a screaming fast 28,800-baud modem if you're connected to a 2400-bit line.

- Use FlashSessions for e-mail. This is perhaps the single most time-saving feature in AOL. Described in much more detail in Chapter 6, FlashSessions essentially automate your e-mail for you. You read and answer messages offline, signing on only to send messages that are ready to go and retrieve new messages that are waiting. FlashSessions themselves can occur automatically.

- Another excellent time saver is the *Favorite Places* feature. Favorite Places is a window where you can add the names of places you like to go often; these can be forums, Web sites, AOL areas, etc. All you have to do is double-click a name in your Favorite Places window, and AOL will take you there. This is especially useful for Web sites with long, complicated names. The Favorite Places feature is covered in more detail later in this chapter.

- Take a few hours to really learn your way around AOL. The better your sense of where things are, the less time you'll waste finding them. Furthermore, take the time to read books like this *before* you sign on, as they can really save you a lot of frustration. For instance, just by skimming this chapter before going online, you might save yourself the cost of the book. Now that's smart! See also chapters 8, 9, 10, and 11 for more instruction about navigating AOL and the World Wide Web.

- If you find you must leave your computer during an online session and you cannot sign off, there is a safety net; you can pop into the Member Services area. *You are not charged for time spent in the Member Services area.* This is very useful to know, because it lets you take a breather without signing off. To reach the Member Services area, choose Members ➤ Member Services. (Member Services is covered in more detail in Appendix A.)

- When you come across lengthy documents or any other information that might take some time to read, just download it or save it to your hard disk. Saving and downloading take relatively little time, and you can read the documents at your leisure after you've signed off. Downloading and saving documents is covered in Chapter 5.

- Allow AOL to download art when it wants to. Downloading as you go is more time-consuming and expensive.

No doubt you will come up with other clever ways to use your online time efficiently, and I encourage you to explore these options. Remember, as an AOL user, your motto should be: more offline, less online.

No More Waiting for Art!

If you've used AOL before, you'll immediately notice that they've eliminated that time consuming "Please wait while we add new art to AOL" dialog box. You used to have to wait for the art needed to update the icons, graphics, etc. that go with the Welcome and Channels areas, which are the first two windows that appear.

Now, windows appear immediately, and any art that needs to be updated is rendered (drawn in) at its own pace. So instead of drumming your fingers impatiently, you are free to click around on anything that looks interesting. As you visit other areas, new art will need to be added there as well, but you will still enjoy a great deal of mobility while you wait for art to appear in all its glory.

Why It's a Good Idea to Download Art

Sometimes, you will enter areas (such as the main Stocks and Finances window) that tend to remain relatively the same once you've downloaded the initial art, and either new art will start to download automatically or you will be given a chance to download new art, as shown in Figure 2.1.

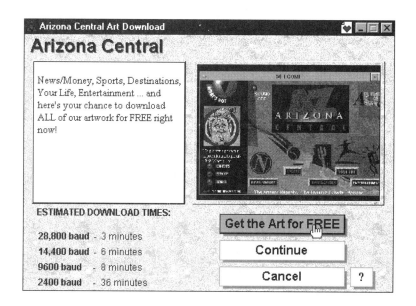

FIGURE 2.1:
You will often be given the chance to download art without using up online time; usually, this is a good idea.

In such instances, it's a good idea to allow AOL to download the art to your hard disk. Why? Well, if you download the art once, even if it takes a little time, then it's there on your hard drive, and you won't have to download it again. Furthermore, downloading all the art at once is free—that is, you're not charged for access time. If, however, you don't download it, then you'll have to go through the same rigmarole every time you access that area, as well as put up with new art being added for each place in the area you enter. And downloading art this way is *not* free, so you use up more online time. If you have a fast computer and modem, the downloading time for art is usually not significant, and the art won't take up much space on your hard disk. There are more important things to worry about, such as viruses.

Viruses and the Importance of Safe Computing

Unfortunately, any book on online services must eventually come around to the subject of viruses. Before you go online, you should have a sense of what they are and how best to avoid them. Viruses are pieces of programming code designed to alter programs, documents, or operating systems. They spread by attaching themselves to other programs or, less often, to other documents. Attached files are just as dangerous as downloaded files because they offer the same vector for viruses to attack your computer.

Some viruses are relatively harmless, such as the merely annoying "Energizer Bunny," a virus that sends that familiar pink bunny drumming his way across your screen. Most viruses, however, are designed to damage or delete portions of your files or operating system. One notorious example is the Michelangelo virus, which erases infected hard drives every March 6, in honor of Michelangelo's birthday. One thing virtually all viruses have in common is that they're designed to spread far and wide. Computer viruses are analogous to real viruses, in that it is impossible to avoid them altogether. But like real viruses, you can take steps to protect yourself against them.

Although you certainly don't have to go online to find a virus, online services offer an ideal environment for viruses to spread. On services like AOL, an enormous number of people sign on and exchange files. A virus gets transferred from one machine to the next through infected files, usually passed on by individuals unaware the virus is even there. For this reason, AOL takes extra precautions to ensure that any files you download from AOL's software libraries are virus-free. In this sense, AOL offers your first line of defense against viruses.

Still, even AOL's best efforts are no guarantee. Here are some important tips to help you avoid computer viruses:

- First and foremost, be sure to have some good virus-scanning software. Disinfectant is a very good program, and it's free from AOL. You can download Disinfectant right to your hard disk, and then scan all files and disks that you introduce to your computer. (You'll learn where to find Disinfectant and other virus programs in Chapter 8.)
- Check out AOL's special area devoted to information about files that help you protect against computer viruses. You can find it by using the keyword **virus**.

- Avoid any disks that you aren't sure about. Don't insert disks into your floppy drives if you're not sure where they came from or if you suspect they might contain pirated (illegally copied) programs. If you must use a disk that you are suspicious about, be sure to use your virus-scanning software on it first.
- Update your virus programs regularly. New viruses are always appearing, and therefore most antivirus programs are updated regularly. It's not enough to install a program and then forget about it for two years.

The WinWord Concept Virus

The WinWord Concept virus is unusual in that it is very selective. The virus quietly attaches itself to Microsoft Word documents using Word Basic, a programming language built into recent versions of Word. If you open a tainted document, your copy of Word gets the bug. Fortunately, Microsoft offers a simple fix for the WinWord Concept virus called **scanprot.dot**. It's available in AOL's software libraries, which we'll visit in Chapter 8. If you're using a recent version of Word on your machine, it's well worth your time to download **scanprot.dot**, open it up in Word, and go through the installation procedure.

The Good Times Virus Hoax

Even longtime computer users can get taken in. A while back, I was fooled by something called the Good Times virus. An e-mail message came in one day about this horrible virus and how it was spread, and I fell for it hook, line, and sinker. I e-mailed everyone on my mailing list (because the file said the virus was spread through mailing lists) and told them about it, only to find out a few days later that it was a hoax. Boy, did I feel stupid!

Some people consider this another kind of virus altogether—a mental virus that spreads through people as they pass the warning along. The point of the Good Times virus joke was that you can't get a virus just by receiving an e-mail message, just as you can't get a virus by just exploring AOL.

Still, I'd rather have been safe than sorry. It was better to look like an idiot than risk my friends' computers and files. This is not a bad attitude for you to adopt, either. Even if you end up looking foolish, you might save a lot of people a lot of time and heart-break down the road if you at least pay attention to all warnings. You can always e-mail or phone AOL if you are worried about a potential virus. Believe me, they are probably more interested in keeping AOL virus-free than you are.

Let's Sign On Already!

Okay, so enough yakking. Let's sign on already!

If you set up your account back in Chapter 1, then you're all ready to begin explor-ing AOL. It might not be a bad idea to follow along with the rest of this chapter as you explore, so you don't get lost. Remember, unless otherwise indicated, during the fol-lowing explorations you will always be using up your allotted online time.

To sign on, follow these steps:

1. Start up AOL, or switch to it if it's already running.

2. Make sure that the screen name in the Screen Name box is the one you designated in Chapter 1 (as opposed to Guest or New Local #). If it is not, click on the drop-down menu and choose your screen name.

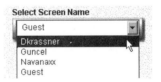

3. Type the password you chose in Chapter 1 into the Password box and click on Sign On, as shown below.

4. You will see a series of sign-on screens, one of which is shown in Figure 2.2. Pay attention to these, because if anything goes wrong, you will be alerted in one or more of the sign-on screens. In any case, it's just nice to know what the sign-on program is doing at any particular time.

5. Once you are connected, the sign-on screens will disappear, and you will probably see a dialog box asking you to wait while AOL downloads new art. Be patient; this will only take a few minutes.

6. Finally, the Welcome window will appear—you're ready to explore.

FIGURE 2.2:
Pay attention to the sign-on screens. If anything goes wrong, they can help you figure out the problem.

TIP   If you get stuck at any time, just click on a Help button (they're all over the place) or choose Help ➤ Contents to find assistance.

Welcome to AOL!

Whenever you sign on to AOL, the first window you'll see is the Welcome window. The format of this screen is always the same, but the contents change frequently. As shown in Figure 2.3, there is a message with its own button at the top of the screen and four icons with some descriptive text to the right. Also, there are icons on the left-hand side that let you reach Channels (discussed next), the People Connection (discussed in Chapter 7), the Internet (more on that in Part IV), and finally, What's Hot, a compendium of new and interesting features. If you have e-mail, the mailbox icon will be illuminated, and the words *You Have Mail* will appear inside it. If you have a sound card and speakers installed, you should also hear AOL say "Welcome" and then "You've got mail."

In Figure 2.3, some of the things going on in AOL include software to download, flowers for all occasions, an online talk show, and a news story. If you've just set up your account, you will probably have mail: a letter of greeting from AOL president Steve Case. What you see will doubtless be different from Figure 2.3, because this screen is always changing.

The nice thing about this window and most other AOL screens is that you can simply click on any of the icons to see more about the topic. For instance, if you were to click

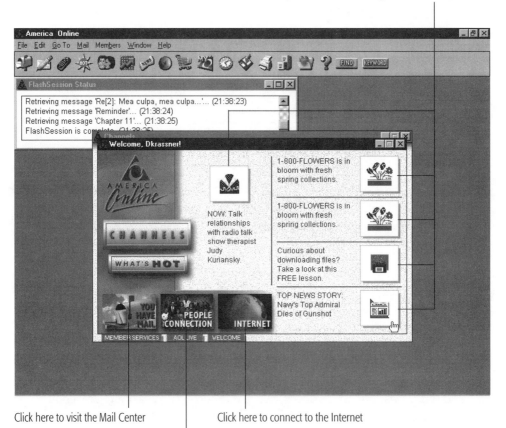

Click on any of these buttons to go to the indicated area

Click here to visit the Mail Center

Click here to visit People Connection

Click here to connect to the Internet

FIGURE 2.3: The Welcome window tells you what's going on in AOL, as well as giving you a chance to see the news of the day.

on the Top News Story icon, you would be transported to one of the news sections of AOL and given a chance to read the story, as shown in Figure 2.4.

The idea behind the Welcome screen is to give you a quick, easy way to access the news items and other bits of information you might be interested in. Let's begin by looking at the screen that's lurking behind the Welcome window, Channels.

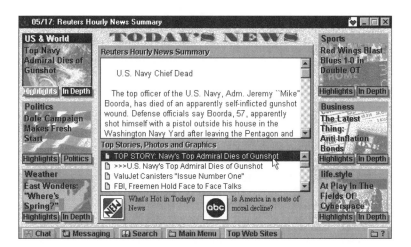

FIGURE 2.4:
Click on the Top News Story icon to open this window, where you can double-click to see photographs and read the story.

> **NOTE** If this is your first time exploring AOL, you're going to encounter art downloads at every turn. This will slow you down a bit, but it's better to get the downloads out of the way (and they're mostly free). As you continue to click around and revisit areas, there will be fewer art downloads.

Checking out Channels

If you click on the screen that's partially hidden by the Welcome window, Channels will surge forward. As shown in Figure 2.5, Channels is your launching pad to many AOL services, including news, entertainment, travel, finance, the Internet, sports, education, and many special-interest sections, such as games, Kids Only, and the People Connection.

FIGURE 2.5:
Channels offers a cornucopia of interesting places to visit.

Like the Welcome window, the items you see in Channels can be reached with a simple mouse-click. (AOL provides many different ways to get around, but we'll start by looking at the simplest approach—clicking until you get where you want to go. This is ideal if you're not sure where you want to end up or if you're in the mood to explore.)

Try clicking on the Newsstand button. The Newsstand window will appear, as illustrated in Figure 2.6, showing the dozens of magazines and newspapers that are

FIGURE 2.6:
The Newsstand window contains dozens of dailies, weeklies, and other periodicals for you to browse.

available online. You might want to take a few moments to scroll through the list. You'll find everything here from *American Astrology* to *Wizard's World*. Just think how much money you can save by not buying as many magazines! Now you can search just those magazines you are interested in and read only the articles that you want to. If you can't make up your mind, AOL provides several ways to narrow your choices. For example, there is the Critics Choice button, which takes you to a list of articles deemed especially interesting or topical. And at the top of the list, there are several separate listings of computer articles.

To access any magazine or newspaper listed, all you have to do is double-click on its name, and a list of articles will appear. To see how this works, double-click on the *Arizona Republic/Phoenix Gazette;* its screen will appear, as shown in Figure 2.7.

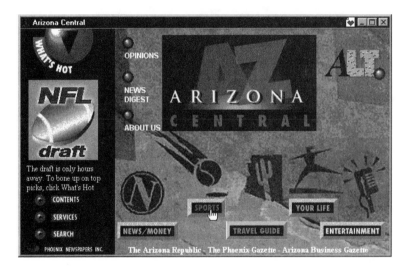

FIGURE 2.7: Double-click on the Arizona Republic/Phoenix Gazette to see this main screen for those daily newspapers.

If you've never visited these publications' area before, you will probably have to download the art. (Don't be surprised if it takes a few minutes to get all the art for this feature. If you really don't want to wait, try clicking on one of the other magazines.) You'll see that the artwork is quite sophisticated and attractive. Once it's downloaded, you can visit an area of interest by clicking on one of the buttons.

For example, let's say you want to catch up on what's happening in the NFL. You could click on Sports to see a list of sporting articles, as shown in Figure 2.8. Click on a headline to read the article, or click on one of the buttons for other choices. Be careful not to open *too* many windows at once, or else you run the risk of running out of memory. If you find that you have a lot of windows open, just click on the close boxes

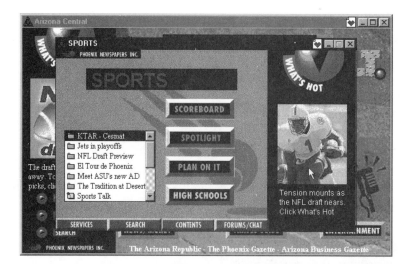

FIGURE 2.8:
You can click on the What's Hot icon to read the day's big story, or scroll the window on the left to see other sporting news.

of any windows that you're not using. (There's also a Close All command on the Window menu.)

By now you may be getting an idea of the wealth of information available through an online service such as AOL. Consider this: we explored just *one* category from the many choices on Channels, and within that category we barely scratched the surface. Remember, too, that as numerous as the possibilities are within AOL, on the Internet, which is much, much larger than AOL, the quantity and variety of information is seemingly infinite.

Searching by Keyword

You might feel a bit overwhelmed in the face of all these choices. But AOL has a number of features designed to help you get around more easily. The first of these is the *Keyword* command. Keyword is a word-search feature designed to let you go somewhere quickly without having to click through a lot of dialog boxes. This can be a huge time saver if the intermediate dialog boxes have a lot of art that takes a while to download. A disadvantage of Keyword is that you have to *know* what the keyword is before you can use it. Sound like a catch-22? Well, AOL tries to make it easier by using intuitive keywords that are easy to guess.

Guessing Keywords

Common sense is your best guide in guessing keywords, but here are a few more tips:

- Try single words rather than phrases. For example, if you were to type **Acid Rock Bands of the Eighties**, you probably wouldn't get anywhere, whereas simply typing **Music** will get you on the right track immediately.
- Guess nouns rather than verbs or adjectives. Usually you will be looking for subjects, so this makes sense.
- Be specific. Keyword doesn't approximate, so if you type *water,* you won't get very far. Better to type in something concrete, like *lake*.
- Be sure to spell words correctly! Keyword does not tolerate misspellings. (Capitalization doesn't matter.)

Searching for areas with Keyword is a lot like using the Find or Find File commands that are so common in programs these days. Let's look at an example of how Keyword can help ease your searching efforts by trying to reach the *Arizona Republic*. Follow these steps:

1. Choose Go To ➤ Keyword, click on the Keyword icon on the flashbar, or use the Ctrl+K keyboard shortcut. The Keyword dialog box will appear, as shown in Figure 2.9.

2. Now, what do you think would be a likely keyword for the *Arizona Republic?* Since it's Arizona news, let's guess the word *Arizona;* type **Arizona,** and click on the Go button. Voila! The *Arizona Republic* page appears.

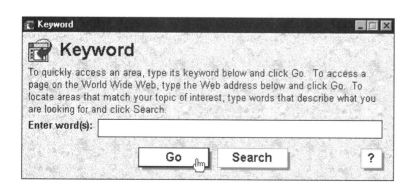

FIGURE 2.9: You can get to an area quickly by typing its keyword in the Keyword dialog box.

Notice that by using Keyword, you've found something in two easy steps that took three or four using click-and-hunt. And you were able to bypass the intermediate screens, saving valuable online time.

Once you know the keyword, you can always use it to return to an area. But what if you plan to visit the *Arizona Republic* a lot? In that case, you might want to use the Favorite Places feature.

> **NOTE** As you explore AOL, you will often be asked to choose a topic in keyword boxes similar to the one shown in Figure 2.9.

Using Favorite Places

AOL has a special folder to keep track of places you visit frequently. It is called the *Favorite Places* window, and it's very easy to use. To visit an area in your Favorite Places list, all you need to do is select it and on click the Connect button. If you've been following along with this chapter and you're still in the *Arizona Republic* area, let's add it to your Favorite Places list.

> **TIP** I'll be taking you to many of AOL's most interesting places in the course of this book. When you find one you want to revisit later, be sure to add it to your Favorite Places list.

Adding Areas to Your Favorite Places List

To add an area to the Favorite Places list, follow these steps:

1. In the title bar of the area window, click on the little folder with the heart, as shown below.

2. A small dialog box will appear (see below), asking you if you wish to add the area to your list of Favorite Places. Click on Yes.

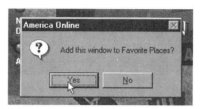

Now, let's see if it worked! To visit your Favorite Places list, Choose Go To ➤ Favorite Places, use the Ctrl+B keyboard combination, or click on the folder with the heart located on the flashbar (shown at left).

As you can see in Figure 2.10, the *Arizona Republic* area (actually called *Arizona Central*) was added to my list just fine. Your list will certainly look somewhat different. But if you look at my list for a moment, you'll see there's quite a variety of places I can visit with a single mouse-click.

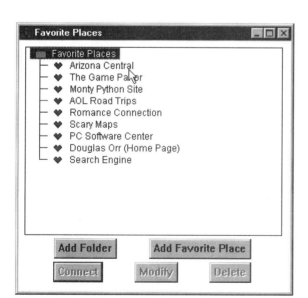

FIGURE 2.10:
Once you add an area to your Favorite Places list, you can reach it anytime with a single mouse-click.

You can also add Internet sites to the Favorite Places list from this window, thereby saving yourself from having to type out long, complicated Internet addresses. Just click

on the Add Favorite Place button, and a dialog box will appear in which you can type in the name of the site.

You *can* use this same method to add AOL areas to the Favorite Places list, but this is a more cumbersome method than the one described above. Generally you'll do this only for addresses that someone has e-mailed to you, which you can then copy and paste into this box.

Adding Folders and Modifying Places

Now that you've seen how to add items to your Favorite Places list, let's look at a few housekeeping commands. First, you can group your items into logical divisions by placing them in different folders. For example, you could group all Internet sites in a folder called *Internet*.

To create a folder called Internet, simply click on the Add Folder button, and type the name **Internet**. A new folder with that name will appear in your window. You can then click and drag items to move them to that folder, as shown below.

You can also modify the names of places (or their addresses). To do so, highlight the place you wish to alter, and click on the Modify button. A dialog box almost identical to the Add Favorite Place dialog box will appear, allowing you to edit the place (or its address, if you got it wrong). This can be useful if you find you have a lot of places with similar but not very descriptive names.

You can remove a place from your Favorite Places list altogether by highlighting it and clicking on the Delete button.

Using the Go To Menu

A slightly different approach to reaching areas you visit frequently is the Go To menu. The Go To menu is a backdoor to Favorite Places, where you can add up to ten areas you visit frequently *and* assign them keyboard shortcuts. This is one purpose of the Go To menu: to provide a place for keyboard-oriented folks to assign shortcuts to favorite places. After all, the Favorite Places list is great, but it still takes a few mouse-clicks to reach it. The Go To menu, on the other hand, allows you reach places with one keystroke.

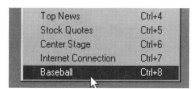

Here's how it works. If you click on the Go To menu to bring down the list of commands, you will see a list of places at the bottom with corresponding keyboard shortcuts.

If you were to execute one of those keyboard shortcuts, you would be whisked directly to the corresponding place. For example, in my system, if I type Ctrl+8 on my keyboard, the next thing I know, I'm at the AOL Baseball window, as shown in Figure 2.11.

But, you say, I can't do that! Well, that's because you haven't added the baseball area to your Go To menu. Let's look at how to add areas next.

FIGURE 2.11:
The AOL Baseball window is just one area you might add to your Go To menu.

Adding Areas to the Go To Menu

To add an item to your Go To menu, follow these steps:

1. Choose Go To ➤ Edit Go To Menu. The Favorite Places window will appear, as shown in Figure 2.12.

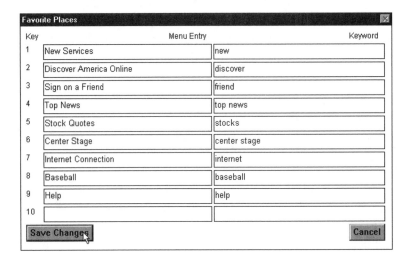

FIGURE 2.12: You can customize your Go To Menu, making it easy to reach the sites you are most interested in.

Now, don't confuse *this* Favorite Places window with the one discussed in the previous section. This window shows a list of favorite places you can reach from the Go To menu. It's confusing, but until AOL thinks of a better name, we're stuck with it.

2. To add an area to the menu, just type the name in an empty box in the left-hand column. Then type the keyword you use to get to the area in the right-hand column.

Note that the name of the area and the keyword are not necessarily the same. For example, the keyword for Stock Quotes is simply **stocks**. You *do*, of course, need to type the correct keyword, so it's wise to find the area and determine its keyword first. (Usually the keyword is spelled out in the upper-left corner of the area's window.) If you're having problems finding areas, see the section "Guessing Keywords" earlier in this chapter.

Signing Off from AOL

Since you are charged for the time you spend connected to AOL, it's important to know how to break the connection, or *sign off*, the AOL equivalent to hanging up on a long-distance call. Fortunately, it's quite simple.

To sign off from AOL, simply choose Go To ➤ Sign Off. You will be asked to confirm this choice.

Click on Sign Off, and you will be disconnected. If you are ready to shut down AOL altogether (perhaps because you're tired and want to go to bed), click on Exit instead of on Sign Off.

NOTE

AOL has a built-in precaution to prevent your wasting valuable online time by forgetting that you are online. If you spend a lot of time reading a document in AOL, or if you work for awhile in another Windows program, you might see a dialog box informing you that you have been online for some time without doing anything. After a certain amount of time spent online with no activity, if you do not respond to this dialog box, AOL will sign off your account automatically. When this happens, you will see a dialog box informing you that your account has been signed off.

Chapter 3

CUSTOMIZING YOUR AOL ACCOUNT

Now that you've signed on and learned a few of the ropes of online browsing, it's time to customize your account, setting it up in the way that's going to work best for you. In this chapter, you'll learn how to find local access numbers, so that you'll be able to access your account if you take your computer to another city. Even if you don't have your own computer with you, you'll see how you can access AOL from any of several computers, or even sign on as a guest from someone else's machine.

Then we'll look at adding more screen names, assigning and changing passwords, and setting Parental Controls. This last feature is especially important if you have children who use your account and you are concerned about what they might have access to. And last but not least, we'll take a look at a typical AOL billing summary and read it together.

Finding Local Access Numbers

One of the nicer features of AOL is that almost anywhere you go in the United States or even abroad, you can find a local access number. As you'll recall from Chapter 1, a local access number is simply a local phone number that connects you to America Online.

Think for a moment how convenient this is. For example, if you are a business traveler, you can sign on in Chicago, New York, Los Angeles—even Wilberforce, Ohio—and not have to pay long-distance charges. Not only that, you can send e-mail messages to another city, or even another country, and you still won't be charged a toll.

Editing Your Home Location

AOL provides for *one* location that you use most often. This is the local access number you use to sign on, and it is probably in the same area code as your business or home. In fact, it is called your home location. When you installed the software in Chapter 1, you set up your home location, but for a variety of reasons it's important to know how to change it. For example, you might run AOL on more than one computer, in which case you will have to set the local access numbers for each machine.

TIP	Before going through the following procedure, you might want to check the front pages of your phone book to compare the costs of calling various prefixes in your local area. It is possible, however, if you live in a rural area, that you will have only one local access number to choose from. You might not even have any *local* access numbers, in which case you'll have to dial into the nearest big city.

To find local access numbers for your home location, follow these steps:

1. Start up AOL, or switch to it if it is already running.
2. In the Screen Name box of the Welcome window, choose New Local #, as illustrated in Figure 3.1.

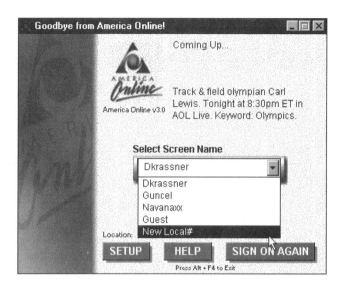

FIGURE 3.1: Choose New Local # in the Screen Name box of the Welcome window.

3. Click on Sign On. A sign-on screen will appear, informing you of AOL's progress. Notice that you are calling a toll-free 800 number.

> **TIP**
> At the bottom of the sign-on screen, AOL informs you of what is happening step-by-step. Pay attention to these messages, because if something goes wrong with the sign-on, you'll have some idea what the problem is.

4. Finally, you'll see a congratulations message, followed by a window that asks you to type in your local area code. Do so.

5. Another window will then appear, offering you a choice of several local sign-on numbers. (The closer you are to a major metropolis, the more choices you are likely to have.) Choose the local access number you wish, and click on the Select Phone Number button, as shown in Figure 3.2.

6. Next, you will be required to choose a second access number, to be used when your primary number is busy or out of service. Follow the procedure in step 5 above.

7. Finally, you will be asked to confirm your numbers. Click on OK.

AOL will then sign you off. From now on, when you wish to sign on, all you have to do is to click on the Sign On button in the AOL Welcome window.

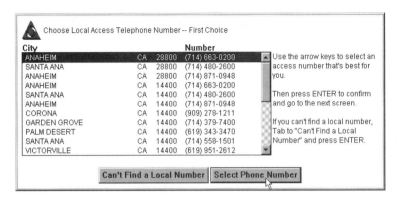

FIGURE 3.2:
Choose a local
access number,
and then click on
the Select Phone
Number button
in the Local
Access Number
window.

Finding Other Locations

If you followed the steps in the previous section, it might have occurred to you to try typing in an area code other than the one from which you were calling. If you did so, you probably saw that you were given a choice of several local access numbers for the area code you typed in, not for your own area code. This option is useful, as it allows you to find local access numbers in cities other than your hometown.

> **TIP**
>
> **If you travel for business, or even if you are just someone who takes a laptop on vacation, find the local access numbers for the places you're going *before* you leave home. While you *can* find access numbers on the road, if you're in a hurry, it's convenient to have the settings files already set up.**

To create settings files with access numbers for other cities, follow these steps:

1. Start up AOL, or switch to it if it is already running.
2. In the Screen Name box of the Welcome window, choose New Local #. Then click on the Setup button.
3. When the Network & Modem Setup dialog box appears, click on the Create Location button to open the Network Setup dialog box; type the name of the city for which you wish to find local numbers, as shown in Figure 3.3. (Notice here that you also have a choice of networks. You can read more about networks later in this chapter, but for now, just leave this option at the current setting.)

Network Setup

Location: San Francisco

Phone Type: ⦿ **Touch Tone** ○ **Pulse**

Phone Number: [   ]   Phone Number: [   ]

Modem Speed: [2400 bps   ▼]   Modem Speed: [2400 bps   ▼]

Network: [AOLnet   ▼]   Network: [AOLnet   ▼]

☐ **Use the following prefix to reach an outside line:** [9,   ]

☐ **Use the following command to disable call waiting:** [*70,   ]

[Save]   [Swap Phone Numbers]   [Cancel]

FIGURE 3.3: Type the name of the new city in the Location box of the Network Setup dialog box.

4. Click on Save, and your new location will now appear in the Network & Modem Setup box.

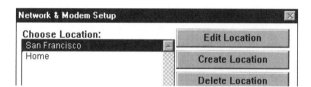

5. To return to the Welcome window, click on OK. Notice that the Current Location is now the name of the city you designated in the Network Setup dialog box.

6. Click on Sign On. You will see the sign-on screen that informs you of AOL's progress.

7. When you reach the window that asks you to type in your local area code, type in the area code of the city for which you wish to create a settings file, *not* your local area code.

8. A window will then appear, offering you local sign-on numbers. Choose the local access number you wish, and click on the Select Phone Number button. Choose a second access number the same way, as instructed.

9. When you are asked to confirm your numbers, click on OK.

Back in the Network & Modem Setup dialog box, notice that your new city has been added to the location list. Now, when you visit another city, or one of several cities if you travel a lot, all you have to do is click on Setup in the Welcome window and choose the correct city name. You do, of course, have to know what city you're in—AOL can't help you with that!

Editing Locations

You may find that, from time to time, you need to alter a settings file for a particular location. For example, you might get a new modem that's capable of faster access speeds, or you might move to a new city where you'll need a new home location. Whatever the case, editing settings files is similar to setting them up in the first place. Follow these steps:

1. Start up AOL, or switch to it if it is already running.
2. Click on Setup to open the Network & Modem Setup dialog box.
   - If you want to find different local access numbers, click on the name of the location, click on OK, and then continue to step 3.
   - To make other changes, select the desired location, and then click on the Edit Location button. This will open the Network Setup dialog box, where you can change the name of the location, change the modem speed, or make other alterations. If that's all you wanted to do, click on OK twice and you're done.
3. Next, choose New Local # in the Screen Name box of the Welcome window. Notice that the Current Location is now the name of the city you chose in the Network & Modem Setup dialog box.

TIP

It makes a lot more sense to create new location files for places you visit than to keep on changing your home location. It's best to leave that alone and create new locations as needed.

4. Click on Sign On. As usual, the sign-on screen will keep you informed of AOL's progress.
5. When you reach the window that asks you to type in your local area code, type in the area code of the city for which you are editing the settings file.
6. The next window will offer you a choice of local sign-on numbers. Choose the local access number you wish, and click on the Select Phone Number button. You will then be asked to choose a second access number in the same way.
7. When you are asked to confirm your numbers, check to make sure they're correct, and click on OK.

Battle of the Networks

In the Network Setup box, there are a number of different *networks* you can use to access AOL. In this context, a network is the maze of phone lines and computers that you use to access an online service. Your choices here are AOLnet, Datapac, AOLGLOBALnet, SprintNet, and Tymnet. (There's also one called TCP/IP, but that has to do with accessing AOL from a local-area network, such as you might have at work or at a university, and it is not applicable in other contexts.)

You will want to choose the fastest network available to you. When you sign on and choose local numbers, AOL will tell you which networks are available with those numbers. AOLnet numbers tend to be high-speed connections (up to 57,000 bps). Such speeds are not of practical use, however, since the fastest rate at which data can flow through a telephone line is 28,800 bps. Given this fact, it really doesn't make sense to purchase a modem that's any faster than 28,800 bps, unless you are going to be signing on from a very fast network (such as a TCP/IP connection).

Running AOL from Multiple Computers

One of the advantages of an online service such as AOL is that you can access it from any computer that has the software and a modem. If you are using someone else's computer, then you sign on as a guest, as discussed in the next section. But if you have more than one computer of your own, you can also sign on to AOL from any of them, using the same screen name. For example, I run AOL from four different computers; you might do so, too.

| NOTE | Running AOL on several machines is a perfectly legal, acceptable, and widespread practice; just don't try to access your account from several machines simultaneously. |

Suppose you have one computer at work, another at home, and perhaps even a laptop you take on the road. Since the only thing you really need to sign on to AOL is your screen name and password, there is theoretically no limit to the number of computers from which you can sign on. You *cannot,* however, sign on to AOL from different machines simultaneously.

To run AOL from multiple computers, all you have to do is install the software on each computer, as described in Chapter 1. Then, just sign on as if you were doing so for the first time (also described in Chapter 1). When you are asked to give the screen name and password supplied with the AOL disk, just use your regular screen name and password instead. Quicker than you can say *Jack Robinson,* you'll be hooked up from that other computer.

Running AOL as a Guest

There may be times when you want to sign on to your own account from someone else's computer. If they have an AOL account, then you need to sign on as a guest. Running AOL as a guest is more or less like using someone else's telephone to make long-distance calls on your own calling card, and it is less complicated than setting up your account on multiple computers. Simply follow these steps:

1. Start AOL, or switch to it if it's already running.
2. In the Welcome window, select Guest from the Screen Name box.

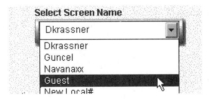

3. Click on Sign on. AOL will go through the usual sign-on procedures, finally connecting you with the window shown in Figure 3.4.
4. Type in your usual screen name; then press Tab and type your password. When you either press Enter or click on OK, you will be taken to your AOL account just like always, where you can do *almost* anything you can do when you sign on from one of your own computers.

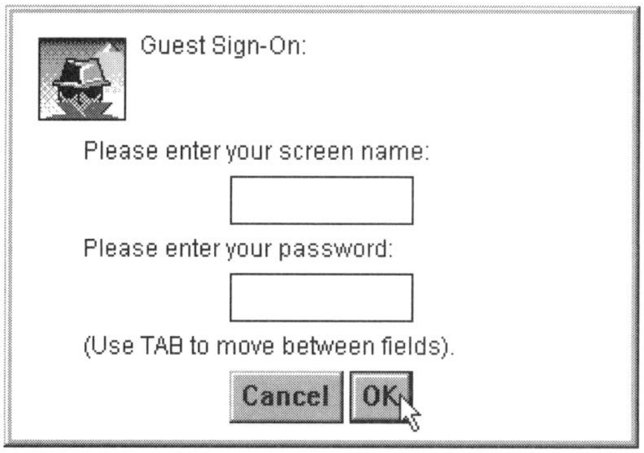

FIGURE 3.4:
You sign on to
AOL as a guest
using this
window.

Things You Can't Do when Signed on as a Guest

Unfortunately, there are certain limitations to using AOL as a guest. Restricted features are mostly those that depend upon information on your hard disk to work properly. After all, when you sign on as a guest, the information on the computer you are using pertains to the person who owns the computer, not to you. Therefore, you cannot access the following:

- Your incoming or outgoing mailboxes
- Your Favorite Places list
- Your Personal Filing Cabinet
- Your Address Book
- Your Download Manager
- FlashSessions

You *can,* however, send and receive messages, browse the Internet, and access AOL's other online features. Generally speaking, when you sign on as a guest, you should still be able to access any features *online* that you cannot access when you are *offline* on your own computer.

Customizing Your Account with My AOL

You can customize many aspects of your account with a feature called *My AOL*. My AOL is really just a dialog box that brings together several commands that it makes sense to have grouped together. These commands include creating and editing screen names, changing passwords, and limiting your children's access to AOL with *Parental Controls*. We'll explore each of these in depth, but first, let's look at the My AOL dialog box.

You can access My AOL only when you are online, so go online now if you are not already there. Then choose Members ➤ My AOL or click on the My AOL icon on the flashbar, as shown below.

This will bring up the My AOL dialog box, shown in Figure 3.5.

FIGURE 3.5:
Here in the My AOL dialog box, you can work with Flash-Sessions, create your own web page, and specify Parental Controls.

Click on Set Up AOL Now and we'll look at a few of My AOL's features in more detail.

Creating New Screen Names

The first time you signed on to America Online, you were asked to choose a screen name; this is known as the Master Account screen name. This name cannot be changed. But you can create up to four additional screen names if you wish. In fact, this is what families do if they want to have an account for each member of the family (assuming the family is limited to five members).

By having a separate screen name, each person has his or her own e-mail account, password, Personal Filing Cabinet, and Favorite Places list; this ensures a certain amount of privacy and mitigates the confusion that could potentially arise with several people using the same AOL account. Furthermore, parents can specify certain restrictions in terms of access for their children's accounts.

In addition, one individual can have more than one screen name, as it allows for a certain amount of anonymity. For instance, you might have one screen name that more or less incorporates your real name, such as *dkrassner,* which you give out for business purposes, and another which you use for chatting, when you want to be a little more mysterious. (I use the screen name *Guncel* to prowl with a greater degree of anonymity than my regular screen name would allow.)

> **TIP**
>
> America Online knows you (and bills you) by the screen name you chose when you signed on, called the Master Account screen name. No one else, however, needs to know that name. You can devise up to five screen names and give out only the ones you want people to know. So if you hate your Master Account name, just create a new screen name, and use that one all the time.

To create a new screen name, follow these steps:

1. In the My AOL Tour window, click on Screen Names, then click on the Set Up Now button. The Create or Delete Screen Names dialog box will appear, as shown below.

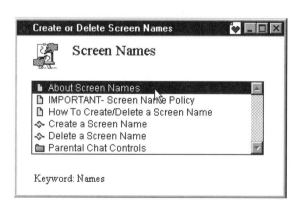

2. Double-click on Create a Screen Name to bring up the Create a Screen Name dialog box, as shown in Figure 3.6.

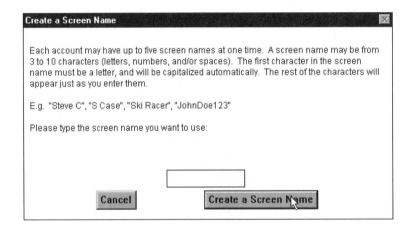

FIGURE 3.6: You create screen names in—surprise— the Create a Screen Name dialog box.

Read the information here carefully. Notice that there are a number of criteria for inventing a screen name:

- Your screen name must start with a letter.
- Your screen name may be no longer than 11 characters.
- You must limit yourself to alphanumeric characters (letters and numbers).
- Your screen name must be unique.

Try to think up an unusual but catchy screen name that will be easy to remember. This is *not* a password, so feel free to make it something obvious like your first initial and last name. Don't worry whether your screen name is unique. AOL will let you know if it's not.

3.   Type in your screen name, and then either press Enter or click on the Create a Screen Name button. If your screen name was already taken, you will see the following dialog box.

> The screen name you have chosen is already in use. You may have the following alternate name, or you may enter another name of your choice:
>
> David67566
>
> Cancel   Create a Screen Name

In this box you will be offered a (probably not very clever) alternative name. You can either accept the suggested name or click on the Cancel button and try another of your own. (For tips on choosing screen names, refer to the following section, "What to Do if the Screen Name You Choose Is Taken.")

4.   If your name was unique, you will see the Set Password dialog box. Here you must enter a password. (For tips on passwords, see the section "Seven Pointers on Passwords" in Chapter 1.) After you type in your password, you will be asked to reenter it. Do so, and then click on OK; you're done. Sign off if you don't wish to do anything else.

When you sign off, notice that in the Screen Name box of the Welcome window, you now have several choices. Guest and New Local # will always be options on the list, but any other items are yours to create.

NOTE   When you want to sign on with a particular screen name, you must first choose it from the drop-down list in the Screen Name box of the Welcome window.

To delete a screen name, open the Create or Delete Screen Names dialog box as described in step 1 above, double-click on Delete a Screen Name, and follow the prompts.

WARNING   When you delete a screen name, neither you nor anyone else can use it again for six months.

What to Do if the Screen Name You Choose Is Taken

Don't be discouraged if the first few screen names you try are already taken. Even unusual names like *Bertolucci* and *Yossarian* seem to be a dime a dozen on AOL. Remember, AOL membership numbers in the millions. This strength can occasionally (quite rarely, really) be a weakness. Here are a few tips on what to do if the screen name of your dreams is already in use:

- Try your own name; if you have a somewhat unusual last name, using the initial of your given name and your entire last name should do the trick. If you have a common surname, though, you might need to include a middle initial as well—or you just might have to come up with something else.

- If you want greater anonymity than a last name affords, consider using your first name (or all your initials) and the city or state in which you reside. For example, **Peoriapam** or **Iowapva**. Just using your initials, though, will probably not work. There are only so many combinations of three letters!

- If you want a mysterious screen name, try to avoid obvious pop-culture monikers like **ThePhantom** or **Batman**; these will almost surely be taken, and AOL will offer a weak alternative such as **Batma7021** or some such nonsense. Choosing names from books will probably prove more productive.

- Try to think up something memorable, since you will probably want to give out your screen name to people so that they can contact you. It's much easier to remember something like **mfkfisher** than **9zamboni21**.

- Try adding to your name a number or numbers that mean something to you. For example, there are lots of Terrys out there, but you might be the only one born in 1946. So you could choose **Terry1946** as a screen name. Of course, that does give away your age!

- Descriptions can be a possible source for screen names. **HappyGuy** is a snappy name, as is **AshBlonde**. These may not prove absolutely unique, but adding a number here or there could help.

- Finally, if all else fails, consider using a hobby or pastime for your screen name: **Chess2000**, for instance. The added advantage of this is that you might be contacted by people who share your interest.

Changing Your Password

It's a good idea to change your password at least every few months to ensure the security of your account. Changing your password in AOL is easy. Just follow these steps:

1. In the My AOL Tour dialog box, click on Your Pasword.

2. Next, click on Set Up Now.

3. Another window will appear with a few instructions on changing your password. Just click on Change Password to continue. The Change Your Password dialog box will appear, as shown in Figure 3.7.

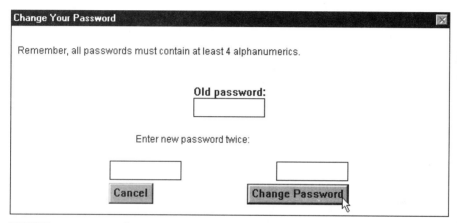

FIGURE 3.7: You can change your password anytime in the Change Your Password dialog box.

4. Type in your old password, making sure you account for any capitalization. Notice that, for security reasons, AOL will display only asterisks (*) rather than the letters or numbers of your password.

5. Now press Tab and type your new password. Press Tab again, and retype your new password. When you are finished, your screen should look like Figure 3.8.

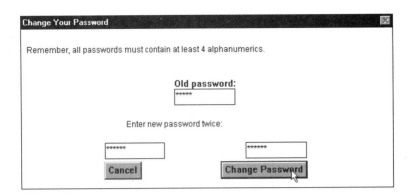

FIGURE 3.8:
When you have
typed in your old
password once
and your new
password twice,
your screen will
look like this.

6. Click on Change Password. If the two passwords you typed in the new password boxes in step 5 are not identical, you will see this dialog box:

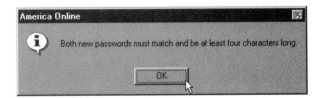

Click on OK and try again.

If the two passwords that you typed in step 5 are identical, you will instead see the following dialog box; click on OK and you're done.

That's really all there is to it. Just be sure to memorize your new password (and keep a written record away from your computer), because you'll need it next time you sign on. If you forget (or lose) your password, you can contact AOL at (800) 827-6364 and, with proper identification, they will give it out over the phone.

> **TIP**
>
> When you change your password, you must remember to also change it in the Stored Passwords area, especially if you use FlashSessions. See Chapter 6 for more details on editing stored passwords.

Parental Controls

Now that you know how to add screen names and change passwords, you might be wondering whether it's all right to add your children to your account. If you're concerned about what they might access, whom they might encounter, and how long they might stay on, your fears are legitimate. For unsophisticated users, there are a lot of pitfalls out there in both AOL and on the Internet. The Parental Controls feature may help allay your concerns somewhat.

> **WARNING**
>
> There are some undeniable perils for youngsters cruising the Internet. One study found that if a young child identifies himself or herself as such and goes into chatting areas, within 40 minutes (on average), some sicko will be trying to get the child's name, phone number, and other information. Such "cyberstalking" is, of course, a felony in all states, but it's very hard to track someone down over the Internet.

The way Parental Controls works is that the Master Account holder can set certain restrictions on any or all of the screen names, both in terms of what they can access and how long they can stay on. You can access Parental Controls only when you are online. This is so that the information resides with AOL, rather than on your computer; if it were the other way around, anyone who was limited by a control could simply sign on from another computer to circumvent your precautions.

To bring up Parental Controls, choose Members ➤ My AOL, or click on the My AOL icon on the flashbar. In the My AOL Tour window, click on Parental Controls, and then click on Set Up Now to bring up the Parental Controls dialog box shown in Figure 3.9.

To specify controls, click on the Custom Controls button to bring up the Custom Controls dialog box. Here, you can click on Chat, Downloading, or Newsgroups. When

FIGURE 3.9: You can police your account in the Parental Controls dialog box.

you do so, a red button will light up near the bottom of the screen. Try clicking on Chat now, and then click on the red Chat Controls button. This will bring up the Parental Control dialog box shown in Figure 3.10.

In this dialog box, you can click to place checkmarks in the appropriate boxes to restrict certain screen names from specific chat areas. For instance, here, I've denied Farooka and Guncel access to instant messages (among other things). When you are

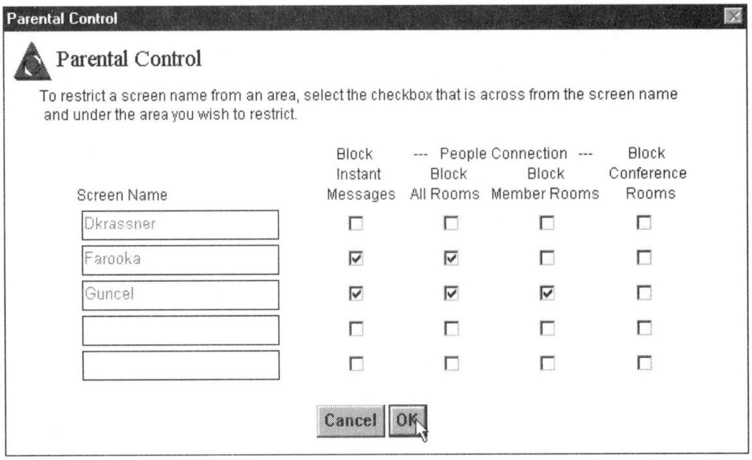

FIGURE 3.10: In this Parental Control dialog box, you can regulate all aspects of chatting for each screen name on your account.

finished placing checkmarks, click on OK. Now those screen names won't be able to use the features you restricted.

> **NOTE** You can also reach the Parental Controls dialog box from the lobby.

Clicking Block All But Kids Only in the Parental Controls dialog box brings up another dialog box, where you can choose screen names for whom *all* AOL services and features are blocked, except the For Kids Only features. (For Kids Only will be covered in Chapter 8.) When you're finished entering your settings, you can leave by clicking on OK or, for windows that have no OK button, by clicking on the close box.

> **WARNING** Only the Master Account screen name can change Parental Control settings. For this reason, it is a good idea *not* to store the password for the Master Account; otherwise anyone who has access to the machine can just go in and make changes.

Setting Your Preferences

Preferences are slightly different from the passwords, screen names, and other account management features we've been looking at up to now. Preferences refer more to how your AOL account looks and to minor options involving various features. For example, for your mailboxes, one option that you can either enable or disable is whether AOL is to retain copies of all e-mail messages you send. Another option specifies whether AOL is to open the Channels window when you sign on.

The rationale behind giving you control over all of these features is that different people will undoubtedly want their accounts to behave differently, depending upon personal preference. At any rate, it makes more sense for us cover Preferences as they arise in context (e.g., mail preferences in one of the chapters on e-mail). Therefore, we will just take a quick look at the Preferences dialog box now.

> **NOTE** Unfortunately, Preferences cannot be set individually for different screen names. The Preferences you set will be the same for all screen names on an account.

Choose Members ➤ Preferences to bring up the Preferences dialog box, shown in Figure 3.11.

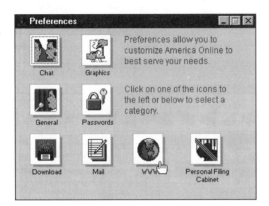

FIGURE 3.11:
You can access all Preferences settings from the Preferences dialog box.

As you can see, this dialog box is composed of buttons, each of which leads you to Preferences for certain aspects of AOL. When you are finished specifying your choices, click on the close box.

Understanding Your Bill

Now that you've gotten a chance to play around a bit with AOL and have learned a little about customizing your account, we'll conclude this chapter by checking "the bad news," as waiters always seem to call it—we'll look at the bill. First, I'll explain to you how to read your bill and understand the charges. Then I'll show you how to change your billing information.

Reading Your Billing Summary

Since your billing summary tells you how much free time you have left, as well as how much you owe, it is a good idea to understand how to read it. Let's take a look at a billing summary to see what the various parts mean. Follow these steps:

1. Access your bill by signing on and choosing Member ➤ Member Services. When you are asked if you want to access the free area, answer Yes.

TIP Whenever you are in the Member Services area, your time is free; that is, you are not charged online time for these services. By accessing Member Services, you can take a break from AOL without signing off. You'll also find a lot of helpful information in the Member Services area.

2. In the Member Services window, double-click on Account Management & Billing, as shown below.

3. This will bring up the Accounts & Billing window. Click on the Current Bill Summary button. This will in turn bring up the Current Bill Summary window, illustrated in Figure 3.12.

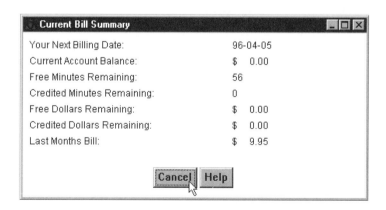

FIGURE 3.12:
You can find out how much free time you have remaining in the Current Bill Summary window.

Each field in this dialog box tells you something useful:

Your Next Billing Date—This tells you when the current billing cycle ends. Use this in conjunction with the Free Minutes Remaining information to plan your online usage.

Current Account Balance—This tells you how much over the basic rate (which is $9.95 per month for 300 minutes) you have spent. The basic rate is automatically added on the next billing date indicated above.

Free Minutes Remaining—This tells you how much of your 300 free minutes you have left to use before the next billing date. Note that you *cannot* roll over free minutes from one billing period to the next. It's a use-it-or-lose-it system.

Credited Minutes Remaining—If you have won extra free minutes of access time, either through promotional giveaways or by signing up friends with AOL, they will appear here.

Free Dollars Remaining—For some accounts, this will indicate how many minutes you have left in terms of dollars. In most cases, this will be $0.00.

Credited Dollars Remaining—If you have won extra free minutes of access time, either through promotional giveaways or by signing up friends with AOL, this amount represents the dollar equivalent.

Last Month's Bill—This indicates how much you were charged for the most recent billing period. Generally this will be $9.95, unless you've exceeded the 300 minutes.

Changing Your Billing Information

As your life changes, your billing information will change along with it. Since the billing information stored in AOL includes your name, address, and credit card or checking account number, it is a good idea to keep this information current. Otherwise, if AOL needed to reach you (because, say, someone was illegally accessing your account), they wouldn't be able to, and you might get stuck with a huge bill.

Be sure to update your billing information when any of the following occurs:

- You change your name
- You change your address
- You cancel your credit card (or bank account)
- You want to switch billing to another credit card (or bank account)

NOTE Only the Master Account name can change billing information. Other screen names will be denied access.

You must update your name and address separately from your method of billing, but the steps for both are almost identical. Let's look at how to update your billing information, as it is a bit more complicated. Follow these steps:

1. If you are not in the Member Services area, go there now.
2. In the Member Services dialog box, double-click on the topic Account Management and Billing. The Accounts & Billing dialog box will appear, as shown in Figure 3.13.

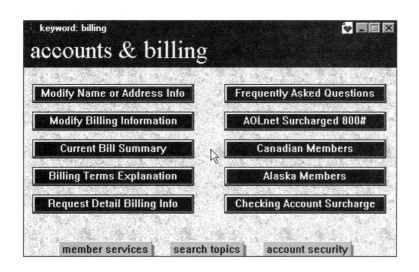

FIGURE 3.13: You can change your name and address as well as your billing information in the Accounts & Billing dialog box.

3. Click on the Modify Billing Information button. The Password Verification dialog box will appear. This is an extra precaution to prevent people from getting your credit card number or other personal information.
4. Type your password and click on Continue; the Your Choice Of Billing Method dialog box will appear, as shown in Figure 3.14.
5. Assuming you want to pay by credit card, click on that button to bring up the Credit Card Billing Option window. Then fill in the information requested.
6. When you are finished, click on Continue, and your account will now be charged to the new credit card you have specified.

TIP   You can reach the Accounts & Billing dialog box by using the keyword billing.

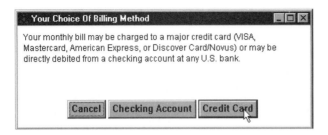

FIGURE 3.14:
You choose how AOL bills your account in this dialog box.

If you had instead wished to update your name and address, you would have clicked on the Modify Name or Address Info button in step 3 to bring up the Account Name/Address Information dialog box, shown in Figure 3.15.

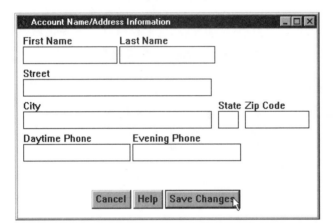

FIGURE 3.15:
If your name or address changes, be sure to update the information using the Account Name/Address Information dialog box.

As with the Credit Card Billing Option dialog box, you must fill in all information requested in the dialog box. When you are finished, click on Save Changes. AOL now has the correct information if they need to reach you. If you decide you don't wish to make changes in the Account Name/Address Information dialog box, just click on Cancel.

Part 2

Communicating
Online

Chapter 4

LEARNING TO USE E-MAIL

FEATURING

- **Addressing and sending messages**
- **Retrieving and reading mail**
- **Replying to messages**
- **Forwarding messages**
- **Setting up your Address Book**
- **Printing and deleting messages**

In Part II, which begins with this chapter, you'll really broaden your horizons as you learn several ways to communicate with others, both within the AOL community and on the much larger Internet. This is a big step, because most of the interactions we've explored so far have been between you and AOL; now you get to reach out and touch someone over the wires! In this chapter and in Chapter 5, we'll cover e-mail and instant messages. FlashSessions are discussed in Chapter 6, and last but not least, we'll cover chatting in Chapter 7.

Electronic mail, or *e-mail,* is one of the primary reasons that many people sign up with online services like America Online. E-mail is similar to regular mail (what some now call *snail mail*), in that your correspondents have addresses where you send correspondence to them. However, e-mail is far superior to the regular mail service in its speed, ease, and consistency.

Whereas a regular, handwritten letter takes a few days, e-mail is almost instantaneous. For instance, I once sent a message to someone in Dunedin, New Zealand, and received a response back within two hours! The only things that slow down electronic messages are *gateways* (see the sidebar, *A Word on Confidentiality*, ahead). Also, for regular mail, if someone moves, you need to get their new address before you can send anything to them. With e-mail, though, the physical location of a correspondent is unimportant; no matter where people are, you always send messages to the same address. Finally, perhaps the biggest advantage of e-mail is that it is so easy to use.

E-Mail Is Easy

Just how much easier is e-mail? Think about all the steps you have to take to write a normal letter. First, you have to find paper and a pen. Then you have to write the letter (and most people write much more slowly than they type). Next, you have to find an envelope, a stamp, and the address book that contains your recipient's address. If you're sending a letter abroad, there's always a chance that you haven't used the correct postage. And, of course, you can't send or receive letters on Sundays and holidays.

E-mail eliminates most of these steps. About the only thing you have to do with e-mail messages is write them. And if your handwriting is anywhere near as bad as mine, the typewritten word is a boon. Furthermore, e-mail allows you to do things that you can't easily do with regular messages, such as sending or forwarding a message to many recipients.

> **NOTE** Don't abandon letter writing altogether. If you handwrite even a few letters now and then, it will probably make you unique in your circle, and handwritten letters can be fun to save and reread years later.

The reason e-mail is so easy is that most of the steps involved in writing a real letter are automated by your e-mail program. AOL has several intuitive e-mail features that make sending and receiving messages a snap. (We'll cover the basic ones in this chapter and the advanced e-mail features in Chapter 5.) And, of course, the only cost

The Drawbacks of E-mail

E-mail is not without its feet of clay. Like regular mail, there is always the risk of your message getting lost or misdirected. Unlike real mail, there are issues of confidentiality, as discussed on the next page. And unlike real mail, you lose that intangible thrill of holding a handwritten note. Even if you print out your messages, it's not quite the same. For this and other reasons, e-mail will never fully replace paper mail, no matter how advanced and minuscule computers may become.

If you doubt this, consider books. Any published book can easily be put on a computer disk. And there are some computers that are now as small as some oversized books. Yet people just don't read books on their computers.

Finally, and perhaps most obvious, are the physical limitations of e-mail: you can generally send only text messages, and of course, you must have a computer. True, you can attach pictures (as files), but you cannot send books, gifts, furniture, or other nonmessage items over e-mail. Furthermore, you *cannot* receive anything you've mail-ordered at your e-mail address. Just try to have L.L. Bean deliver snowboots to you over the Internet and see how far you get!

associated with any message, no matter whom it is directed to, is the time it takes to send it.

Okay, enough lecturing. Let's get on to the nuts and bolts of e-mail, starting with composing messages.

Composing a New Message

Most of the time, when you start a message, you will simply choose the recipient's e-mail address (or the addresses of multiple recipients) from a list you've set up in your AOL Address book. Or perhaps you've found an address in a magazine, or someone has given you an e-mail address on a business card. To get into these topics, though, would be putting the cart before the horse, because you really need to understand how to send messages before moving on to setting up your Address Book.

A Word on Confidentiality

Nothing on the Internet is confidential. Period.

This may sound like a sweeping generalization. In fact, it *is* a sweeping generalization. Unfortunately, it's also true. Just look through the "header" information in an Internet message some time to see how many electronic hands (called *gateways*) your message has passed through. If that's not enough to convince you, consider this. Many companies *routinely* read messages sent to and from employees. This practice, though nefarious, has been upheld in the courts; electronic mail sent and received at a business is considered the property of that business. It is therefore not a violation of your constitutional rights for your employer to read your messages. For this reason, it's better not to receive personal messages at work.

And if you think coding (encrypting) your messages is the answer, think again. A couple of years ago, the military hired some crack hackers to try to break their new "unbreakable" encryption scheme, which they'd been working on for years. Military intelligence had estimated it would take the hackers two weeks to break the code. They broke it in 45 minutes. I'm not certain what this proves about the relative intelligence of computer hackers and military programmers; it does, however, prove that nothing is confidential on the Internet. For the same reasons, nothing is confidential on AOL.

The best practice to follow, therefore, is never to send anything out over the Internet that you wouldn't mind seeing posted to the lunchroom bulletin board or your local post office—with your name on it. Generally speaking, people who read other people's romantic e-mail messages are not the ones to worry about. The people you *should* worry about are those who intercept private and possibly confidential business information. So when in doubt, send it by regular mail. Then you only have to worry about the FBI.

So, as an exercise, why not try sending a message to someone you know will respond: me! If you've never used e-mail before, my address might be the only one you know. Never fear, though, you will soon have so many addresses you won't know what to do with them.

Before you begin addressing and composing messages, though, you'll need to start a new message in AOL. There are several ways to do this, the easiest of which is to simply click on the Compose Mail icon in the flashbar.

Alternatively, you can choose Mail ➤ Compose Mail, or use the Ctrl+M keyboard shortcut. Either way, you'll see the Compose Mail window shown in Figure 4.1. The important parts of this window are labeled to guide you. We'll go over each part in detail.

TIP You don't need to go online to compose messages. In fact, it's better to compose them *offline*, because then you're not using up valuable online time while you're thinking and typing. Once you're finished, you can sign on and send all new messages or use FlashSessions (discussed in Chapter 6).

Addressing Messages

E-mail addresses come in many shapes and sizes. Generally, though, they follow certain rules. All addresses have this basic structure:

`username@site.servicename.type`

Let's break this down into its component parts:

Username—This is the unique name (at that service) that designates the person to whom you are sending the message. You might have people on different services (e.g., CompuServe and AOL) with identical usernames, but you will never find two individuals with the same username on the same service. (Your username in AOL is your screen name.)

@—The "at" sign separates the username from the service and site information.

Site—An optional portion of the address, the site might be the server that is dedicated to e-mail or it might be someone's own computer. Often, the people

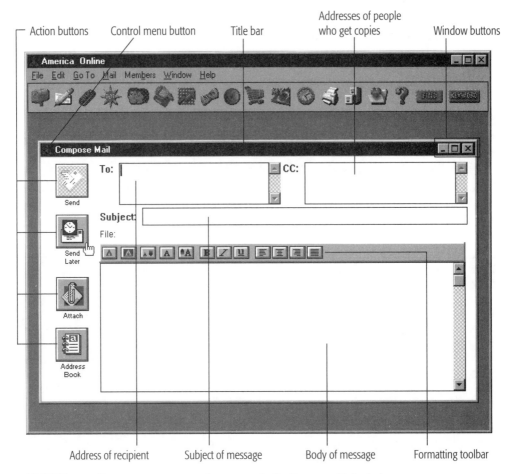

FIGURE 4.1: You compose new e-mail messages in the Compose Mail window.

in charge of e-mail servers come up with creative and amusing names for them, such as *gandalf* and *mailserve*.

NOTE The site, servicename, and type—in other words, everything *after* the @ sign—is often called the *domain* of the address.

Servicename—This is a necessary but variable part of the address. If the individual to whom you are writing is on one of the online services, this is where the name of that service goes. For example, the *aol* in my address designates it as being on the America Online service. If your addressee is on CompuServe, this part will read *cserve*. If the person is at a business or institution (such as a university or foundation), then *that* information will appear here. For example, in a message to the publisher of this book, the servicename would be *Sybex;* if you're writing to someone at Bryn Mawr College, it would be *brynmawr.*

Type—The type is determined by what appears in the servicename slot. If the address is at a university or college, usually the type will be *edu*. If the address is at a business or service, the type will usually be *com*. Government agencies have the type *gov*. For instance, Bill Clinton's e-mail address is *president@ whitehouse.gov. President* is his unique username, *whitehouse* is the server, and *gov* is the type. Bet you never imagined it would be so easy to write to the President! Go ahead, write him a message; tell him how you feel about some issue or other. You'll learn how in a few moments.

There will be variations to this structure, because there are few hard-and-fast rules about e-mail addresses. The most important aspect of an address is, of course, that it be unique, so that your messages don't end up going to the wrong people. And any unusual aspects of addresses will often be quite intuitive. For instance, if it is a foreign address, you might see a country code (such as *uk* for the United Kingdom).

Okay, let's get back to the Compose Mail window. The To box is where you tell AOL who is to receive the message, keeping in mind the addressing structures we just discussed. The cursor always starts in this box when you bring up the Compose Mail window. If you had any addresses in your Address Book, you could open it now and automatically insert one or several addresses. But let's keep it simple. Address the message either to me or to yourself, by simply typing in your own screen name, or by typing **dkrassner@aol.com**.

Since you are sending a message within AOL, you technically don't need the part of the address after the screen name (*@aol.com*); you could get away with simply typing my or your own screen name. It doesn't hurt to put it in, though.

You might be wondering how your recipient will know whom the message is coming from. Well, when he or she retrieves the message, there will be an additional From line with your e-mail address. As you will soon see, this makes it easy for the person to respond to your message. When you are finished typing, press Tab to take the cursor to the CC box.

> **TIP**
> You can send e-mail to more than one recipient. To do so, simply separate different e-mail addresses with commas.

Cc'ing Messages

The Cc box works the same as the To box, but its function is slightly different. In the Cc box, you place the addresses of people whom you wish to receive the message but who don't necessarily need to respond to it. For instance, you might Cc your boss on a message to a client, just so he or she knows what you're doing. It's also considered good etiquette to Cc someone if you mention them in a message to someone else. And then there are all the usual reasons you would Cc people on a regular paper memo: keeping them abreast of projects, keeping a paper trail, etc.

> **TIP**
> There are times when you might want to send a *blind Cc* to someone. A blind Cc is a copy you send that you don't want the main recipient (the person in the To field) to know about. To send a blind Cc, surround the recipient's name in the Cc box with parentheses.

To place an address in the Cc field, simply type it in. If you typed my address in the To box, try typing in your own address in the Cc box. Now you will get a copy of the message you are sending to me.

> **NOTE**
> There is actually a better way than Cc'ing yourself to ensure that you have a copy of a message you send out; AOL has a settings option that allows you to automatically keep copies of all messages you send. See Chapter 5.

When you are finished typing the name, press Tab again to send the cursor into the Subject area.

The Subject Line

In the AOL Compose Mail window, you must type a subject line for your message. Some mail programs allow you to leave this blank (in which case, the recipient gets a message called *untitled* or some such), but not AOL. And it really is a courtesy to your addressee to give the message a meaningful subject line. Many people get dozens or even hundreds of messages every day. It's a real nuisance to them if they get messages that give no indication of how important they are or what they're about. So always try to think up a short but descriptive subject line. This can range from *Price quote you requested* to *Thursday okay for lunch?*

For now, fill in the subject line in such a way that the recipient (probably me) will know what the message is about. When you are done, press Tab to move the cursor into the large text box of the Compose Mail window.

Typing the Body of the Message

Now that you've got your message properly addressed and designated with a good, descriptive subject line, you can get to the real point of the whole thing, which is the body of the message itself. There are no limits to what you can write as the body of the message, although good taste might dictate some parameters. There are, furthermore, no space limitations, as the box will expand as you type.

For business e-mail, you should try to be as formal as you would be if you were typing a paper memo or letter. Keep in mind that it is very difficult to express *tone* in electronic messages. I've learned the hard way that people often cannot tell if you are joking. The reason for this limitation is that, with e-mail, the only thing the recipient sees is the text. That's all. Often there is no formatting to highlight words the way you can do in a paper memo. Also—and this might be obvious but it is worth stating—the recipient has no idea what mood you were in when you wrote the message, because they cannot see your facial expressions or hear the inflection in your voice. Better safe than sorry is a good philosophy to follow, by spelling things out clearly and simply rather than risking offense.

Personal e-mail comes down to your individual tastes and discretion. If you know someone well enough, you can probably get away with anything you want to say. But once again, be aware of people's feelings and realize that they cannot hear how you are saying what they are reading in cold type.

With these caveats in mind, let's look at a few methods that you actually *can* use to highlight words or otherwise add some tone to your messages.

Highlighting Words and Phrases

AOL comes with a wonderful collection of formatting options that you can use to liven up your e-mail messages. There's one drawback, though: many e-mail services will be unable to interpret this formatting. Thus, sending formatted messages to other AOL members is fine; but don't be surprised if formatted messages you send to any-one else arrive with the formatting stripped out or turned to gibberish. Given this limi-tation, we'll defer a full discussion of AOL's formatting features until Chapter 5, focusing here on some highlighting options that always work.

There are several accepted ways to highlight words and phrases in e-mail mes-sages. Remember, it's very likely that your message will reach its recipient with none of your original formatting, perhaps not even correct line breaks. But if you want to highlight a word, the best way to do so is to surround it with asterisks, like *this*. This is not exactly pretty, the way italics or boldface would be, but as mentioned above, such formatting is often lost; so to be on the safe side, use this method. It's best to avoid using ALL CAPITALS to get attention, as capital letters, by convention, indicate that you are YELLING, and you might offend someone.

WARNING Avoid using special characters in your e-mail messages. The Internet is not kind to some of them, and uses others for its own purposes. Even symbols like £, ®, and $^1/_2$, which are easy to insert in most word-processing programs, will probably not survive the trip through cyberspace.

Acronyms

Since everyone seems to be pressed for time these days, an e-mail shorthand of *acronyms* has sprung up, along with *emoticons* (discussed next), to make the task of message writing go more quickly. An acronym is a word made up of the initial let-ters of other words. For instance, the word *scuba,* as in scuba diving, is an acronym for **s**elf-**c**ontained **u**nderwater **b**reathing **a**pparatus. Since the latter phrase is a mouthful, especially underwater, enthusiasts of the pastime have shortened it to simply *scuba.* There are scads of e-mail acronyms, and many people like to invent their own.

Following is a list of common acronyms, and a few I've made up:

Acronym	Meaning
ASAP	As soon as possible
ATB	All the best
BTW	By the way
CMF	Crossing my fingers
CU	See you
CUL8R	See you later
CYM	Clear your mind
DIY	Do it yourself
FYI	For your information
GMTA	Great minds think alike
IMHO	In my humble opinion
LOL	Laughing out loud
MYOB	Mind your own business
RTFM	Read the [colorful epithet] manual
SOW	Speaking of which
TTFN	Ta-ta for now
WRT	With respect to

TIP   If you receive a message from someone that includes an acronym you don't recognize, just ask! Most people are proud of their acronyms.

Emoticons

No one knows who invented *emoticons,* but they are clever little composites that you can use to convey a certain mood. These are quite useful, given that there is no other nonverbal way to express moods with e-mail. An emoticon is several typed characters that are intended to resemble an icon. The most common is the happy face:

:^)

To see this emoticon properly, tilt your head to the left. See the eyes, nose, and smiling mouth? Here is a list of a few of the more common emoticons:

Emoticon	Name	Meaning
:^)	Happy face	I'm happy!
:^(	Sad face	I'm bummed
:^|	Unemotional	I'm on an even keel
:^D	Laughing	That's funny!
;^)	Winking	We have a secret
|^O	Sleepy face	I'm tired
:^*	Kissing	(Obvious…)
:^p	Sticking tongue out	Nyah, nyah, nyah!
*<:^)	Party hat	Let's celebrate!
:^?	Confused	What?
:^#	Lips sealed	Keep this in confidence
:)	Simple face	I'm simply happy!
:*)	Clown face	Just kidding around

There are hundreds and hundreds of emoticons. In fact, there are entire books dedicated to them! Feel free to invent your own, although if they're somewhat obscure, you might have to explain them. Also, be aware that some e-mail users *hate* emoticons and will tell you so in no uncertain terms.

Signing Your Messages

When you are satisfied that the body of your message is acceptable, you must decide how to sign off. Once again, if the message is a business message, you'll probably want to be formal and sign with your full name on one line, and your title on the line below. If it's not clear from the message, you may even want to add a third line with the name of your company, as shown here.

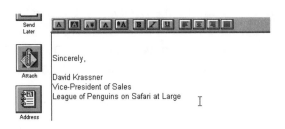

You can sign personal messages with just your first name or even a nickname, since your recipient probably will know whom the message is from by reading the From line. Right now, sign off your message using your full name and your company name or the city and state in which you live.

Sending a New Message

When you are satisfied with your message and have filled in all of the text fields, you are ready to send your message. You can either send the message later if you composed it offline or send it right away if you composed it online.

Using Send Later Offline

If you've been composing the message offline, as I recommended, click on the Send Later button on the left-hand side of the Compose Mail window.

When you do this, you will see a small dialog box informing you that you can send this message using a FlashSession. You will learn more about FlashSessions in Chapter 6. For now, just click on OK. If you want to write more messages, repeat the steps you followed to compose the first message.

When you are ready to send your message, follow these steps:

1. Start AOL, or switch to it if it is already running.
2. Be sure that your regular sign-on name appears in the Screen Name box of the Welcome window, enter your password, and click on Sign On.
3. Once you're online, choose Mail ➤ Read Outgoing Mail. The Outgoing FlashMail window will appear, as shown in Figure 4.2.

NOTE   Even if you're not using FlashSessions, you will still see your outgoing mail in the Outgoing FlashMail dialog box. Using FlashSessions, however, will automate this entire operation. See Chapter 6 for details.

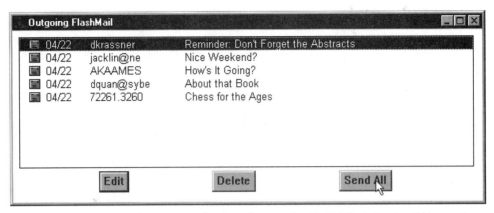

FIGURE 4.2: You can send messages online from the Outgoing FlashMail window by clicking on the Send All button.

4. Click on the Send All button to send the messages.

5. Unless you wish to browse further, choose Go To ➤ Sign Off, and then click on Yes in the dialog box.

Sending while Online

If you were composing the message online, click on the Send button, and the message will be on its way. You will see a little dialog box telling you that your message has been sent.

> **NOTE** If you are not signed on to AOL and you click on Send, nothing will happen. Furthermore, until you actually sign on to AOL and send the message, it resides on your computer's hard disk and doesn't go anywhere.

Sending Mail to Internet Sites

Take a look at my Incoming FlashMail window, shown in Figure 4.3. Notice that all the messages but one are from services other than AOL. For instance, the first message is from someone at CompuServe. Two other messages are from servers at universities (the University of Maryland and Bryn Mawr College). The others are from business sites, except for the ones marked *Mailer-daemon* with subject lines reading

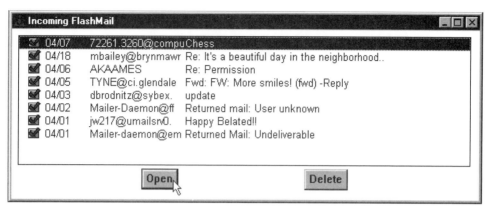

FIGURE 4.3: Most of these messages originated outside AOL.

Returned mail: User unknown and *Returned Mail: Undeliverable*. We will look at what to do with these last two items a little bit later.

NOTE As always, your screen will look slightly different from mine, since we will have sent and received messages from different people.

For now, consider that most of these messages did not come from AOL. You might be wondering how they got to me in the first place. The answer is that they traveled via the Internet to reach their destination. As a general rule, when you're sending e-mail from within AOL, any other site apart from AOL is called an *Internet site*. For these sites, you must know the correct servicename to ensure your mail gets to the right person.

NOTE A *bounced* message is one that is returned to you without the recipient ever having seen it. Naturally, you want to avoid having messages bounced back to you.

Following is a list of the proper way to address messages (sent from within AOL) to some of the more popular services:

AOL—*username* (you do not have to include the *aol.com*)

CompuServe—*nnnnn.nnnn*@compuserve.com, where *nnnnn.nnnn* is based on the username *nnnnn,nnnn*. Notice that the comma in the CompuServe address is replaced with a period when addressing that person from within AOL.

Delphi—*username*@delphi.com

MCI Mail—*nnn-nnnn*@mcimail.com, where *nnn-nnnn* is the phone number

Prodigy—*username*@prodigy.com

Most Companies—*username*@*company*.com

Most Universities and Colleges—*username*@*university*.edu

In case you're wondering, when you send messages to other AOL users, the messages are *not* traveling via the Internet; they are simply traversing the AOL network of computers. This is why you don't have to include the name or type of service in messages to other AOL users. A screen name will suffice (the part before the @ sign), because every AOL screen name is unique, so there's no chance of a message going to the wrong person.

TIP	If you are unsure about how to address a message, ask the individual to e-mail you first; then you can reply to that message without even having to know how to address your message.

Reading Mail

Now that you've learned how to send e-mail, you can almost certainly expect to get replies to your messages. Assuming you have some e-mail waiting (and if you're using AOL for the first time, there is always some kind of welcome message sent to your address), let's now look at how you can read it. If you don't have any mail, either write to me and I'll write back, or send yourself a test message, as described earlier in the section "Sending a New Message."

To read your new messages, follow these steps:

1. Start AOL, or switch to it if it is already running.
2. Be sure that your regular sign-on name appears in the Screen Name box of the Welcome window, enter your password, and click on Sign On. Once you're online, you'll know right away whether you have mail by looking at

Headers

It is worthwhile stepping back for a moment to look at *headers*. A header is an information table about a message that tells you, among other things, who sent you the message, when they sent it, to whom it was addressed, when it was retrieved, whether it's been forwarded and from whom, what route it took to get to you, and the subject line.

In an AOL message, the header always appears at the bottom, separate from the rest of the message by the word *Headers,* as shown here.

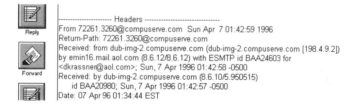

The utility of headers is that, if a message has been returned to you as undeliverable, as the one shown above has, you can trace it to see what went wrong. Sometimes, you won't be able to tell what the problem was, but it's still worth checking before resending or trying the help line. And even if much of the header information is indecipherable to you, it might be of use to a network manager trying to spot a problem.

Mailer-Daemons

If you look closely at two of the messages in the dialog box pictured back in Figure 4.3, you will see two *mailer-daemons* in action, as shown below.

A *daemon* is a small program that usually serves some mundane function. A *mailer-daemon* is a program that automatically checks messages coming into (or going out of) a site to ensure that there is in fact someone with the username indicated or that there is a service with the indicated site name.

When a mailer-daemon comes across a message that has an unrecognized username (i.e., one not assigned to anyone at its site) or site name, the program *bounces* the message back to the sender for repairs. Often, the problem will just be a mistyped address. This problem can be eliminated by using an Address Book, discussed toward the end of this chapter.

The two types of daemons shown in Figure 4.3 are labeled *User unknown* and *Undeliverable*. The former means that the message reached the site (the business or institution where it was supposed to go), but there was no user there by that name. The latter indicates that the message never even reached the site, usually because the site's server was down or because you typed it in wrong. In either of these cases, the usual remedy is double-checking the address to make sure you typed it correctly.

If you correct a message, resend it, and get it back again, you might have some wrong information about the address. Try calling the recipient or asking someone else who might have the correct address. If worse comes to worse and you just can't find the proper address, you might be able to locate the person using the Internet feature called Netfind, discussed in Chapter 11.

Replying to Messages

Replying to an e-mail message is similar to answering a letter. Someone writes you to say hi; you write back. Someone writes you with a question; you reply with an answer. You get the idea.

There are several variations on replying. The first is to incorporate the original message into your reply. To do this, highlight the original message in its window (or at least as much as you'd like to have in your reply), and click on the Reply button.

Another message window will appear, where you can type your responses to the original message, as shown in Figure 4.6.

As you can see in Figure 4.6, several things have happened. First, you now have a message box that is almost identical to the one you saw when you were first learning how to send new messages. Second, the To field is already filled in with the address of the individual who sent you the original message. Also, the subject line of the original

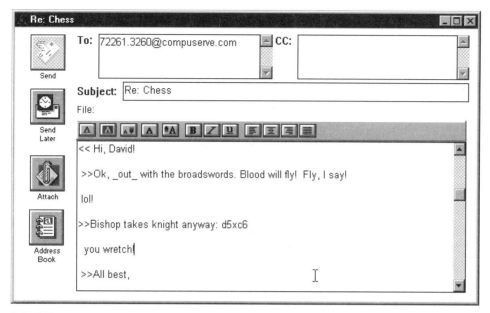

FIGURE 4.6: You can type your response to a message in another message box like this one.

message has been placed in the Subject field with the letters *Re:* in front of it. The rationale behind this is that, if you reply to this message using conventional methods, when the person who sent you the original sees your message, they will immediately know it is an answer to *their* message.

Notice also that whatever you highlighted in the original message window before clicking on Reply is now in your message, set off by angle brackets (<< >>) at the beginning and end. You can do a couple of things at this point: you can intercalate (insert) your own responses in between lines of the original message, as I have done, or you can place your entire message after (or before) the copied message.

> **WARNING** Always be sure to ask your correspondents if they mind the intercalation method. Some people find this annoying or distracting, so it's best to ask first.

A simpler way to respond to a message is to just click on the Reply button. This also opens a message window, but without any of the text of the original message. This makes for cleaner messages (i.e., it's easier for your recipients to see immediately what you're saying), but if your recipient has forgotten what he or she wrote, it might be confusing!

However you do it, once you've typed your response, just click on the Send Later button, and then follow the steps outlined earlier in the section "Using Send Later Offline."

Forwarding Messages

The difference between replying to a message and *forwarding* a message is that, when you reply to a message, you are sending a response to the person who sent you the message; when you forward a message, you are sending the original message to a third party.

Forward

To forward a message, you must have it open. Open a message now by double-clicking it. Then click on the Forward button.

You will again see a message window, only now the To field is empty; unlike replies, where the reply went to the originator of the message, AOL cannot guess whom you wish to forward the message to. Fill in this box with the address of the person to whom you wish to forward the message, as shown in Figure 4.7. If you don't know anyone else's address, just forward the message to yourself or to me.

Also unlike a reply, there is no text in the window. So where's the forwarded message, you ask? Well, you don't actually see it. What you can type in the text area of this window are prefacing comments to the message. These will be separated from the forwarded message in such a way that it will be clear to your recipient which are your comments and what constituted the original message.

When you have typed your prefacing comments (if you wish to include any), click on Send Later, and then follow the steps outlined earlier in the section "Using Send Later Offline."

Setting Up Your Address Book

Just as you have an actual address book in order to look up phone numbers and mailing addresses, you can also have an electronic address book in AOL to keep track of e-mail addresses you use often. This feature is very handy, since it saves you the effort of having to remember and type up addresses for every message you send, and

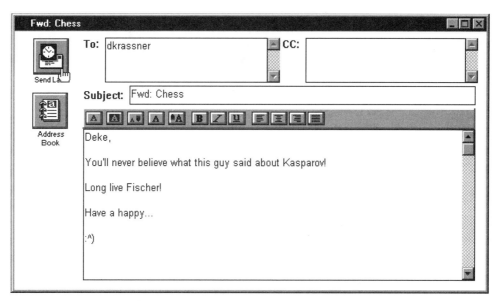

FIGURE 4.7: You can type prefacing comments in the forwarded message window.

it should cut down on the number of messages bounced back to you because of typos in the address.

Adding Names to Your Address Book

To add names to your AOL Address Book, follow these steps:

1. Start AOL, or switch to it if it's already running.
2. Choose Mail ➤ Edit Address Book. The Address Book dialog box will appear, as shown in Figure 4.8.

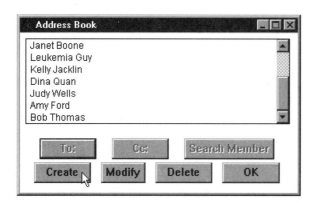

FIGURE 4.8:
You add names and addresses in the Address Book dialog box.

3.   Click on the Create button to open the Address Group dialog box.

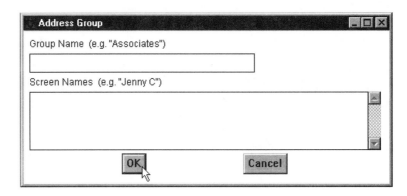

4.   Type the name of the person in the Group Name box. Or, if you wish to have several people grouped under one name, type the name of the group (e.g., *Marketing*).

5.   Type the e-mail address of the individual, or type multiple addresses if it is a group with more than one screen name.

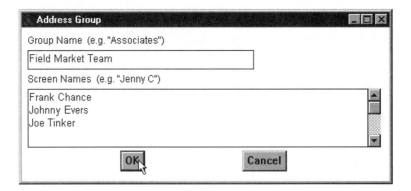

6.   Click on OK. The name (or names) you have added will now appear in your Address Book, as shown below.

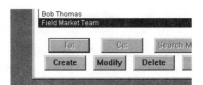

Editing Your Address Book

From time to time, you'll need to remove names from your address book that you no longer use, or update any names or addresses that have changed. To delete a name from your address book, choose Mail ➤ Edit Address Book to open the Address Book dialog box; then simply select the name, and click on Delete.

To edit a name, select it and click on Modify; this will open the Modify dialog box, where you can make your changes. Click on OK when you're finished.

Using Your Address Book

To use your Address Book to place an address in a message, follow these steps:

1. Start AOL, or switch to it if it's already running.
2. Either choose Mail ➤ Compose Mail, or click on the Compose Mail icon to bring up the Compose Mail window.
3. Click on the Address Book icon to bring up the Address Book.

4. Click on the name you wish to place in the To box, and then click on the To button. (Note that if mail is sent to a group name, all individuals who have been defined as members of the group will receive the message.)

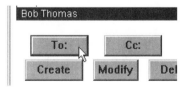

5. If you wish to add other names, repeat step 4.

6. If you wish to add a name to the Cc box, select it and click on the Cc button.

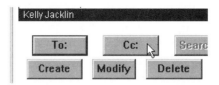

7. If you wish to add other names to the Cc box, repeat step 6.
8. When you are finished, click on OK.

WARNING You cannot insert an address into any field other than the To or Cc field. If you try to do so, AOL will give you an electronic wrist slap.

Printing Messages

There are many reasons why you might want to print out a message. The most obvious is that you want to keep a hard copy of the message for your records. But you might also want to print out directions someone has sent you so you can take them with you, or you might wish to post a funny or informative article on the lunchroom bulletin board. Regardless of your reason, printing an e-mail message is easy.

NOTE You must be hooked up to a printer to get a hard copy of your message. Just because you're hooked up to a modem doesn't mean you're hooked up to a printer.

To print an open message, either choose File ➤ Print (Ctrl+P), or click on the Print icon on the flashbar.

Your message will then print out to the default printer (the printer your computer is hooked up to, if any).

> **WARNING** Use common sense when printing out messages, especially if you are printing private messages at work. You never know who might get to the printer before you do or when your message will get sent to the wrong printer.

Deleting Messages

Eventually, you will receive so many messages that you will want to delete some or all of them. You can delete messages in piecemeal fashion, in bulk, or even as you read them. There are three ways to delete messages: in the Personal Filing Cabinet, in the Incoming FlashMail window, and in the actual message windows themselves. Let's look at all three.

We'll look at the Personal Filing Cabinet in a lot more detail in Chapter 5. For now, let's just see how to delete a message in the Personal Filing Cabinet. Choose Mail ➤ Personal Filing Cabinet; then select the message you wish to delete and click on the Delete button, as shown here.

To delete a message from the Incoming FlashMail window, choose Mail ➤ Read Incoming Mail. Then select the message you wish to delete and click on the Delete button, as shown below.

To delete a message from a message window, open the message (either from the Personal Filing Cabinet or from the Incoming FlashMail window) by double-clicking on it. Then click on the Delete button, as shown here.

Whichever way you choose to murder the message, you will get the following confirmation dialog box.

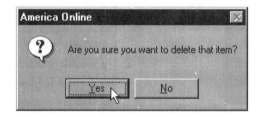

Click on Yes to delete the message.

Chapter 5

BECOMING AN E-MAIL POWER USER

FEATURING

- **Formatting your messages**
- **Editing and saving messages**
- **Attaching documents to messages**
- **Rereading mail you've already sent or received**
- **Sending and responding to instant messages**
- **Sending faxes and paper mail**
- **Using the Download Manager**
- **Archiving messages with Personal Filing Cabinet**
- **Setting Mail Preferences**

In Chapter 4, you learned the rudiments of e-mail, including how to compose and send messages, read and respond to incoming mail, and forward messages. In this chapter, we'll look at some more advanced e-mail features. You'll learn how to format your messages with AOL's many text-attribute options, edit messages you've already finished, attach files to messages, and review mail that you've already sent, even if you didn't keep a copy.

You'll also find out how to send and receive instant messages, send faxes, and organize your downloads with the Download Manager. Finally, we'll look the Personal Filing Cabinet, an excellent way to organize all your archived messages. Let's dig right in with formatting.

Formatting Your Messages

As mentioned in Chapter 4, formatting will often be lost as your messages wend their way across the Internet. If you are sending messages to other AOL members, though, you have an impressive array of formatting options at your fingertips. As you can see in Figure 5.1, there are no fewer than 12 formatting options.

When you position the cursor over one of the formatting icons, a Tooltip pops up to let you know what that icon does. Let's look at each option in some detail so you get a sense of what they do and how you can make the best use of them. For sake of simplicity, I'm going to assume that you have the Message Compose window open and are writing a new message.

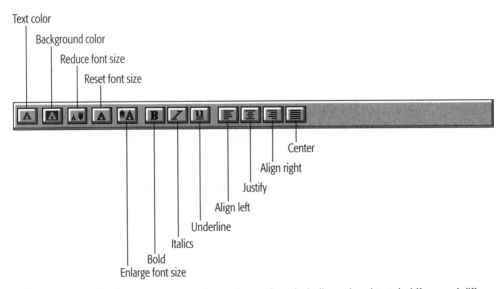

FIGURE 5.1: AOL offers you numerous formatting options, including colored text, boldface, and different font sizes.

Colors

Your first choices are the color of your text and the color of your background. While text color is obvious, background color might not be. The background is everything inside the box where you type your messages.

WARNING Use common sense when changing the background and text colors. For instance, it is not a good idea to make them the same color, because then the text won't be visible.

To change the color of the text in an open message, highlight the text you want to change, and click on the Text Color icon on the toolbar. This will bring up the Color dialog box shown in Figure 5.2.

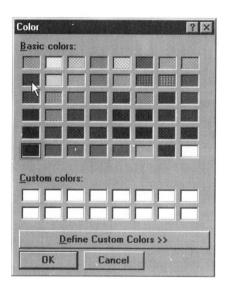

FIGURE 5.2:
You can change the color of your text in the Color dialog box.

Since the customary use of text color is to highlight a word or phrase, your best bet is to choose a bright red or orange. Darker colors tend to be hard to distinguish from black. Yellow doesn't show up well on a white background, but it does show up wonderfully on a blue background. For now, click on one of the basic colors, and then click on OK. Notice that your text has now taken on the color you assigned.

Now let's change the background. Click on the Background Color icon on the tool-bar to bring up the same Color dialog box shown in Figure 5.2. Choose a color, and click on OK. Your background will change, as shown below.

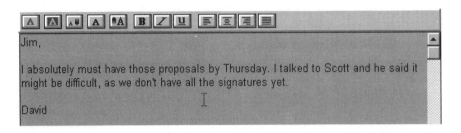

As you experiment, you'll find that some backgrounds are hideous, others annoying, and others make your text downright illegible. But a few work nicely. For example, blue provides nice contrast, especially with white or yellow text.

TIP You can choose a custom color in the Color dialog box by clicking on Define Custom Colors >>. When you do this, another palette will appear. Click to select a color, and then click on Add to Custom Colors. Your chosen color is added to the Colors dialog box, where you can then choose it as you did the basic colors by simply clicking to select it and clicking on OK.

Font Size

If you've ever used a word processing program, you're probably familiar with font sizes. The Enlarge, Reset, and Reduce Font icons all do exactly what you'd expect them to do: change the size of your text. If you have a hard time reading small print, you might try enlarging the text. To do so, simply highlight the text and click on the Enlarge Font icon.

Similarly, you can shrink down text that you may be trying to fit within one screen with the Reduce Font icon. If you don't like your changes, you can always click on Reset Font to change everything back to its original settings.

Boldface, Italic, and Underline

These are the options you use to highlight words and phrases of particular importance. In the example here, the word *must* has been emphasized by putting it in boldface.

To use these formatting options, highlight the text you want to emphasize, and click on the appropriate icon on the toolbar.

Alignment

Another way to make phrases stand out is to use one of the four alignment options:

- Left align
- Right align
- Center
- Justify

Left align (the default setting) and right align are similar in that they run the text right up to the left or right edge of the box where you type messages. The center option is just what it sounds like—the text will be centered within the text box, with an equal amount of space on either side. Justify is a little more difficult to explain in words, so let's look at a picture:

The paragraph shown above has been justified. Notice that all the words on both the right- and left-hand sides reach all the way to the edge of your text box. This is accomplished by adjusting the amount of spacing between the words. Keep in mind, however, that many people find justified text hard to read. So unless you have a very good reason, it's difficult to (ahem) justify using justified text in an e-mail message.

Right-Clicking Shortcuts

As you may know, when you right-click (that is, click the nonprimary button on your mouse) in many programs, you often see pop-up menus with a number of options.

AOL is no exception. You can use these *right-clicking shortcuts* to perform many different functions, including formatting messages. If you find yourself in the midst of composing a message and want to highlight a word, just select it and right-click. A pop-up menu will appear with all of the formatting options we discussed above, as shown in Figure 5.3.

TIP

There is a nifty way to send your e-mail friends hypertext links within messages. As you are composing a message, select the text you wish to serve as the hypertext; then right-click and select Create Hyperlink. This will bring up a dialog box where you can type the URL (see Chapter 10 for more on URLs and hypertext). Then your correspondent can simply click on the text to be taken directly to the site you have specified as a link in your message.

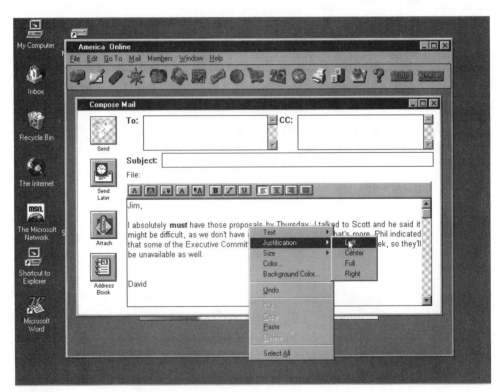

FIGURE 5.3: When you right-click, a menu will pop up with a variety of formatting options and other commands.

To choose any option, just slide the highlight bar up to the desired format and click. Notice that the commands also include Cut, Copy, and Paste, making it easy for you to move text around in your messages.

> **TIP**
>
> If you are left-handed (or perhaps just a nonconformist), you might have reconfigured your computer such that your *right* mouse button is your primary button, in which case you need to *left-click* in the above instructions.

Editing and Saving Messages

As you were learning the ins and outs of composing messages, you might have wondered whether there was any way to make changes to a message already clicked into the Outgoing FlashMail window. Or, better yet, if there was a way to save messages (especially lengthy ones) to avoid losing your work in the event that your computer hung up.

The answer to both of these questions is yes. And it's really quite easy.

> **NOTE**
>
> Even though you won't be learning about FlashMail until Chapter 6, I'll be referring to it throughout this chapter, as that is what AOL calls almost all of the Mail windows.

Editing and Saving Outgoing Messages

A common scenario might be the following: you have composed a message and clicked on Send Later, only to realize that you forgot to include some vital piece of information. This is painless to remedy. Follow these steps:

1. Choose Mail ➤ Read Outgoing Mail. The Outgoing FlashMail dialog box will appear, as shown in Figure 5.4, looking almost identical to the Incoming FlashMail dialog box. The two mail windows function the same way; you can open or delete a message in either window. What we want to do, of course, is to open an outgoing message and make changes.

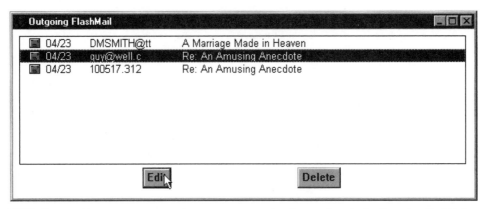

FIGURE 5.4: You can reopen outgoing messages to make changes here in the Outgoing FlashMail dialog box.

2. To open an outgoing message and make changes, either double-click on the message of your choice, or select the message and click on Edit. A window that looks like the Compose Mail window will open. There are a couple of important differences, though. First, the title bar of the window will reflect the subject line, reading *Re:* and then whatever you had typed as the subject. The other difference is that, instead of Send and Send Later buttons, there is a Save Changes button.

3. Edit any aspect of your saved message, including the To and CC boxes, the same way you composed it in the first place. You can also add text to the body of the message. This window includes the Address Book button so that you can easily change the address of the message.

4. When you are finished making changes, click on the Save Changes button; a dialog box will appear, confirming your action.

A convenient use of this editing feature is to save long messages and then continue them later. This way, if your computer hangs up, you don't lose the whole message. Or you just might want to take a break from writing messages. There are plenty of reasons to save a message that you intend to keep working on. Whatever the reason, the steps are the same as those you followed above.

WARNING   **The one danger of saving messages to the Outgoing FlashMail window is that, if you forget you still have work to do and you run a FlashMail session, either manually or automatically, you'll be sending half-finished messages!**

Saving Any Message

An alternative to the above method of saving messages is to use the Save command. This command will work for any message, whether incoming or outgoing. To save any message, first open the message, and then choose File ➤ Save (or use the Ctrl+S keyboard combination); the Save File As dialog box will appear, as shown in Figure 5.5.

Give the file an appropriate name in an appropriate location, and click on OK.

Saving messages this way, however, has three main disadvantages:

• You have to remember where the message is on your hard drive.

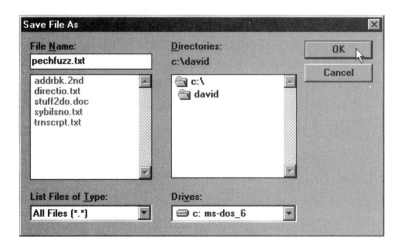

FIGURE 5.5:
You can also save messages using the File ➤ Save command, which brings up the Save File As dialog box.

- When you save the message, it is not placed in the Outgoing FlashMail window, where you can easily send it the next time you do a FlashMail session or go online.
- You now have the message cluttering up your hard drive, even after you send it.

For the preceding reasons, I do not recommend saving messages using the Save command. If you really want to keep copies of your messages, it's better to have AOL do it for you automatically, as described in the section "Automatic Permanent Archiving" later this chapter.

Composing Messages in a Word-Processing Program

An obvious but seldom-used alternative to saving unfinished messages to the Outgoing FlashMail window is to simply compose your messages in a word-processing program, such as Word or WordPerfect. But even an unassuming program like Windows WordPad works just fine, as shown in Figure 5.6.

Using a word-processing program to compose your messages has several advantages:

- You have all the text-editing tools of the word-processing program, which may be more sophisticated than those in AOL.
- You can save your work frequently, thereby avoiding the risk of losing work due to a computer crash.
- You don't have to worry about accidentally running FlashSessions before your messages are finished.
- If AOL hangs up, you can quit out of it without losing any changes to your message, since the word processor is a separate program.

There also are a few disadvantages, the most obvious of which is that any formatting or special characters in your text may be obliterated when the message ultimately gets sent. The Internet is not kind to formatting, and it eats special characters for breakfast. (For tips on how to highlight words and phrases in Internet-bound messages and what to avoid, refer back to Chapter 4.)

Once you've finished your message, just select all the text, copy it to the clipboard (Edit ➤ Copy), and then switch back to AOL (Alt+Tab) and paste it into the message window (Edit ➤ Paste).

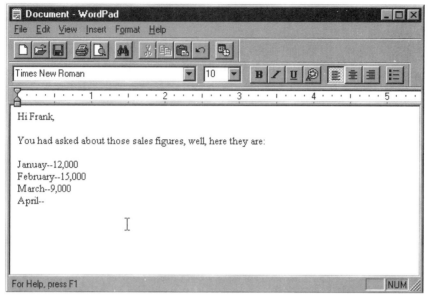

FIGURE 5.6: Using a word-processing program, such as Windows WordPad, to compose messages avoids the risk of losing your work or sending out unfinished messages.

> **TIP**
>
> In any Windows 95 application, the following shortcut keys will always work the same: Ctrl+C to copy; Ctrl+X to cut; Ctrl+V to paste; and Alt+Tab to cycle through applications.

Attaching Documents to Messages

If you use e-mail a lot, you will soon find yourself wanting to send files along with your messages. In the previous section, you learned how easy it was to compose messages in a word-processing program and then copy it to an AOL message window. As you might imagine, it's sometimes even easier to compose a message and then simply include it with an AOL message as an attached document. One advantage of this method is that an attached document, unlike an AOL message, *will* retain any formatting.

Like many other features of AOL, the Attach Document option is very easy and intuitive to use. Follow these steps to attach a document to a message:

1. Open the Compose Message window, either by clicking on the Compose Mail icon, choosing Mail ➤ Compose Mail, or using the Ctrl+M shortcut combination.

2. Once the Compose Message window is open, address the message and give it a subject line, just as you would with any other message.

3. You can place body text in the message if you like, or you can just type something like **See attached file** if the information you're really interested in sending is in the attached file.

4. When you are finished filling in the Compose Message window, click on the Attach icon.

5. The Attach File dialog box will appear, as shown in Figure 5.7.

6. This dialog box is very similar to the Open File dialog boxes you are used to seeing in AOL and other Windows programs. If you type ***.***, then you'll see a list of all files in the open folder. If you want to see other folders or drives, select them in the Folders and Drives boxes. You may need to go into several folders to find the file you are looking for.

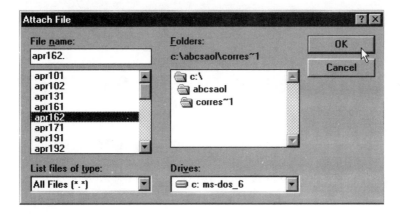

FIGURE 5.7:
You choose the file to attach to your e-mail message in the Attach File dialog box.

TIP   Even though Windows 95 normally doesn't show file extensions, if you want to see files of a certain type, you can enter an extension to filter out all other files. For example, if you want to find only Word documents, type *.doc.

7. When you've found the file, either double-click it or select it and click on the OK button.

8. Notice that the name of the file (and the folder containing it) now appears in the File area of the Compose Message window, as shown in Figure 5.8. Also, notice that the Attach icon has changed into a Detach icon.

9. After making sure you have attached the correct file, click on the Send Later button to send the message the next time you go online, just like any other message.

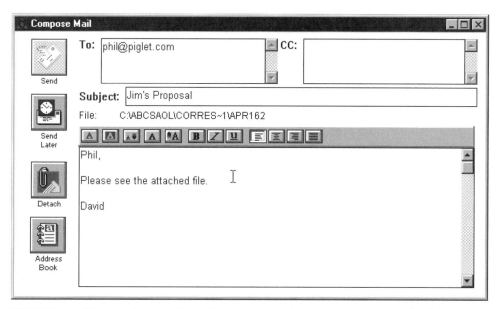

FIGURE 5.8: When you have attached a file to a message, its name appears and the Attach icon changes to Detach.

TIP If you decide you don't want to attach a file after all, just click on the Detach button, and the file will no longer be attached to the message.

You can tell that a message has an attached file by looking at it in the Outgoing FlashMail window. Choose Mail ➤ Outgoing Mail to bring up this window. If the icon next to the message has a little disk on it, then it has an attached file. The same is true for incoming messages with files attached.

Rereading Mail You've Already Received

If you regularly delete mail from your Incoming FlashMail window, eventually you will accidentally delete something that you need. It might simply be a message that you want to reread, or it might be something more important, such as directions to someone's house or a business proposal. There are several ways to avoid finding yourself in this dilemma:

- You can manually archive messages with your Personal Filing Cabinet, discussed later in this chapter.
- You can have AOL automatically save copies of all messages you read.
- You can save messages to your hard disk, as described earlier in this chapter.
- You can *reread* your mail on the AOL service.

Let's look at this last option right now.

WARNING Time you spend browsing through your old mail online is *not* free time. The clock is running, so work as quickly as you can.

AOL saves copies of all your incoming and outgoing messages for a brief period of time (three to five days). While this is not a fail-safe way to keep backups, it will work in a pinch. Here's how.

Sign on to AOL in the usual way. When AOL has finished downloading any new art, choose Mail ➤ Check Mail You've Read. The Old Mail dialog box will appear, as shown in Figure 5.9. Notice that this looks a lot like the Incoming and Outgoing FlashMail windows. It works almost the same way, with a few exceptions.

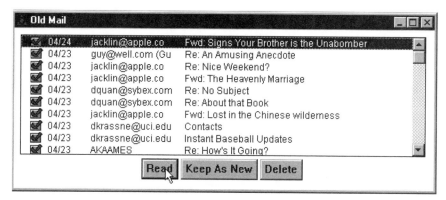

FIGURE 5.9: You can read old messages in the Old Mail dialog box, and you can even keep messages as new.

> **NOTE**   You might notice that I have mail in my Old Mail dialog box that has come from me. Sounds crazy, no? No! These are messages I have sent to myself from *other* machines. This is a good way for me to send myself reminders from work that I can read at home. Chapter 3 explains how to run AOL on multiple computers.

As in the FlashMail windows, you can read messages by double-clicking on them or by selecting them and clicking on the Read button. You can also delete messages by selecting them and clicking on Delete. But this window has an added feature, the Keep As New button, discussed next.

Keeping Messages as New

If you think you might want to reread a message later, you can highlight it in the Old Mail dialog box and click on the Keep As New button, as shown below.

AOL places any highlighted messages into your New Mail window, as if you had just received them (see Figure 5.10). Then you can read them online, or even offline at your leisure if you retrieve them with a FlashSession. (See Chapter 6 for more about FlashSessions.)

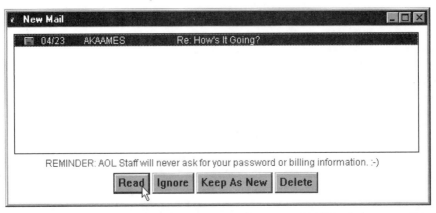

FIGURE 5.10: When you click on the Keep As New button, any highlighted messages will be saved to your New Mail window, where you can read them as if they were new.

> **TIP**
>
> When you keep a message as new, it will stay in your New Mail window until you delete it. There is no time limit on the messages in this window.

Rereading Mail You've Already Sent

Just as you can reread messages that you've received, you can also reread mail that you've sent. Again, there are several ways to do this:

- You can save the messages to a disk as described earlier in this chapter.
- You can manually archive messages with your Personal Filing Cabinet.
- You can instruct AOL to automatically keep copies of all outgoing messages, as described later in this chapter.
- You can *reread* your outgoing messages online.

We will discuss the last method in this section.

Just as with incoming messages, AOL saves outgoing messages for a brief period. Again, if it's important for you to have copies of outgoing messages, it's better to have AOL keep copies of them automatically. However, the following method will work as a stopgap measure.

Sign on to AOL in the usual way. When AOL has finished downloading any new art, choose Mail ➤ Check Mail You've Sent. The Outgoing Mail dialog box will appear, as shown in Figure 5.11. It looks a lot like the Incoming and Outgoing FlashMail windows and works almost the same way.

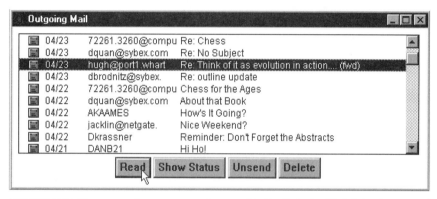

FIGURE 5.11: You can read messages you have sent in the Outgoing Mail dialog box; you can even unsend messages.

As in the FlashMail windows, you can read messages by double-clicking them or by selecting them and clicking on the Read button. You can also delete messages by selecting them and clicking on Delete. Where this window differs from the others, though, is that it has *Unsend* and *Show Status* options.

WARNING Time you spend browsing through your sent mail online is *not* free time. The clock is running, so work quickly.

Retrieving Messages You've Already Sent

When you highlight a message or messages in the Outgoing Mail dialog box and 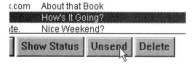 click on Unsend, as shown at left, AOL removes any highlighted messages from the mailboxes of the individuals to whom they have been sent.

Unsend will work, however, only if two conditions are met: first, the message has to still be unread by the recipient; second, the recipient must be an AOL member. AOL cannot plunge its icy hand of death into the Internet to extract messages. If you try to unsend such a message, you will see this dialog box:

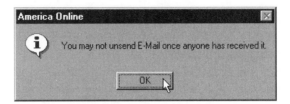

Just click on OK, since there's not much else you can do.

Showing the Status of a Sent Message

Show Status works the same way as Unsend in that you can use it only for messages you send to other AOL members. If you highlight a message you've sent to another AOL member and click on Show Status, a dialog box similar to Figure 5.12 will appear, telling you whether or not the individual has read the message.

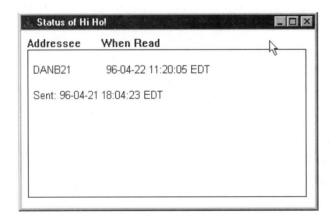

FIGURE 5.12:
You can check to see if someone has read your message yet in the Status dialog box.

With this feature, you can keep tabs on people and find out if they are really reading your messages or just ignoring them. When you are finished browsing in this window, close it by clicking on the close button.

Instant Messages

Since AOL is itself a large network of computers, there are things you can do online with other AOL members that you cannot do with nonmembers. You've already seen, for example, that you can unsend as well as check the status of messages you've sent to other AOL members. In Chapter 7, you will learn about chatting, another feature reserved for AOL members. For now, let's look at *instant messages*.

Sending Instant Messages

An instant message differs from a regular message in that the text of an instant message, sent to another AOL member, appears immediately on his or her screen in a special dialog box. The disadvantage, of course, is that the other member needs to be signed on; otherwise you have to send the message conventionally.

That's why it's not a bad idea to check to see if your intended recipient is online before you start sending an instant message. Let's go through an example right now.

> **NOTE**
> **Unlike other features, sending instant messages will only work if you have a buddy with whom to exchange messages. So before you work through this exercise, try to find someone—a friend or coworker, perhaps—with whom you can practice.**

Sign on to AOL in the usual way. When AOL has finished downloading any new art, choose Members ➤ Send an Instant Message (or use the Ctrl+I keyboard shortcut). The Send Instant Message dialog box will appear, as shown in Figure 5.13.

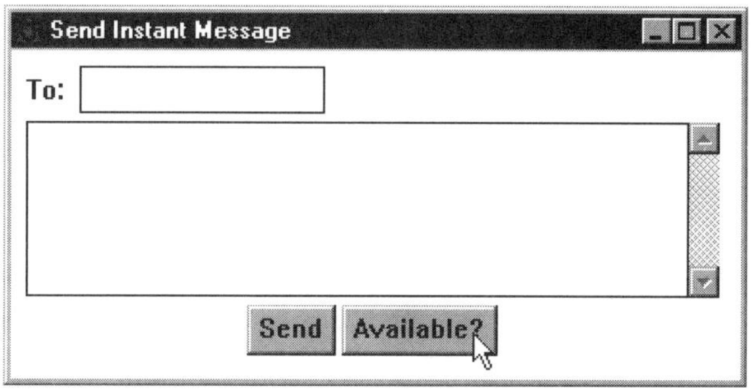

FIGURE 5.13:
You can send messages to other AOL members instantly (provided they are online) using the Send Instant Message dialog box.

Before you try sending an instant message, let's first check to make sure your recipient is online and available to receive instant messages. Type in  the screen name of the AOL member to whom you wish to send the instant message and click on the Available? button. If the other member is online and available to receive instant messages, you will get this message:

If not, you will see this message:

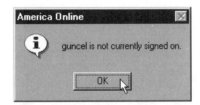

If the other member is online, you can now try sending an instant message. The Send Instant Message window should still be open, showing the screen name you just tested for availability. Thus, all you have to do is press Tab to move the cursor into the message area and type the text of your message. Click on the Send button to send the message on its way. If all goes according to plan, your message will appear immediately on the other member's screen.

TIP In Chapter 7, you will learn about a feature called Buddy Lists that lets you check to see if several people are online with just one command.

Responding to Instant Messages

Naturally, if you send instant messages, you can expect to receive some in return. Responding to instant messages is as easy as sending them. When you receive an instant message, it will appear in a dialog box very similar to the one you saw when you sent the message, as shown in Figure 5.14.

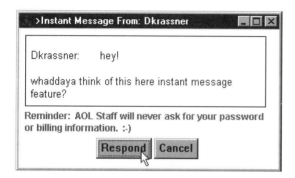

FIGURE 5.14:
When you receive instant messages, they appear in the Instant Message From dialog box.

If you would like to respond to the message, click on the Respond button. The box will expand, providing you with a place to type a response (see Figure 5.15). Notice that you can still read the original message in the scrolling marquee above; this is quite handy, as it reminds you what you're responding to!

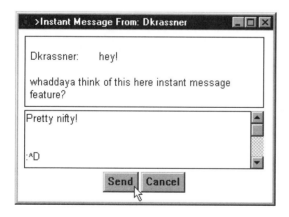

FIGURE 5.15:
When you click on the Respond button, it changes to the Send button, and the Instant Message dialog box expands to make room for your response.

When you have crafted your response, click on the Send button, just as you did before, to launch the message into cyberspace. Your reply will be added to the scrolling marquee.

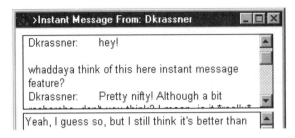

In this manner, you can have a "running" dialog with another member using instant messages. Since everything written will appear in the scrolling marquee, you can check at any time to see what you've said and how your interlocutor has responded.

> **TIP**
>
> **If you're just dying to try out the Instant Message feature, you *can* send instant messages to yourself. Don't be surprised, though, if you see your responses to yourself shown *twice* in the scrolling marquee (once for you as sender and the other for you as recipient).**

The Instant Message dialog box will stay on your screen until you close it, even if you open up other windows. If another window is covering up the Instant Message dialog box and you want to get back to it, just choose Window ➤ Instant Message.

Blocking Instant Messages

Just as you might get crank phone calls on your telephone, you can also get crank instant messages. Of course, you can always see who sent you the message, so the analogy isn't perfect, but it's nice to know you can always block instant messages if you want to. Another scenario might be that you're working on something online or even just browsing and don't wish to be interrupted. Whatever the reason, follow these steps to block instant messages:

1. If you are offline, sign on in the usual manner. After AOL has finished downloading new art, choose Members ➤ Send an Instant Message (or use

the Ctrl+I keyboard shortcut). The Send Instant Message dialog box will appear.

2. Instead of typing in a screen name, type in the text string **$im_off**, as shown below.

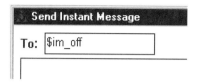

The dollar sign (**$**) tells AOL that a command is coming, rather than a screen name. The rest of the string tells AOL to turn **off** your availability to instant messages (**im**).

3. You must also type something in the message box (one character is enough). When you have typed the text string and your message, click on the Send button.

Now, when people try to send you instant messages, they will be informed that you are currently unavailable to receive them.

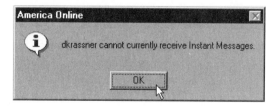

When you are ready to receive instant messages again, repeat the above steps, substituting the string **$im_on**, which will turn your availability to receive instant messages back on.

TIP

If you receive harassing instant messages, the best thing to do is to save the message to your hard disk (Ctrl+S) and then forward the message to the powers that be at AOL. Use the keyword (Ctrl+K) **TOS**, click on the **Write to Terms of Service Staff** button, and then click on the **IM Violations** button. You'll see a dialog box where you can enter your complaint.

Sending Faxes and Paper Mail

Sometimes an electronic message is not enough. You may be pleasantly surprised to discover that AOL offers both fax and paper mail services. So if you want to send someone hard-copy text, you can choose between these two alternatives. There are, of course, many fine fax programs available, but faxing from within AOL is particularly convenient if you work in AOL a lot or if you don't have something like WinFax Pro. The paper mail feature, on the other hand, allows you to easily send messages you've received or articles you've found to individuals who don't have e-mail.

Sending Faxes

As with most other messages, it's best to prepare your faxes offline to save time (which, after all, on AOL, is money). Here's how to prepare a fax.

> **WARNING** The fax service is *not* part of the basic AOL service. You will be charged $4.95 for each fax you send. If you have access to a fax machine, sending faxes conventionally is almost certainly cheaper.

First, start up AOL, or switch to it if it's already running. Then either click on the Compose Mail icon, choose Mail ➤ Compose Mail, or use the Ctrl+M keyboard short-cut to open the Compose Mail window. Normally, you would type a screen name (for AOL members) or an e-mail address (for other Internet addresses) into the To box. This time, though, you want to type the name of the person to whom the fax is going, followed by the fax number. For example, let's say you wanted to send a message to Sherlock Holmes at (800) 555-1212; you would type **S. Holmes@800-555-1212**.

> **TIP** You can send a fax to more than one recipient. Separate the different addresses (names and numbers) by commas, just as you do when sending e-mail messages.

Complete the rest of the message window as you normally would, and click on the Send Later button to add the fax to your Outgoing FlashMail window. If you want your full name (as opposed to a screen name) to appear somewhere on the fax, you will have to incorporate it as part of the body of the text.

> **NOTE**
>
> A few limitations: The name and fax number combined can be no more than 20 characters. Also, you won't be able to use the fax service or the paper mail service within 45 days of opening your account.

The next time you go online to send messages or run a FlashSession, your fax will be sent along with the rest of the mail.

Sending Paper Mail

As with most other messages, it's best to prepare your paper mail message offline. Let's look at how to send paper mail messages now.

> **WARNING**
>
> The paper mail service is *not* part of the basic AOL service. You will be charged $2.95 for each piece of paper mail you send. If you have the time, addressing the envelope and sending it conventionally is still cheaper.

First, start up AOL, or switch to it if it's already running. Then either click on the Compose Mail icon, choose Mail ➤ Compose Mail, or use the Ctrl+M keyboard shortcut to open the Compose Mail window. Normally, you would type a screen name (for AOL members) or an e-mail address (for other Internet addresses) into the To box. This time, though, you want to type the person's name to whom the message is going, followed by the text string **@usmail**. For example, let's say I wanted to send a message to my Uncle Walt, who doesn't have e-mail. I would type **Walt@usmail**.

Complete the rest of the message window as you normally would, and click on the Send Later button to add the message to your Outgoing FlashMail window.

The next time you go online to send messages or run a FlashSession, you will see the U.S. Mail Return Address dialog box, as shown in Figure 5.16, followed by the U.S. Mail Send To dialog box. Just fill in the information, and click on OK to send your mail on its way. It will take a few days to get there, just like any other regular mail.

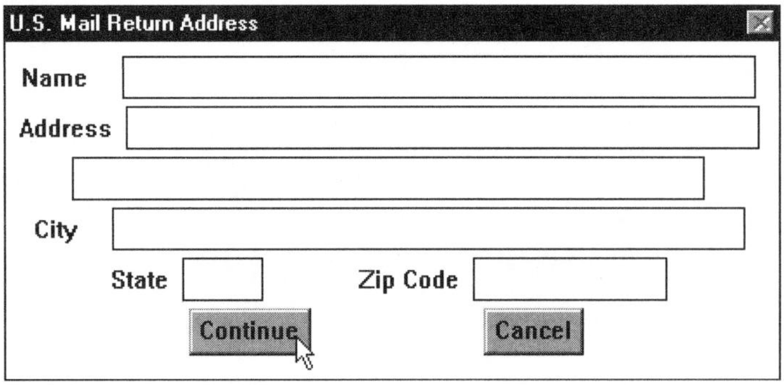

FIGURE 5.16:
Fill in your return
address and then
click on Continue
to fill in the
address of the
recipient of
your letter.

The Download Manager

The *Download Manager* keeps track of files attached to e-mail that you download. The utility of the Download Manager is that it helps you keep track of what you've downloaded, as it keeps a list of all files you've copied to your computer. If you download a lot of stuff, this can save you time you might otherwise waste double-downloading.

NOTE

To *download* a file means to take it from somewhere out on the Internet or from AOL where it is stored and place a copy of it on your own computer. The reasons you might wish to do this are many: you might find a program you want to try out; you might want to read a long document offline to save yourself some online time; or it might be downloaded art. Your e-mail items are essentially downloads. Indeed, you might be downloading files along with your messages.

Just to get you up to speed with downloading in AOL, you should know that you can

- designate files to be downloaded later.
- download files in the background while you work on other things.
- specify exactly where on your hard disk downloaded files are to be placed.
- delete downloaded items.

- view descriptions of downloaded files.
- specify various aspects of how your Download Manager works.

With these possibilities in mind, you should know that most users specify that files be downloaded automatically during FlashSessions (described in Chapter 6); with this method, much of the downloading you do will be behind the scenes, and you really won't have to do much after you are happy with the preferences you've set.

Let's now take a look at the Download Manager. Start up AOL, or switch to it if it's already running. Choose File ➤ Download Manager, or use the Ctrl+T keyboard short-cut. The Download Manager window will appear, as shown in Figure 5.17. Note that your Download Manager will undoubtedly look different than mine, since we will have downloaded different files.

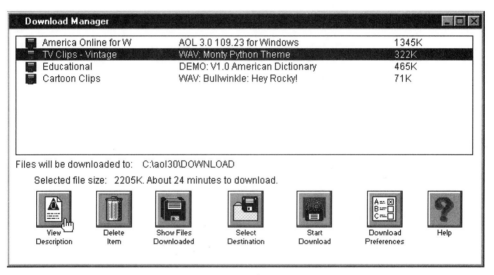

FIGURE 5.17: You can keep track of your downloads with the Download Manager.

In my Download Manager, there is a list of several files that are designated to be downloaded later. All that "later" means, as far as AOL is concerned, is "not now." It can be a day or a month or a year later. Where do the files that are to be downloaded later come from? Well, any time you see one of those *Download Free Art* windows and click on Download Later, that download is added to your list of files to be downloaded later.

To find out more about a particular download (such as how large the file is and what it contains), select it and click on the View Description button. To delete a download scheduled for later, click on Delete Item. To see a list of files that you've already downloaded, click on the Show Files Downloaded button, and AOL will bring up the Files You've Downloaded dialog box, as shown in Figure 5.18.

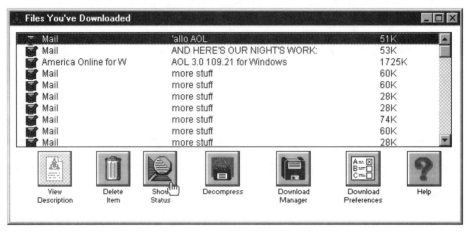

FIGURE 5.18: You can view a list of files already downloaded in the Files You've Downloaded dialog box.

The options in this dialog box are self-explanatory. Going back to the Download Manager dialog box, you can instruct AOL to begin a download by selecting a file and clicking on the Start Download button. AOL will sign on and download the file. If you prefer, you can select all files and download them together.

Let's look at some of the other options you have in this window.

Selecting a Download Destination

If you've performed a normal installation of AOL, then by default downloaded files go into a folder called Download, located in the AOL folder on your hard disk. You can change this destination anytime, though. Follow these steps:

1. In the Download Manager window, click on the Select Destination button. The Select Path dialog box will appear. As you can see in Figure 5.19, this dialog box looks very much like an Open or Save dialog box. You navigate your folders the same way you would in an Open or Save dialog box, too.

2. Click around until you find the folder where you want to have your downloads go. Then just select it and click on OK. That's all there is to it! From now on, all downloads will funnel into your newly designated folder.

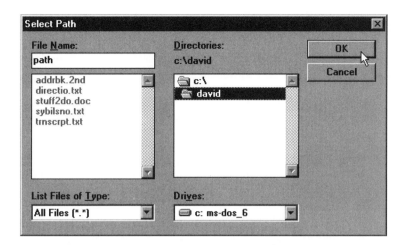

FIGURE 5.19:
You can select a different destination folder for downloads in the Select Path dialog box.

Download Preferences

There are a number of useful options that can make downloading work more smoothly. To access them, click on the Download Preferences button in the Download Manager window. The Preferences dialog box will appear, as shown in Figure 5.20.

This is what each option means:

Display image files on Download—This option, when checked, tells AOL to display images that you download.

Automatically decompress files at sign-off—In order to cut down on the time it takes to transfer files, most large files are *compressed* to make them smaller. The smaller a file, the less time it will take to download. This option, when checked, automatically *decompresses,* or expands, the files back to their normal size when you sign off from AOL.

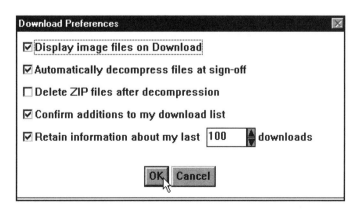

FIGURE 5.20:
You can specify your download preferences in this dialog box.

Delete ZIP files after decompression—This option, when checked, automatically deletes the compressed version of a file after AOL has expanded it (compressed files often have the extension *ZIP* or *ARC*). Don't worry, though; you won't lose the expanded file when the compressed file is deleted.

Confirm additions to my download list—This option, when checked, instructs AOL to ask your permission before adding downloads to your download list.

Retain information about my last *nnn* downloads—This option, when checked, instructs AOL as to how many downloads it needs to keep information on. You can change the *nnn* if you like; the default is 100.

When you are satisfied with your preferences settings, click on OK. Click on Cancel to close the dialog box without making any changes to your preferences.

Background Downloading

Downloading files in the *background* simply means having AOL download the files while you are doing other things in AOL. To download in the background, all you have to do is wait for the download to begin, and then click outside the window that shows you its progress. The download will continue as you work on other tasks (messages, browsing, chatting, etc.).

 **WARNING** Background downloading can significantly slow down other operations for the obvious reason that your computer is doing do two different things at once.

Archiving Messages with Your Personal Filing Cabinet

AOL provides a handy tool for managing your downloaded files called the Personal Filing Cabinet (PFC). In the PFC, you can view all archived messages, as well as move them around, rename them, and delete them. *Archiving* messages and files simply means storing them on your hard disk for later use. You can use the PFC to organize your archives. You can also use it to search for and open files, activate FlashSessions, and create folders. Let's look at the Personal Filing Cabinet in more detail and learn how to perform each of these tasks.

Bring up the PFC window by starting AOL (or switching to it if it's already running) and either choosing Mail ➤ Personal Filing Cabinet or clicking on the PFC icon in the flashbar. The PFC window will appear, as illustrated in Figure 5.21.

Your PFC will look different from mine, of course, but there are several things we'll probably have in common, including folders for the Download Manager, Favorite Places, Mail, and Newsgroups. Notice that mail you've read will have a checkmark, as opposed to unread mail items, which have no checkmarks.

There are all sorts of things you can do to reorganize the files to your liking. To delete a file or folder, just click on it and then click on the Delete button.

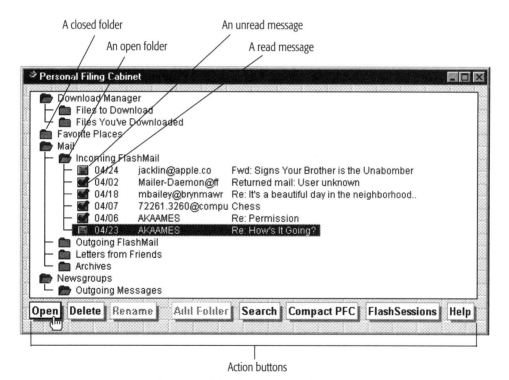

FIGURE 5.21: You can organize your archives in your Personal Filing Cabinet.

TIP
You can always select more than one file by holding down the
Shift key or the Ctrl key and clicking on multiple files. Using
the Shift key while clicking selects any number of contiguous files;
using the Ctrl key selects multiple files whether or not their names
are side-by-side.

To open a file or folder, either double-click on it or click on it and then click on the
Open button. You can also close an open folder by double-clicking on it. (Closing
a folder means hiding all of its subfolders and files.) In Figure 5.21, the Favorite Places
folder is closed.

To rename a folder, click on it, click on the Rename button, and then type in the
new name.

To move a file, click on it and drag it to its destination folder, like so:

When the destination folder has a box around it, release the mouse button to place
the file in its new home.

You can also create other archive folders. For example, let's say you want to create
an archive folder for messages about a certain project or from a special friend. Just
select the folder where you want the new archive folder to appear (for instance, the
Mail folder) and click on Add Folder. A small dialog box will appear where you can type
the name of the new folder. Do so, and then click on OK.

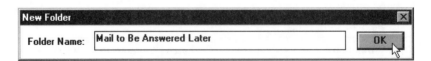

Now, whenever you receive a message pertaining to that project or from that special friend, all you have to do is drag it into the new archive folder, and the message
will then have been moved from the Incoming FlashMail folder to the archive folder.

Searching for Files

The Search utility in the Personal Filing Cabinet is very handy, because you can search for files containing specific information even if you can't remember what the files (or mail messages) are called. To search for a file, click on the Search button. The Search dialog box will appear. Type in a few key words of the information you are looking for. For example, let's say you know that someone has sent you a message telling you what time to meet them for a hockey game, but you have so many messages, you can't remember which one it's in. You might type the words **Hockey game**, as shown here:

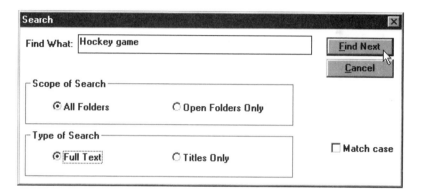

Notice that, in this situation, you would also select the Full Text option under Type of Search. If you don't have a lot of folders, you would probably also click on the All Folders option under Scope of Search. Don't check the Match Case box unless you think there might be some confusion with other cases of the searched text ("Hockey" versus "hockey"). When you are ready, click on Find Next, and AOL will find the desired file or files.

Automatic Temporary Archiving

As mentioned earlier in this chapter in the sections on rereading mail, AOL automatically retains copies of both incoming and outgoing messages for three to five days. You must go online to reread messages, but it's a valuable resource if you accidentally delete a message that you really wanted to keep. If you think you'll usually want to keep copies of incoming and outgoing messages, though, it's best to have AOL archive them automatically, as described next.

Automatic Permanent Archiving

You can instruct AOL to permanently archive incoming and outgoing messages. To do so, start AOL or switch to it if it's already running. Then choose Members ➤ Preferences. In the Preferences dialog box, click on the Mail button to bring up the Mail Preferences dialog box, as shown in Figure 5.22.

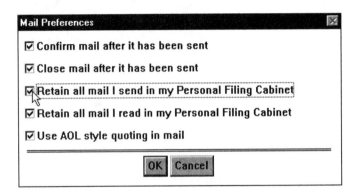

Mail Preferences

☑ Confirm mail after it has been sent

☑ Close mail after it has been sent

☑ Retain all mail I send in my Personal Filing Cabinet

☑ Retain all mail I read in my Personal Filing Cabinet

☑ Use AOL style quoting in mail

OK   Cancel

FIGURE 5.22:
You can keep copies of all incoming and outgoing messages by choosing those options in the Mail Preferences dialog box.

To keep copies of outgoing messages, click on the checkbox next to the option "Retain all mail I send in my Personal Filing Cabinet." To keep copies of incoming messages, click on the checkbox next to the option "Retain all mail I read in my Personal Filing Cabinet." When you are satisfied with the settings, click on OK.

Next time you open the PFC, you will notice that an additional folder called *Archives* has been added in your Mail folder. Within this folder, there are two new folders called Mail You've Read and Mail You've Sent.

From now on, a copy of all messages you send and read will be archived in your PFC.

TIP

You're not limited to the simplistic "sent" and "received" arrangement described here. *Within* your archive folders you can place other folders to keep meticulous track of messages from, say, your boss, your spouse, your friends, your family, etc.

Mail Preferences

You can, to some degree, customize the way your mail system works. To do so, choose Members ➤ Preferences to bring up the Preferences dialog box. Then click on the Mail button.

This will bring up the Mail Preferences dialog box, shown in Figure 5.23.

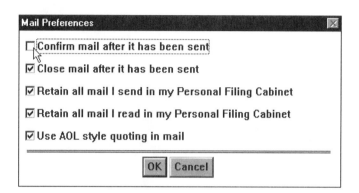

FIGURE 5.23:
The Mail Preferences dialog box.

Just click on an option (so that the checkmark appears) to activate it. To deactivate it, click again to remove the checkmark. The options work as follows:

Confirm mail after it has been sent—Requests that AOL inform you when it sends mail.

Close mail after it has been sent—Tells AOL to close a mail message after you've clicked on Send or Send Later.

Retain all mail I send in my Personal Filing Cabinet—Instructs AOL to keep copies of all messages you send.

Retain all mail I read in my Personal Filing Cabinet—Instructs AOL to keep copies of all messages you receive.

Use AOL style quoting in e-mail—When this option is checked, you can select text in an original message, click on Reply, and the selected text will appear in the reply message.

When you are finished making your selections, click on OK. If you want to exit without making any changes, click on Cancel.

Chapter 6

AUTOMATING E-MAIL WITH FLASHSESSIONS

I've teased you with hints about FlashSessions here and there in previous chapters of this book; now you're finally going to learn about them. Possibly one of the most useful and intelligent features in AOL, FlashSessions make signing on and e-mailing so easy that you may never again sign on conventionally or send another message manually.

In this chapter, you'll learn how to set up your account's FlashSessions feature to best meet your needs. You'll see how to activate FlashSessions, both manually and automatically, as well as how to read your FlashMail. And finally, we'll discuss a few limitations of FlashSessions.

What Is a FlashSession?

A *FlashSession* is an automated online session. By comparison, a conventional online session usually involves the following:

- Specifying a screen name
- Typing a password
- Signing on
- Opening the Outgoing Mail window
- Sending outgoing mail
- Opening the New Mail window
- Reading and responding to incoming mail
- Going to your newsreader
- Downloading new postings
- Responding to old postings
- Signing off
- Confirming that you want to sign off

Believe it or not, AOL's FlashSessions feature can automate *all* of these steps. As its name implies, you can set up AOL to take care of the usual clicking, sending, and retrieving in a flash. There are at least six other very good reasons to use FlashSessions:

- To minimize online time, which equals savings (the best reason)
- To simplify mail sending and retrieving
- To save you from having to remember to check your mail
- To allow for message sending and retrieval at convenient times (i.e., when no one is likely to be using the telephone)
- To allow you to read and compose mail offline
- To automate downloading

We'll explore all the possibilities of FlashSessions in this chapter.

A Lesson on Online Costs

Let's face it, time is money. The more tasks you do offline, the more online minutes you'll have to do things like browsing the Web and other fun stuff you *can't* do offline. Also, the faster you sign on, send and retrieve mail and files, and sign off, the better.

I find that, with a fast modem, an average FlashSession lasts about a minute. Doing the same stuff (reading mail, etc.) manually that a FlashSession does automatically often takes 2 or 3 minutes. If you sign on two or three times a day, over the course of a month, you're looking at the difference between, perhaps, 90 online minutes for e-mail with FlashSessions as opposed to *270 minutes* for manual mailing sessions.

WARNING   The above estimate is a liberal one gauged for fast readers; if you have lots of mail to read and respond to, you could spend 5 to 10 minutes *per session* doing just that. If you assume 10 minutes per session, your monthly online time starts ballooning into the 600–900 minute range. Ouch!

The standard AOL account allows for 5 hours (300 minutes) at the $9.95 flat rate, after which you get charged on an hourly basis. Anyone can do the math and, based on the 270-minute estimate above, figure out that the manual approach leaves you only about 30 free minutes for all other browsing, while the FlashSession approach leaves you about 210 free minutes. So if you use FlashSessions, you're effectively buying yourself about 3 extra hours of browsing time.

Not to beat a dead horse, but it should be pretty obvious that, unless you don't mind using up your free online minutes with e-mail, you should use FlashSessions; even if you are only using AOL for e-mail, FlashSessions can greatly refine your use of online time.

Setting Up FlashSessions

There are several aspects to setting up FlashSessions. First, you can specify *which* tasks you want AOL to do during your automated sessions. Next, you can schedule *when* you want your FlashSessions to occur. You can also set up AOL such that any or all of your screen names can take advantage of FlashSessions. Finally, you can store passwords for any screen names for which you run FlashSessions. Let's look at all of these possibilities.

Headquarters for all FlashSession operations is found in the FlashSessions dialog box. Let's bring it up now, since we'll need it for the next few sections. Start AOL, or switch to it if it's already running. Then choose Mail ➤ Setup FlashSession. The FlashSessions dialog box will appear, as shown in Figure 6.1.

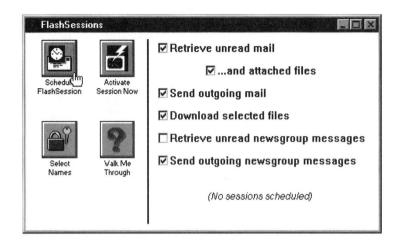

FIGURE 6.1: The Flash-Sessions dialog box is your starting point for all matters relating to FlashSessions.

FlashSession Options

On the right side of the FlashSessions dialog box is a list of five options. These specify what AOL is to do when it runs a FlashSession for you. Let's look at each option in detail:

Retrieve unread mail—This asks AOL to check your "in" mailbox to see if there is mail there you haven't read. If it finds unread mail, AOL moves it into your Incoming FlashMail window, where you can peruse it offline.

...and attached files—This tells AOL to download any files that might be attached to mail messages. If you do not check this option, then attached files are placed in a holding area and designated in the Download Manager as files to be downloaded later. One caveat with respect to automatically downloading files is that it can sometimes take a while for long files.

Send outgoing mail—This instructs AOL to check your "out" mailbox to see if there is mail there to be sent. If it finds outgoing mail, it sends it on its way.

Download selected files—This directs AOL to download any files that you have selected to be downloaded in the Download Manager. (Remember, files are placed in the Download Manager when you choose *not* to have them downloaded during an online session.)

Retrieve unread newsgroup messages—Similar to the "Retrieve unread mail" option, this option asks AOL to find unread postings that you have received from newsgroups. If it finds any unread postings, AOL downloads them to a folder on your hard disk, where you can peruse them offline.

Send outgoing newsgroup messages—Similar to the "Send outgoing mail" option, this option instructs AOL to look in the folder on your hard disk that contains responses to newsgroup postings to see if there are any to be sent. If it finds outgoing postings, it sends them out into cyberspace.

These options work like any others in AOL: to enable an option, you click on the checkbox to place a checkmark there. To disable an option, click again to remove the checkmark. When you are finished making your choices, either click on the close button to save your changes, or click on one of the action buttons to make more choices.

Scheduling FlashSessions

One of the advantages of FlashSessions is that you can specify when they are to run and set them to run automatically, a bit like an automatic sprinkler system. To schedule FlashSessions, you must be in the FlashSessions window. If you are not there, choose Mail ➤ Setup FlashSession to bring up the FlashSessions window. Then click on the Schedule FlashSession button.

This will bring up the Schedule FlashSessions dialog box, shown in Figure 6.2.

FIGURE 6.2:
You can specify when Flash-Sessions are to take place in the Schedule Flash-Sessions dialog box.

The first thing you need to do is select the days you want FlashSessions to run. If you have AOL at work, you might just want them to run on weekdays. If you use AOL at home, though, you might want FlashSessions to run every day of the week, so you don't miss a single message.

Next, choose the time that you want FlashSessions to *start*. Keep in mind that the time you choose to have your first FlashSession run is different from how often they run. To select a time other than the default starting time (7:15 a.m.), click on the up and down arrows to change the time.

Starting time: 15 : 15

☐ Sunday

The hours are in military time, so 3:00 p.m. will appear as 15 in this dialog box. Generally speaking, it's best to let FlashSessions start running in the morning; that way, you can catch any messages sent to you overnight that much sooner. If you want to run FlashSessions according to your convenience, however (when no one is likely to be using the phone, for instance), you might want to schedule them to start at a time such as 2:00 a.m.

WARNING If you've scheduled a FlashSession for an unusual hour (say, 3:15 a.m.), you'll either have to make sure your computer and AOL are up and running in time for the session, or leave them on when you go to bed. The first alternative is inconvenient. The second can increase the chance of problems—anything from a really big online bill to damage to your system from power surges during an overnight thunderstorm.

In the How Often box, you tell AOL how frequently you want it to run FlashSessions. Frequency can range from every half hour to once a day for each day you've designated. To specify an interval other than the default (every hour), click on the down-pointing triangle to reveal the drop-down menu, as shown below, and make your new selection.

If you find yourself going online a lot—enough to really cause conflicts over use of the phone line—you might want to consider getting a second phone line just for online use. Such a line is sometimes called a *dedicated* line.

Schedule Flashsessions

☑ Enable Scheduler

When you are satisfied with your settings in the Schedule Flashsessions dialog box, make sure you click on the Enable Scheduler checkbox so that a checkmark appears. If you forget to do this, your new settings will not go into effect.

Finally, click on the OK button to save your settings and close the dialog box. If you decide you don't wish to make any changes after all, click on Cancel.

Near the bottom of the FlashSessions dialog box, there is a line that tells you when the next automatic FlashSession is scheduled, or if there are no FlashSessions scheduled.

FlashSessions for Multiple Screen Names

You can run FlashSessions for any or all of your screen names. You might want to do this if, for example, different members of your family have different screen names. Whatever the reason, here's how you do it.

To set up FlashSessions for multiple screen names, you must be in the FlashSessions window. If you are not there, choose Mail ➤ Setup FlashSession to bring up the FlashSessions window. Then click on the Select Names button.

This will bring up the Select Screen Names dialog box, shown in Figure 6.3. To select a screen name, just click next to it to place a checkmark in the box.

To unselect a name, click again to remove the checkmark.

FIGURE 6.3:
You can specify the screen names for which AOL is to run Flash Sessions in the Select Screen Names dialog box.

You must also store passwords for any or all selected screen names. The disadvantage of storing passwords is that anyone who uses your computer can run FlashSessions without having to know your password, but you've got to do it to use the feature. To store a password for any of the screen names you've selected, just click on the Password box next to the name, and then type the password. When you are finished, click on the OK button.

If you decide you don't wish to make changes, click on Cancel.

NOTE
When you set options for FlashSessions, those options apply to all screen names in your account. You cannot independently set options for different screen names.

Now when you run FlashSessions, either manually or automatically, AOL will run a separate FlashSession for each selected name. For any name for which you did not store passwords, you will see a dialog box informing you of this.

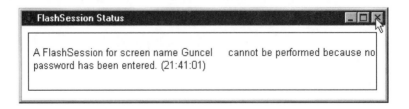

When you see this dialog box, you must go back to the Select Screen Names dialog box to store a password for that screen name before you can run a FlashSession.

Storing and Editing Passwords

As discussed in the previous section, another time-saving feature related to FlashSessions is the ability to store passwords. Storing passwords in AOL is easy. Follow these steps:

1. Start AOL, or switch to it if it's already running.

NOTE If you store passwords, there is always a risk that someone will sign on to your account from your computer without your authorization; so consider carefully before you store passwords.

2. Choose Members ➤ Preferences and click on the Passwords button to bring up the Edit Stored Passwords dialog box, shown in Figure 6.4. Notice that this dialog box is almost identical to the Select Screen Names dialog box. The major difference is that you cannot choose *which* screen names to run FlashSessions for in the Edit Stored Passwords dialog box.
3. Click in the box next to the screen name for which you wish to add, delete, or change a password, and type the correct password (or delete the one that's there, if you want to get rid of it). Click on OK when you are finished.

From now on, when you sign on with the screen name whose password you've added, you won't have to go back to give the password.

FIGURE 6.4:
You can add or change stored passwords in the Edit Stored passwords dialog box.

WARNING   When you change your password, as described in Chapter 3, you must also change your stored passwords, as explained here. Otherwise, you won't have the correct password stored the next time you run a FlashSession or sign on using the corresponding screen name.

Setting Your Offline Newsreader

In order to have AOL retrieve unread newsgroup messages during FlashSessions, you must first set one particular option in the newsgroups preferences. To do this, you must be online, so start AOL or switch to it if it is already running, and sign on in the conventional manner.

Next, either choose Go To ➤ Keyword, click on the Keyword icon, or use the Ctrl+K keyboard combination to bring up the Keyword dialog box. Type the word **Newsgroups** as shown below.

Now click on the Go button to bring up the Newsgroups window, as shown in Figure 6.5.

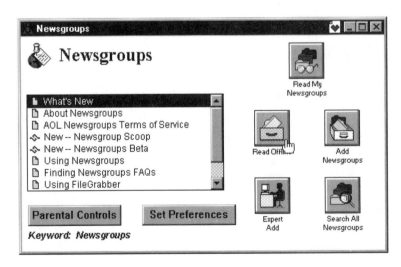

FIGURE 6.5:
In the Newsgroups window, you can specify that newsgroup messages are to be read offline.

Newsreaders and Newgroups Explained

You'll learn about newsgroups in detail in Chapter 11, but here's a quick primer for the curious. The first thing to understand is the difference between *newsgroups* and *mailing lists*.

A mailing list is a generic term for any area on the Internet where people exchange messages on a specific subject. For example, you might belong to a mailing list whose subject is hang gliding. When someone posts a message to this mailing list, it is delivered directly to your e-mail mailbox (irrespective of whether you use AOL, CompuServe, or another service). You can then write a reply and post it back to the mailing list; the original message, along with your reply, will be posted to everyone else on the mailing list. In this sense, a mailing list is like a conference.

The term *newsgroup,* on the other hand, is reserved for special mailing lists on the service called Usenet. Like AOL, Usenet is a service, but its function is completely different. We'll see why in Chapter 11. For now, all you need to know is that newsgroups differ from mailing lists in one fundamental way. Messages posted to newsgroups do *not* go to your mailbox. Rather, they go to a holding area out there in cyberspace, and you won't see them until you actually download them to your computer. This is actually more convenient, because it means you don't have your mailbox all cluttered up with messages. On a practical level, however, these distinctions will make little difference to you as you read and respond to messages, since AOL makes your interaction with both newsgroups and mailing lists seamless.

Since newsgroup messages are *not* sent directly to your mailbox, you must have some way of reading them. This is where *newsreaders* come in. A newsreader is a program that allows you to read newsgroup messages. There's a lot more to it, of course, but if you think in the terms I've just outlined, you can't go far wrong.

Click on the Read Offline button.

This will bring up the Choose Newsgroups window, where you can specify which newsgroup messages you wish to read offline (see Figure 6.6).

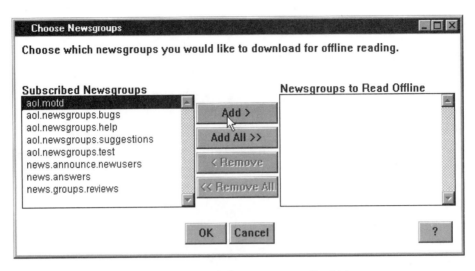

FIGURE 6.6: In the Choose Newsgroups window, you can specify which newsgroup messages are to be read offline, and therefore downloaded during FlashSessions.

To add a newsgroup to the offline reading list, select it in the left-hand window and click on the Add button.

Do the same for each newsgroup whose messages you want to read offline. If you want to read messages from all newsgroups offline, click on the Add All button.

If you later decide you want to remove a newsgroup from the list, select it in the right-hand window and click on the Remove button.

You can remove all newsgroups from the right-hand window by clicking on the Remove All button.

When you are finished, click on the OK button. If you have no more browsing to do, you may now sign off.

TIP   For details on how to sign up for newsgroups, see Chapter 11.

Activating FlashSessions

There are two ways to activate FlashSessions: manually and automatically. The two methods are not mutually exclusive; you can and probably will use both of them in conjunction.

Automatic FlashSessions

You've actually already seen how to set automatic FlashSessions in the section "Scheduling FlashSessions," even if you didn't realize it at the time. The setting that  governs whether or not automatic FlashSessions take place is in the Schedule FlashSessions dialog box, shown back in Figure 6.2. You reach this dialog box by choosing Mail ➤ Setup FlashSession and clicking on the Schedule FlashSessions button. Once there, all you have to do to tell AOL to run automatic FlashSessions is click to place a checkmark in the box next to Enable Scheduler.

AOL will then run FlashSessions according to the schedule you have set in the Schedule FlashSessions dialog box. If you later decide you don't want to run automatic FlashSessions, just go back into the Schedule FlashSessions dialog box and uncheck the Enable Scheduler option.

Manual FlashSessions

There are many ways to start FlashSessions manually, and many reasons for doing so. Even if you run automatic FlashSessions, manual FlashSessions are still the fastest and easiest way to sign on. As an added benefit, your mail will be checked automatically, so you don't have to remember to do it.

Here are the ways you can activate a FlashSession manually:

- Choose Mail ➤ Activate FlashSession Now.
- In the FlashSessions dialog box (Mail ➤ Setup FlashSession), click on the Activate FlashSession Now button.
- In the Personal Filing Cabinet, click on the FlashSessions button to bring up the FlashSessions dialog box, and then click on the Activate FlashSession Now button.

TIP

You can even run FlashSessions while already online. This is still quicker than manually checking your mail. Plus, if you click to enable the "Sign off when finished" option, you don't have to sit there and watch the download so that you can be ready to sign off the minute it's over.

However you do it, once you have manually activated a FlashSession, you will see the dialog box shown in Figure 6.7.

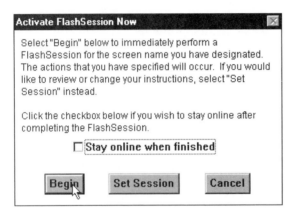

FIGURE 6.7:
You activate a FlashSession from this dialog box.

If you need to adjust any of your FlashSession settings, you can click on the Set Session button to open the FlashSessions dialog box. If you want to stay online when the FlashSession is over, click to activate the "Stay online when finished" option. (If you are running a FlashSession while online, the text of this option changes to "Sign off when finished.") If you decide you don't want to run a FlashSession after all, click on Cancel.

WARNING

If you enable the "Stay online when finished option," be sure to stick around. If you run a FlashSession with this option enabled and then wander off, you might lose valuable online time by not being there when the FlashSession is done. AOL will *not* sign off automatically, and you'll be charged for all your online time, whether you're doing anything with it or not.

If you're all ready to try it out, click on the Begin button to start your FlashSession. You will see the usual sign-on screens, the usual art downloading, and a little window that tells you the progress of your FlashSession (called the FlashSession log).

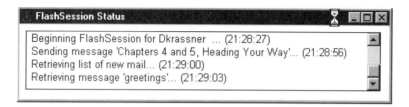

After it does its thing, AOL will sign off and take you back to a sign-on screen (unless you've checked the "Stay online…" option, in which case you'll see the line "FlashSession is complete" in the FlashSession log). If you do check the option to stay online, be sure you sign off at some point, as you will be charged online time for your session, whatever its length.

A Walk-Through for First-Timers

Walk Me Through

Some kind soul at AOL figured that, since FlashSessions are so useful, there ought to be a sort of guided tour of FlashSessions, specifically designed to show neophytes how to use them. To take this tour, you must be in the FlashSessions window. If you are not there, choose Mail ➤ Setup FlashSession to bring up the FlashSessions window. Then click on the Walk Me Through button.

This will bring up the FlashSessions Walk-Through dialog box, shown in Figure 6.8.

Clicking on the Expert Setup button just brings back the FlashSessions dialog box, with which you are already familiar. Clicking on Continue takes you through a number of prompt screens where you answer yes-or-no questions. If you wish to leave the tour at any time, just click on the Cancel button.

NOTE **Since signing on with a FlashSession—that is, by using a stored password—is the most expedient way to sign on to AOL, from now on, when I want you sign on, I'll just say "Run a FlashSession to get online."**

FIGURE 6.8:
AOL will walk you through FlashSessions if you're feeling uncertain about how to use them.

Reading Incoming Messages and Files

You read your incoming messages and files from FlashSessions the same way you would read messages and files that you downloaded in the usual way. In fact, the names AOL has given to your windows make more sense under FlashSessions (the Incoming FlashMail and Outgoing FlashMail dialog boxes, for instance).

After your FlashSession is complete, you can read your incoming mail in one of two ways. You can choose Mail ➤ Read Incoming Mail to bring up the Incoming FlashMail dialog box, as shown in Figure 6.9. To read a message, either double-click on it, or select it and click on Open.

Alternatively, you can read mail in your Personal Filing Cabinet. Choose Mail ➤ Personal Filing Cabinet, and then double-click on messages you wish to read. If your Incoming FlashMail folder is closed, double-click on it to open it.

For either method you use, once you have the mail window open, you can select the next message by clicking on the Next button.

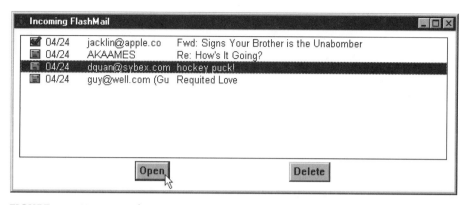

FIGURE 6.9: You can read your messages in the Incoming FlashMail dialog box.

 To select the previous message, click on the Prev button.

TIP See Chapter 4 for more tips on reading your mail.

Limitations of FlashSessions

As great as FlashSessions are, they aren't perfect. The following highlights the downside to using FlashSessions:

- You can't use FlashSessions when you're signed on as a guest.
- FlashSessions work only if AOL is running.
- There is a limit to the size of messages you can transmit using FlashSessions (64K bytes maximum).
- Automatic FlashSessions can interrupt telephone calls, which is a nuisance.
- Telephone calls can interrupt automatic FlashSessions, which is a different kind of nuisance.
- FlashSessions (either manual or automatic) can interrupt other data transfer.
- FlashSession settings apply to all screen names.
- You must store your password to use FlashSessions.

In spite of these limitations, FlashSessions are still the best way to do a lot of the basic housekeeping functions in AOL.

Chapter 7

PEOPLE CONNECTION AND CHATTING

FEATURING

- **Locating other AOL members online**
- **Buddy lists**
- **Member profiles**
- **Creating your own member profile**
- **Rooms and where to find good ones**
- **Netiquette**
- **The How-To's of Chatting**

One of the big selling points of AOL is its huge member base. There are many advantages to joining an online service with lots of members. For one thing, it means you're more likely to encounter other people with interests similar to yours. AOL makes it easy to find members with shared interests through chatting, instant messages, and member profiles. And once you've found them, you can easily check anytime to see if they are online.

You might be wondering to yourself, why is AOL so special with its huge installed member base? Isn't anyone who has an Internet address accessible to me? Well, yes; but not *instantly*. AOL offers several features that allow you to interact with other members in *real time*. Real time simply means that there is no lag time in the communication. As you type your responses, your recipient reads them, and vice versa. In this sense, it's a little like talking on the phone, but without the nuances of voice, tone, volume, and inflection. At any rate, you can exchange thoughts with other AOL members in ways that are impossible with people not on the AOL service.

> **WARNING** The same caveats that hold for e-mail hold for chatting as well. Be aware of what you're saying, since the only thing your recipient sees is your words. Better to play safe than sorry: if you're joking, it's not a bad idea to put the word *joke* in parentheses, at least until you're sure your interlocutor has a good sense of humor!

Chatting, covered extensively in this chapter, is the most interactive of AOL's many features designed to get members in touch with each other. It's also the best way to meet new people whom you might not encounter otherwise. In AOL terms, to *chat* with someone means to converse with them in real time. Even faster than instant messages, where you have to send each response, chatting is instantaneous. You type your message and press Enter, and your text appears on your recipients' screens instantly. Think of chatting as being like a virtual telephone conversation (or if there is more than one recipient, like teleconferencing).

So let's dive right into the pool of AOL members—you're sure to find some interesting net-mates!

Locating a Member Online

As you might expect, the first thing to do when you want to "talk" to someone online is to make sure they're out there and signed on. There are many ways to do this (and many ways to interact once you've found the person), but the three most efficient methods are the Instant Message feature, the Locate Member feature, and the Buddy List feature.

I am assuming here that you know the member's screen name. (We'll explore techniques for finding members whose screen names you *don't* know later in this chapter in the section "Member Profiles.") Since we covered instant messages in Chapter 5, let's look at the other two methods, locating members and buddy lists.

Using the Locate Member Feature

Like the Instant Message option, the Locate Member feature works only if you are signed on. So sign on using a FlashSession, clicking on the "Stay online when finished" box. When you're ready, choose Member ➤ Locate a Member Online (or use the Ctrl+L keyboard shortcut). The Locate Member Online dialog box will appear.

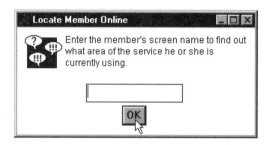

Type the member's name and click on the OK button.

As you can see, the Locate Member approach is a little more sophisticated than the Instant Message method. Not only does the Locate Member feature tell you whether someone is signed on, it also tells you whether they are in a chat area.

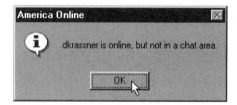

If the person is not in a chat area, Locate Member will tell you so. In that case, even though you can't chat, chances are you can send an instant message to catch up with someone. See the section "Sending Instant Messages" in Chapter 5 for details.

Buddy Lists

The *Buddy List* feature is like the Locate Member feature on steroids. Your buddy list contains the screen names of individuals with whom you like to chat, exchange instant messages, and otherwise communicate online. The main function of this feature is to inform you whenever someone on one of your lists signs on or signs off. Additionally, you can send instant messages directly from the Buddy List dialog box, as well as locate members in chat rooms. If for some reason you don't want people to know when *you* sign on or off, you can specify in your preferences that people cannot add you to *their* buddy lists. Let's look first at how to create a buddy list.

Creating Your Buddy List

To utilize the Buddy List feature, you must first create your list. To do so, choose Members ➤ Buddy Lists to bring up the Buddy Lists dialog box.

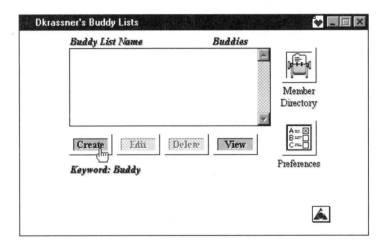

Click on the Create button to bring up the Create a Buddy List dialog box, shown in Figure 7.1.

The first thing you have to do is think of a name for the buddy list. When you have one, type it into the Buddy List Name box. For now, let's just choose the name **Online Buddies**. As you get to know more people online, you will learn who likes to talk about what and refine your list by dividing it into many lists, each with a meaningful name. But for now, let's just stick to one. When you've typed the name of the list, click in the Enter a Screen Name box and type in the screen names of several people you know in AOL. If you don't know anyone else, as practice, try entering your own name or my screen name: **dkrassner.**

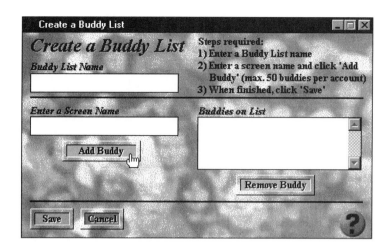

FIGURE 7.1:
You add names
to your buddy
lists in the Create
a Buddy List
dialog box.

Next, click on the Add Buddy button to add the screen name you have just typed to your buddy list. Add other screen names if you know any. You could even try entering some names at random (such as *eco* or *hamlet*) to see if people with such names are out there. After you type each screen name, click on Add Buddy to add it to the list. When you have added all the screen names you want to add, click on the Save button in the lower-left corner of the dialog box.

TIP

You can easily add or delete individuals from buddy lists by opening the Create a Buddy List dialog box; once there, double-click on the name of the buddy list you wish to alter to open up that list. Then you can add individuals as described above, or delete them by selecting names and clicking on Remove Buddy.

Using Your Buddy List

Your buddy lists work automatically (unless you've specified that they should not, as discussed shortly). If you've changed the default, you must go look to see who is online. To do so, choose Members ➤ Buddy Lists to bring up the Buddy Lists dialog box. Click on the buddy list from which you wish to find other members, and then click on the View button to bring up the BuddyView window, shown in Figure 7.2.

This screen will tell you if any of the individuals on your list are online (and where).

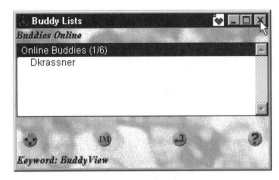

FIGURE 7.2:
You choose which buddy lists you want to look at in the BuddyView window.

Buddy List Preferences

While buddy lists might sound like a neat idea to you, maybe you're a bit nervous about other people having the ability to keep track of when you sign on and off from AOL. If so, lay your fears to rest, because you have complete control over who can check on you with their buddy lists. You can specify your desires in the Buddy List Preferences dialog box, shown in Figure 7.3. You reach it by choosing Member ➤ Buddy Lists and clicking on the Preferences button.

As always, to enable an option you click to place a checkmark next to it (or, for the radio buttons, you click to place a black dot inside the button). Click again to remove the checkmark (or dot) and disable the option. If you check the first option, the BuddyView window will appear automatically when you sign on. The next two choices specify whether AOL should audibly advise you (assuming you have a sound card installed) when buddies sign on or off. Below these are two options that let you specify whether or not people are allowed to add you to *their* buddy lists.

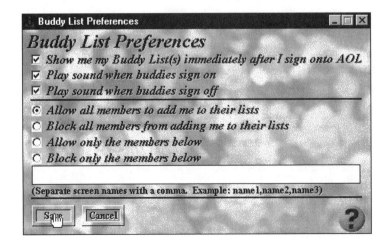

FIGURE 7.3:
You specify who can check on you in the Buddy List Preferences dialog box.

For the final two choices, you can allow only certain people to add you to their buddy lists, blocking all others; alternatively, you can block only certain people from adding you to their buddy lists, allowing all others. They both work the same way. You click on one of the options and fill in the appropriate screen names in the text box below. When you are finished, click on Save to record your preferences.

If you're itching to add some individuals to your buddy lists, read on. In the next section, we'll look at how to find other AOL members who share your interests.

Member Profiles

All this talk about buddy lists might sound really great, and you might be really excited about all the ways you can communicate with other AOL members—but what if you don't actually *know* anyone else on the service? That's where *member profiles* come in. A member profile is a stat sheet that any AOL member can fill out, and many do. A profile provides places for you to fill in any of the following information:

- Your real (as opposed to screen) name
- Your hometown
- Your gender
- Your marital status
- Your birthday
- What kind of computer you use
- Your interests and hobbies
- Your occupation
- A quote that sums up your philosophy of life

AOL does not require you to fill in your member profile. Furthermore, no one polices member profiles, so what you enter as your own information and what you read in others' member profiles may be lies, exaggerations, or just plain wishful thinking. Nevertheless, it's worthwhile filling in your member profile, for at least three reasons.

First, if people who know you (but don't know you're on AOL) happen to be clicking around AOL looking for friends, they might stumble across your name (assuming, that is, you included your real name in your member profile). In fact, it's even a useful way for people who *do* know you're on AOL to find your name, especially if they've forgotten or lost your screen name.

Second, it's a great way for other members who have similar interests to find and contact you. For instance, if you like chess and you list this as an interest in your member profile, someone browsing through profiles to find people with similar interests might see that you're interested in chess and—boom!—next thing you know, you've got a red-hot e-mail chess match going on.

Third, if you meet someone in the chat rooms (covered later in this chapter) who finds you interesting, that person may very well look up your member profile to learn more about you. (This is just one way for e-mail friendships to blossom.) On the other hand, if someone goes to look up your profile and there's nothing there, they will probably think that (a) you haven't figured out how to fill out the form, or (b) you have something to hide and therefore are probably not worth knowing. We'll take care of overcoming (a) together; however, you're on your own for (b)!

Creating Your Own Member Profile

By now, you're probably eager to create your own member profile, so let's do that now. To create (or edit) your member profile, you must be signed on. So if you're not signed on, sign on now using a FlashSession, clicking on the "Stay online when finished" box. When you're ready, choose Member ➤ My AOL. In the Personal Choices dialog box, click on Edit Online Profile. When you do so, the Create or Edit Online Profile dialog box window will appear. Double-click on Create/Modify Member Profile to bring up the Edit Your Online Profile dialog box, shown in Figure 7.4.

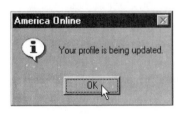

If you are creating your member profile (as opposed to editing it), just fill in each box, pressing Tab to move to the next box. As you can see in Figure 7.4, mine is already filled in, so if I want to change things, I make the changes and then click on the Update button. Don't click on the Update button until you've made *all* your changes. When you do click on Update, you'll see a message like the one above telling you that your profile is being updated.

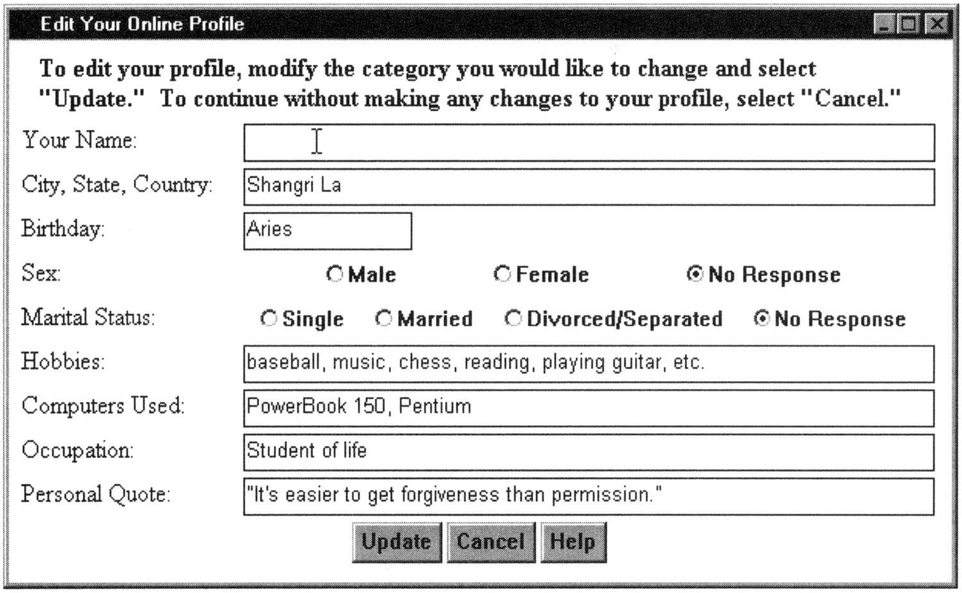
Edit Your Online Profile
To edit your profile, modify the category you would like to change and select "Update." To continue without making any changes to your profile, select "Cancel."
Your Name:
City, State, Country: Shangri La
Birthday: Aries
Sex: ○ Male ○ Female ◉ No Response
Marital Status: ○ Single ○ Married ○ Divorced/Separated ◉ No Response
Hobbies: baseball, music, chess, reading, playing guitar, etc.
Computers Used: PowerBook 150, Pentium
Occupation: Student of life
Personal Quote: "It's easier to get forgiveness than permission."
Update
Cancel
Help

FIGURE 7.4: You can either create or edit your member profile in this dialog box.

To exit your member profile without making changes, just click on the Cancel button.

TIP

The time you spend creating and updating your member profile is *not* free. Therefore, it is smart to plan what you're going to type in before you actually sign on and do it. If you get really stuck and just can't think of anything, click on the Member Services icon in the flashbar to go into that free area to do some pressure-free thinking.

Finding a Member's Profile

There are two ways to search for member profiles. The first involves finding profiles for screen names you already know. This is very easy and works just like the Locate a Member Online command, discussed earlier in this chapter. Choose Member ➤ Get a Member's Profile (or use the Ctrl+G keyboard shortcut). The Get a Member's Profile dialog box will appear.

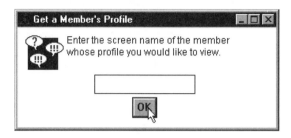

Type the member's screen name and click on the OK button. AOL will then display the profile in a dialog box similar to the one shown in Figure 7.5. Notice that this looks a bit different from the dialog box in which you edit your member profile.

 **The time you spend searching for and viewing member profiles is _not_ free. So plan what you're going to look for ahead of time.**

The second way to search for member profiles is to find them for people you _don't_ know. The rationale is that, by searching member profiles, you might find people with

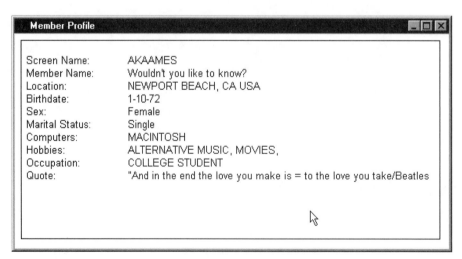

FIGURE 7.5: When you display member profiles, they look like this.

similar interests. You base your search on some kind of text string (such as *tennis* or *photography*), and you can search for just about any text. You can also use this method to search for people you do know, but whose screen names you don't know; you simply search for a person by their real name. To search for member profiles this way, follow these steps:

1.   Sign on to AOL if you're not already signed on.

2.   Choose Members ➤ Member Directory. The Member Directory dialog box will appear. Double-click on the Search the Member Directory option to bring up the Search Member Directory dialog box, shown in Figure 7.6.

3.   You can type almost anything in the keyword box near the top of the dialog box. If you type a hobby (such as *surfing*), you will see a list of other AOL members who list surfing as a hobby. If you type in a city, you will see a list of other AOL members who live (or at least who *say* they live) in that city. If you type a name, the search utility will find any individuals who have that name listed as their real name. For now, type in the name **Ludovico Settembrini** to see if there's anyone by that name.

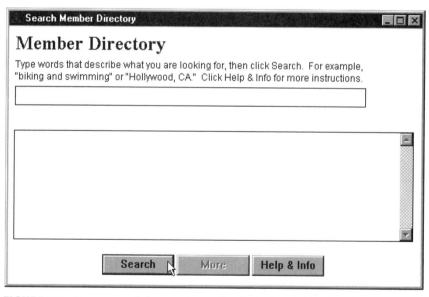

FIGURE 7.6:   You can search for member profiles in the Search Member Directory dialog box.

4. After mulling over your request, AOL will return a list (this can be large, small, or anywhere in between) of matches to your keyword or words. In our example, AOL has returned just one AOL member with the name *Ludovico Settembrini,* as shown in Figure 7.7.

5. Double-click on the one name to see more about this person. Another Member Profile dialog box will pop up with the information. As you can see in Figure 7.8, this is my member profile! Yes, even nice guys like me lie about their real names.

6. If there are more individuals whose member profiles you'd like to browse, close the current one and double-click on another to open it.

7. When you are finished, sign off unless you wish to do further browsing.

TIP If you are searching for folks who share your interests and find a lot of people, you can use the Edit ➤ Copy command (Ctrl+C) along with the Edit ➤ Paste command (Ctrl+V) to copy screen names to your Address Book for later use.

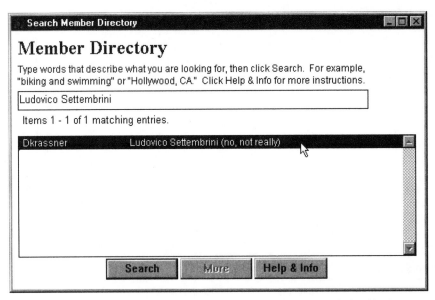

FIGURE 7.7: AOL will return a list of members who in some way match the criteria you typed into the keyword box.

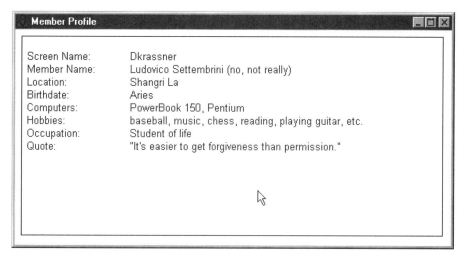

Member Profile

```
Screen Name:       Dkrassner
Member Name:       Ludovico Settembrini (no, not really)
Location:          Shangri La
Birthdate:         Aries
Computers:         PowerBook 150, Pentium
Hobbies:           baseball, music, chess, reading, playing guitar, etc.
Occupation:        Student of life
Quote:             "It's easier to get forgiveness than permission."
```

FIGURE 7.8: Double-click to display any member profile that AOL has found for you to learn more about that person.

Now that you know how to find people, you can *chat* with them, which is the real fun. Before we explore the subtleties and etiquette of chatting, though, we must first discuss the concept of a *room*. All chatting takes place in rooms, whether they be pre-existing ones or ones you've created (yes, you can create your own chat rooms), so you must have at least some sense of what a room is before you can learn about chatting.

What Is a Room?

To define a virtual room on AOL, we must abandon some traditional notions of rooms. First, a room on AOL has no dimensions or physical reality. Rather, it is a common address where members can "gather" and type messages to each other. The following are usually true about a room:

- It is a place where members go to discuss matters of common interest (such as current events or sports) and even to flirt.
- What you type is seen by all other members in the room.
- You see whatever is typed by other members in the room.
- There is sometimes an AOL guide (called the *OnlineHost*) in the room who sees all that is typed and ensures that no one threatens or harasses anyone else in the room; often the guide will greet you as you come into the room.

- When you enter or leave the room, all other members in the room receive a message informing them of this.
- When another member enters or leaves the room, everyone else in the room receives a message informing them of this.

If the notion of a room still seems somewhat opaque to you, here's how I like to think of it. You know those old reels of NASA space launches from the '50s and '60s, where there is this huge control room with all those crew-cut guys in white shirts and ties in front of computer monitors? Well, that's my personal metaphor for understanding what a room is. It is the virtual equivalent of those old NASA mission control rooms, where everyone sits in front of a computer and sees what everyone else is saying. The obvious difference is that, instead of all being in the *same* physical location, all members in a room are in *widely dispersed* physical locations. I've been in chat rooms where there were members from California, Oregon, Minnesota, Massachusetts, Maryland, and Florida, all at once. (We also had better haircuts.)

Of course, the best way to understand a room is to find an interesting one and go there. Let's go find some rooms now. For this first session, we'll just eavesdrop; that is, we'll just go into a few rooms to see what sort of things people are talking about, but we won't participate in any conversations yet. Sign on now in the usual way if you are not already signed on.

How to Find an Interesting Room

There are three quick and easy ways to find chat rooms:
- Click on the People Connection button in the Channels window.

- Click on the People Connection icon in the flashbar.

- Choose Go To ➤ Keyword, type **Lobby**, and click on Go.

Enter word(s): Lobby

Go

Any of these commands will take you into a lobby.

Hanging Out in the Lobby

Like the notion of a room, the idea of a virtual lobby has a few things in common with your conventional sense of a lobby. Maybe the best way to think of an AOL lobby is to imagine yourself entering a giant movie theater complex. You enter the lobby or foyer, and you see dozens of doors, each of which leads to a movie theater playing different movies. An AOL lobby is very much the virtual equivalent.

When you enter a lobby using one of the above commands, an AOL guide tells you what lobby you are in. You also see a list of other individuals in the lobby (that is, their screen names) and are informed how many people are there. As shown in Figure 7.9, once you're in a lobby, there are a number ways you can find interesting places to chat. Since each button leads to a world of options, we'll look at each one separately.

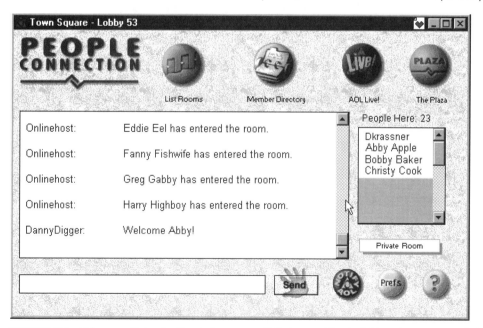

FIGURE 7.9: When you first enter the chat areas, you'll find yourself in the lobby, where you can find interesting chat rooms.

List Rooms

Clicking on the List Rooms button brings up the Public Rooms dialog box, shown in Figure 7.10.

The list on the left-hand side of the dialog box shows all available rooms. There are essentially three different kinds of rooms: public, private, and member. What you will see first are public rooms, which are rooms created by AOL for public debate on a variety of issues. They usually have descriptive names such as Game Parlor Teen, Garden Center, Sports, or the Flirts Nook. There is even one called New Member Lounge, where you can meet other new members and ask questions. You can see who is in a room by selecting it and clicking on the Who's Here button. We'll explore this option in more detail later, in the section "Getting Info about People."

Most of the rooms will have a number after them (such as Teen Chat 70), since there can be more than one room with the same name. It's not much fun having lots and lots of people in the same room (yes, virtual rooms get crowded, just like real ones), so it makes more sense to have several rooms of the same type. The number on the far left of the list in Figure 7.10 is the number of people in the room. For reasons that will become clear when you see chatting in action, it is not practical to have more than about twenty people in a room; realistically, this number should be even smaller if the members in the room are unusually garrulous!

If you click on the Member Rooms button, you will see another list of rooms that were created by AOL *members,* as illustrated in Figure 7.11. There are many, many more member rooms than there are public rooms, and the list changes constantly.

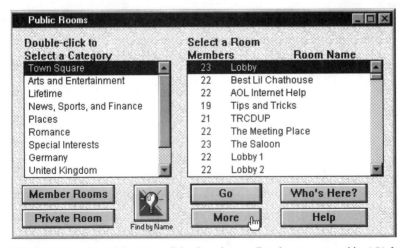

FIGURE 7.10: The Public Rooms dialog box shows a list of rooms created by AOL for discussion of general-interest topics.

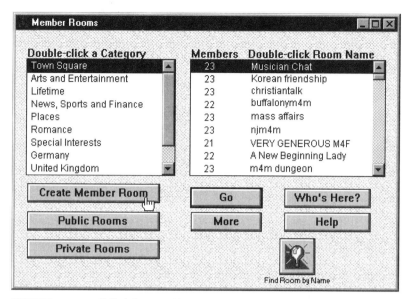

FIGURE 7.11: You'll find dozens of interesting rooms in the Member Rooms area of the chatting service.

These rooms accommodate an incredible variety of interests, personalities, and lifestyles. For example, if you like the pop singer Tori Amos, there's a room for you and other like-minded individuals. You will find more broad-minded and divergent opinions in the member rooms than in the public rooms.

You can even create your own room by clicking on the Private Room button. You might do this if you find a kindred spirit in one of the chat rooms and wish to have a private conversation with him or her. Alternatively, someone might also ask you to join them in a preexisting private room. To go to a private room, you not only have to click on the Private Room button, but you also must enter the name of the room. There are no lists of private rooms that you can access, so you'll have to wait for someone to invite you to a private room or create your own. We'll cover private rooms in detail in the section "How to Ask Someone to Join You."

The other buttons in the Public Rooms dialog box are fairly self-explanatory. Clicking on Help brings up a file that tells you all about chatting, rooms, online etiquette, and so forth. Clicking on More simply lists more rooms. If you see something that disturbs you, you can always tell AOL about it. There is a button back in the People Connection dialog box called Notify AOL. If you click that button, you'll see the Notify AOL dialog box, shown in Figure 7.12, where you can report problems. By problems, I mean instances of harassment.

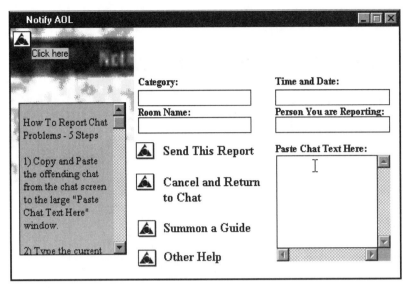

FIGURE 7.12: You can use the Notify AOL dialog box to report problems such as harassment.

When you have decided which room you wish to visit, simply select it and click on the Go button. Go ahead and choose a room right now.

You should see a window similar to the one shown in Figure 7.13. This is where the action is! You'll learn all about how to chat and how to read what people are saying a little later in this chapter. For now, just watch for a few minutes to get a sense of the sorts of things people chat about.

When you are ready to leave this room, choose Window ➤ Public Rooms to return to the list of rooms. If you'd like to see what other public rooms are like or you'd like to go explore the member rooms, feel free to do so now. When you are finished, return to the lobby by clicking on the People Connection icon on the flashbar to exit whatever chat room you are in.

AOL Live!

Now I hate it when people gush about computers and computer stuff, but the Center Stage seems to me to be an example of online services at their best. If you click on the Center Stage button in the lobby, you'll bring up the AOL Live! window, shown in Figure 7.14.

The AOL Live! area is essentially a group of talk shows in virtual auditoriums. Just as AOL rooms have a few things in common with real rooms, AOL auditoriums have

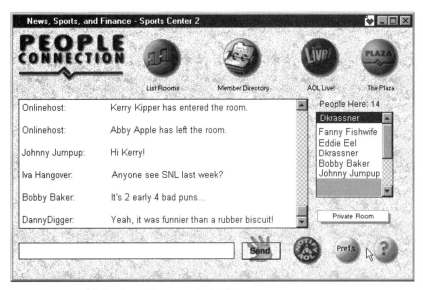

FIGURE 7.13: This is what a chat room looks like.

FIGURE 7.14: The AOL Live! window is your entry into the world of online talk shows.

some things in common with real auditoriums. Imagine yourself in a lecture hall listening to someone conduct a question-and-answer session. This is what AOL Live! is all about, with a few obvious exceptions; instead of you and your fellow audience being in the same physical location as each other and as the speaker, you are all in different places. Another way that AOL Live! auditoriums differ from real auditoriums is that you can hear only three things:

- Responses and comments from the main speaker—called the *guest*
- Comments from the moderator (or the *host,* basically, an AOL guide)
- Comments from other members in your row

Any questions you wish to ask the guest must be directed toward the host, who then announces to everyone in AOL Live! that "so-and-so [a screen name] asks the following question," and poses your question to the guest. The guest then responds for everyone to hear. As for an AOL Live! *row,* as you might imagine, it's analogous to a row in an auditorium; it is a group of people all in more or less the same place, seeing and hearing the same thing. The number of people who can occupy a row is somewhat arbitrary; however, the reason for having a limit, like room size, is one of practicality. It would just be too hard to follow the dialog of your row (interspersed with comments from the guest and questions from the host) if there were more than, say, fifteen people.

NOTE Often, the Welcome window will tell you who are going to be guests on AOL Live! that day.

All right, you say, so what's the big deal? Sounds like a bunch of big chat rooms! Well, you're right, they are just big chat rooms; the big deal is *who* AOL finds to be guests. Since a guest doesn't have to be *physically* present to be on AOL Live! (i.e., he or she can sign on from anywhere—home, work, the road) there are none of the usual logistical problems that come with having entertainment personalities, politicians, athletes, and other luminaries as talk show guests. Furthermore, many individuals seem to be more candid on AOL Live! than they might be in a television interview, and they seem to prefer the relative anonymity of fielding questions via computer. They cannot be attacked or heckled, and they don't have to jet from coast to coast. They can even do the gig if they are not feeling well or are bedridden.

TIP You can reach AOL Live! from the Go To menu (if you haven't changed it) or by using the Ctrl+6 keyboard shortcut. You can also reach it by clicking on the Center Stage button in the flashbar.

All kinds of celebrities and experts have been AOL guests, ranging from the actress Sean Young to Senator John Ashcroft (R-Missouri) and running the whole gamut in between.

If you refer back to Figure 7.14, you can see that you have a number of options in the AOL Live! window. If you click on the Today's Live Events button, AOL will show you a list of the day's events, as shown in Figure 7.15. If you wish to join an event in progress, just select it and click on the Go button. If you try to join an event scheduled for later, you will be informed of the starting time. There will also be several other buttons listing the headline guests of the day. If you want to go back to the main AOL Live! menu, click on Return to Main at the bottom of the window.

Once you have joined an AOL Live! event, you have several options. If you want to ask the guest a question, click on the Interact with Host button and follow the instructions. If you don't want to see what your rowmates are saying (which is often more entertaining than what the guest is saying), click on the Chat button, and then click on Turn Chat Off. Alternatively, you can change rows at any time if you think what your rowmates are saying is persiflage.

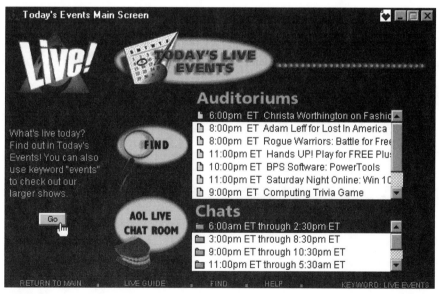

FIGURE 7.15: The Today's Events Main Screen has a list of all events scheduled for AOL Live!

Back in the AOL Live! Main Screen, click on Coming Attractions to see who is scheduled to appear on AOL Live! in the next few days. This is a great way to get a sense of this feature. You'll see that upcoming guests include everyone from computer gurus to comedian Dennis Miller, rock bands to baseball managers. To read more about a guest, select his or her name and click on Open. To see an even more detailed list of guests, click on More. Chances are, if you're not on life-support, you'll find something interesting on AOL Live!

You can find transcripts of past events by clicking on the Find button in the Today's Events window. If you click on Search for Transcripts, a dialog box will appear called DataTimes. Type a word into the search box, such as *recent,* and press Enter. A list of all recent guests who have appeared on Center Stage will come up, as shown in Figure 7.16. You can select any of the files and then double-click on them to see a transcript (a text log of all that the person said) from their appearance on AOL Live!

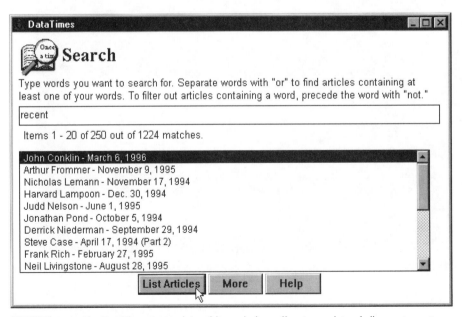

FIGURE 7.16: The DataTimes transcript archives window offers transcripts of all recent guests on AOL Live!

Even better is to download it to your hard disk; that way you can read it offline and save yourself some online time. To do so, click on the Download button.

Clicking on Intermission in the AOL Live! window brings up the Intermission Main Screen, as shown in Figure 7.17. This is the gateway to a variety of services. The idea is that you can visit here during breaks from AOL Live! events.

Let's look at each of the options in the Intermission window:

About AOL Live!—This tells you all about AOL Live! You can always save a document like this to a disk to read offline.

Sponsors—And now, a word from our sponsor… Here you can find, according to AOL, "interesting and valuable information" about the companies that make the special events in AOL Live! possible.

Special Event Coverage—A list of upcoming special events on AOL Live!

Auditorium Entrances—This takes you to the window that lists the various auditoriums and the events scheduled.

Suggestion Box—You can click here to offer feedback.

Backstage Buzz—This brings up a list of the last ten individuals who have appeared on AOL Live!

Games and Contests—Rules and explanations of the games and quiz shows on AOL Live!

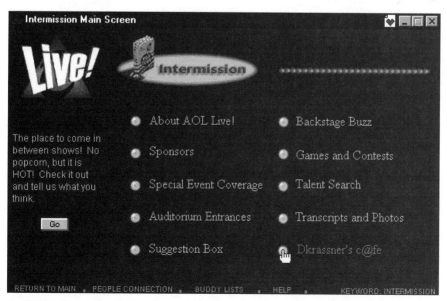

FIGURE 7.17: You can find out more about AOL Live! events in the Intermission Main Screen.

Talent Search— You (yes, you!) can have a say in who appears on AOL Live! Click on this button to make a suggestion.

Transcripts and Photos—This takes you to the Transcript window, where you can read about (and find pictures of) individuals who have appeared on AOL Live!

***Username's* C@fe**—Your username will appear here. It's like having your own coffeehouse where you can hang out with friends and relax.

The Plaza

Back in the People Connection box, if you click on the Plaza button you will bring up the Plaza dialog box, shown in Figure 7.18. The Plaza is a bit of a catch-all area for a collection of services and features that don't neatly fit either the AOL Live! or chat room categories.

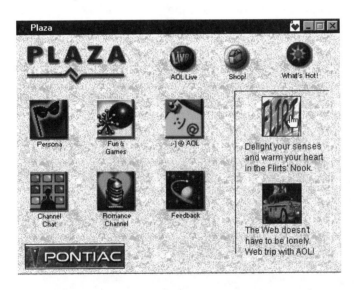

FIGURE 7.18: The Plaza dialog box is your gateway to a variety of other People Connection areas.

In The Plaza, you'll find a number of services, including the Persona Café and :^) @ AOL, both of which lead to chat rooms and bulletin boards. These chat areas cater to no particular interest; in a sense, they are like coffee houses. In fact, within :^) @ AOL there is something called Le Pub, which is the virtual equivalent to an English pub (only the ale's a bit flatter). There is also a Fun & Games area, where you can find some great diversions. The Plaza also includes the new AOL Road Trip, a terrific guided tour of the World Wide Web.

In addition, The Plaza includes a Romance Channel where you can meet your match, in more ways than one. The Channel Chat area is an attempt to overcome the somewhat arbitrary division of topics in the Channels window. For instance, you can go here to talk or read about music, without having to worry about whether it should fall under entertainment, lifestyles, digital city, or whatnot. You can offer feedback by clicking the Feedback button. Finally, there is a link to AOL Live! in the Plaza.

Prefs

Clicking on the Chat Preferences button in the lobby brings up the Chat Preferences dialog box, shown in Figure 7.19. These are just simple options you can check or uncheck to customize your chatting.

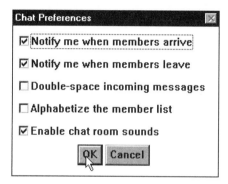

FIGURE 7.19:
Customize your chatting in the Chat Preferences dialog box.

The first two options, if checked, will tell you when members enter and leave chat rooms you are in. If you have trouble following the scrolling dialogs that appear in chat screens, check to have incoming messages double-spaced. Click on the next option to alphabetize the list of people in the room, which appears in the top-right corner of the window. Finally, you can bounce multimedia sounds to other people in chat rooms if you've checked the last option (see the section "Bouncing Sounds" toward the end of this chapter).

TIP You can also reach the Chat Preferences dialog box by choosing Members ➤ Preferences and clicking on the Chat button.

Parental Control

Now is the time to revisit the Parent control dialog box (Members ➤ Parental Control). We explored this dialog box in detail in Chapter 3, so if you'd like to learn more about it, please turn there. Suffice to say, if you have children who use your AOL account, the options in Parental Controls let you closely monitor what your kids can and cannot access, both in AOL and on the Internet. So if you're concerned about security, or if you really don't want your kids to go to certain sites, you can specify this using the Parental Controls.

> **TIP** You can also reach the Parental Controls dialog box by choosing Members ➤ Parental Control.

Now that you've got some idea of how the chatting features work, you're probably feeling ready to try them. But before you do, there are some things you should know about acceptable behavior in chat rooms.

Netiquette

As online chatting has grown as a form of communication, a code of acceptable behavior has grown up alongside it. Chatting is governed by a well-defined canon of acceptable conduct and has its own vocabulary as well as an aggregation of shorthand symbols (emoticons) and acronyms. When you are online, other members will expect you to be cognizant of these standards and to practice them.

Network etiquette, or *netiquette,* as it is often called, is neither complicated nor overly restrictive, but it is an excellent idea to learn at least the basics of netiquette before you spend a lot of time in the chat areas. I've been in chat rooms where most of the members have agreed to ignore all comments from another member whom they found offensive or scabrous. It's no fun being ostracized, so use a little common sense and learn the principles of netiquette; you'll enjoy chatting a lot more if you do

Proper Procedure

Many of the same rules that apply to e-mail also apply to chatting. For instance, the best way to highlight words and phrases is to surround them with *asterisks*. Avoid using ALL CAPITALS to get attention, as capital letters, by convention, indicate that you are YELLING, and nobody likes being yelled at. Also, it is considered the height of incivility to continually press the Enter key, which makes the screen scroll so fast that no one will be able to read it. This is called *scrolling,* and it's a sure-fire way of making enemies.

If someone uses a phrase, emoticon, or an acronym you don't know, feel free to ask. Most people are happy to help out a neophyte in the chat rooms. It's fine to use your own emoticons, acronyms, and other chatting shorthand, provided you are prepared to explain them to anyone who doesn't understand them.

It's inappropriate to ask someone to join you in a private room in front of everyone else, as it can make others in the room feel excluded. Instead, send them an instant message as described in the section "How to Ask Someone to Join You" later in this chapter.

Polite Conversation

The AOL chat areas should be a "marketplace of ideas." You should never feel obligated to back down from an argument, even a heated one. But try to avoid *ad hominum* arguments (that is, arguments that criticize your opponent personally), instead questioning and criticizing his or her *opinions*. You'll find that this will lead to spirited, but not *mean*-spirited, debate. It's no fun for your opponent or for anyone listening in if you just call him or her a bunch of names. This is not debate, it is diatribe. There is even a special name for deliberately offensive or personal attacks: *flaming*. It's usually best to ignore flaming, as it is usually just meant to incite anger and rarely leads to enriching discourse.

Furthermore, any behavior designed to unfairly exclude members from a chat is not kosher. For example, just because you don't agree with someone, you shouldn't try to turn the entire room against him or her.

Finally, whatever chat-room beef you might have with someone, leave it in the chat room. It's churlish to track someone down with their screen name and send e-mail or instant messages to them after you or they have left a chat room. As someone once said, everyone is entitled to his right to be wrong. For a more formal charter on online behavior, refer to the following section, "Reading the Terms of Service."

Along with knowing the appropriate behavior, you can also avoid misunderstandings in chat rooms if you are familiar with the shorthand that is often used: emoticons and acronyms. Although we looked at both of these elements briefly in Chapter 4, we'll do so again here just as a refresher.

Reading the Terms of Service (TOS)

You might have heard about the Terms of Service (TOS) agreement. Whether you knew it or not, you agreed to abide by the terms of this agreement when you signed up for AOL, so it's a good idea to read through it at least once. To do so, either choose Go To ➤ Keyword, click on the Keyword icon on the flashbar, or use the Ctrl+K keyboard shortcut to bring up the Keyword dialog box. Type in **Terms of Service** (or **tos**), and the Terms of Service dialog box will appear.

Click on the Terms of Service button in the lower-left corner of the box to see the Terms of Service agreement. This outlines all of the terms of the AOL service, which you must abide by or risk having your membership rescinded. You can read through the TOS or save it to your hard disk to read later (choose File ➤ Save, click on the Save button on the flashbar, or use the Ctrl+S keyboard shortcut). If you want to see more advice on how to conduct yourself online, go back to the Terms of Service dialog box and click on either the Online Conduct or Rules of the Road buttons.

Chatting Emoticons

Since the people with whom you chat cannot see you or hear you, if you are sending a message that might be misconstrued, it is a good idea to include some kind of indication that you are joking, happy, sad, serious, etc. The best way to do this is with *emoticons*.

An emoticon is a series of symbols intended to make a small picture. For instance, if you type a colon, a caret (Shift+6), and a closing parenthesis, you will make the "happy face" emoticon, as shown here:

:^)

You can see it properly if you tilt your head to the left and use a little imagination.

There are hundreds of emoticons (real power chatters seem to have one for every emotion). If you don't know what a particular emoticon is supposed to mean, just ask!

Here is a list of some useful emoticons:

Emoticon	Name	Meaning
:^)	Happy face	I'm happy!
:^(	Sad face	I'm bummed
:^|	Unemotional	I'm on an even keel
:^D	Laughing	That's funny!
;^)	Winking	We have a secret
|^O	Sleepy face	I'm tired
:^*	Kissing	(Obvious…)
{}	Hug	I'm giving you a hug
:^p	Sticking tongue out	Nyah, nyah, nyah!
O:^)	Angel	I'm an angel
}:^>	Devil	I'm a little devil
*<:^)	Party hat	Let's celebrate!
}:^)	Longhorn	I'm bullish on that
:^?	Confused	What?
:^#	Lips sealed	Keep this in confidence
:^X	Lips sealed	My lips are sealed
:)	Simple face	I'm simply happy!
:*)	Clown face	Just kidding

Chatting Acronyms

Unlike emoticons, which are intended to convey an emotion or mood, chatting acronyms are used simply to save space and typing time. Since chatting is not free, anything that speeds it up conserves precious online minutes.

As with emoticons, there are hundreds of acronyms; if you see one you don't recognize, just ask. Here is a list of some of the more commons acronyms:

Acronym	Meaning
ASAP	As soon as possible
ATB	All the best
ATVB	All the very best
AWK	Away from keyboard

Acronym	Meaning
BAK	Back at keyboard
BRB	Be right back
BTW	By the way
CMF	Crossing my fingers
CU	See you
CUL8R	See you later
DIY	Do it yourself
FAQ	Frequently asked question
FYI	For your information
GLT	Get a load of this
GMTA	Great minds think alike
IMHO	In my humble opinion
LOL	Laughing out loud
MYOB	Mind your own business
NRN	No reply needed
ROTF	Rolling on the floor (laughing)
RTFM	Read the [colorful epithet] manual
SO	Significant other
SOW	Speaking of which
TTFN	Ta-ta for now
WB	Welcome back
WRT	With respect to
WTG	Way to go!

The How-To's of Chatting

All right, enough preparation! Let's give this chatting thing a try.

When we get to the section on private rooms, you might want to either try this with another friend who has an AOL account or just try creating private rooms to practice.

It's probably *not* a good idea to just ask someone at random to join you in a private room, as this might be taken the wrong way.

In order to chat, you must, of course, be in the chat area, so if you're not already signed on, sign on now in the usual way. Then click on the People Connection icon in the flashbar to reach a lobby.

The Real Shockwave Riders

John Brunner once wrote a book called *The Shockwave Rider*, the title of which alludes to those who are at the forefront of any quantum leap in conventional thinking and behavior (those who ride the shockwave of change). Virtual interactions, predicted in that book, are now a reality; people who have mastered the new medium, through such interactions as chatting, are riding this shockwave. But to what purpose?

Well, chatting can be a rewarding and enjoyable way to meet people, discuss ideas, and learn about subjects that interest you. Furthermore, and perhaps more important, as our society becomes increasingly fractured and fast-paced, many people find online discussions their only opportunity to interact with others. Chatting and other forms of online communication should not and (I hope) will not replace more immediate and intimate human interactions, but if we want to keep in step with the trends, it seems we must acquire some fluency in the language of virtual exchanges.

Isaac Asimov took the notion of chatting to the *n*th degree in his book *The Naked Sun,* in which people never interact, other than through holographic images. Let's hope it never comes to that.

How to Tell Who Is Saying What

In both lobbies and chat rooms, you can tell who is "speaking" by looking at the left side of the screen. In a format much like the dialog of a play, screen names (or the word *OnlineHost*) will appear, followed by a colon and then the text of the message.

For instance, if you've just entered a lobby, you will see a message from the OnlineHost looking something like this:

```
OnlineHost: ***You are in  Lobby 53■.***
```

The number will probably be different, as each time you go into the People Connection area, you usually go into a different lobby. If you watch for a few moments, the Online Host will announce the entrance and exit of other members. You might

```
Harry Highboy
Dkrassner
SamSpode
TerryMajor
```

also see messages from other members who are talking to each other in the lobby. Remember, you can see who's in the lobby by scrolling the list in the upper-right corner of the window.

Now let's take a look at some more complicated chatting. Click on the List Rooms button, and then select one of the rooms and click on Go to enter it. Let's try the New Members Room in the Public Rooms list. Notice that you've entered in the middle of the conversation, as it were. You might want to watch for a few minutes, just to get an idea of what the chatting's all about.

> **TIP**
>
> **If you find that the screen scrolls too fast to read, go into the Chat Preferences dialog box and click to enable the "Double-space incoming messages" option.**

Notice that the arrangement is the same in the chat room as it was in the lobby. A screen name will appear on the left, followed by a colon, followed by the message. As always, there is a list of the room's occupants in the upper-right corner. As people add their two cents to the discussion, the screen will scroll down (i.e., the words will move up, like the credits at the end of a movie). If you miss something or want to reread what someone has written, just click on the scroll button at the top of the screen. This will scroll the text *down,* allowing you to see what came before. If you're feeling brave, try typing a response (being as polite as possible) and then either press Enter or click on the Send button. Your comment will appear, as mine has in Figure 7.20.

As you can see, my screen name appears so that everyone in the room knows who made the comment. Since it is always clear who is saying what, don't say things you might regret. Members police the chat rooms almost as vigilantly as the AOL guides. Furthermore, if someone knows your screen name, they can, of course, look up your profile (if you filled one out) to see who you are.

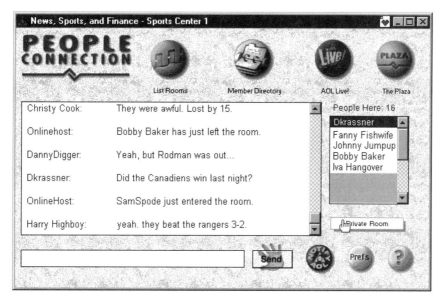

FIGURE 7.20: My screen name appears next to my comment, so there is no anonymity in a chat room (as far as screen names are concerned).

Getting Info about People

If you find someone in a room intriguing—or obnoxious—you might want to know more about them. Or, someone may ask you to join them in a private room, and you might want to know more about them before doing so. There are several easy ways to get information on any individual in a room.

If you haven't yet entered a room, you can click on the Who's Here? button to see who is in the room.

The People dialog box will appear, as shown in Figure 7.21.

FIGURE 7.21: The People dialog box lists all individuals in a room.

Click on Message to send an instant message to the selected individual, or on Info to see the individual's member profile (if they have one).

Once you are in a room, you can find out about a member in the room by double-clicking on his or her screen name in the upper-right corner. When you do this, a dialog box like the one in Figure 7.22 appears.

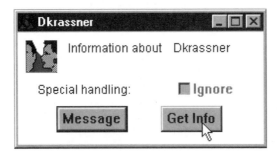

FIGURE 7.22: In a room, when you double-click on an individual's screen name in the upper-right corner, this dialog box appears.

Notice that this dialog box has the person's screen name at the top and indicates whether he or she has chosen to block instant messages; if the Ignore box is unchecked, you can send an instant message by clicking on Message. This brings up an instant message dialog box with the screen name filled in. All you have to do is type the text of the message and click on Send. This is one way to send private messages to someone in a room without the other members seeing it.

If you click on the Get Info button in the dialog box shown in Figure 7.22, the individual's member profile will appear. This is a good way to find out more about the person. If there is no member profile for the screen name you've selected, you will see this message:

TIP
If you want to get information at any time about a member whose screen name you know, you can always use the Get a Member's Profile command (Ctrl+G) and type in the person's screen name.

How to Ask Someone to Join You

Someone once asked a dining Groucho Marx if he could join him, to which Groucho responded, "Why? Am I coming apart?" If you find someone whom you would like to chat with privately—assuming it's not Groucho—the best way to ask is to send an instant message. This way, you avoid making other members feel excluded. To send a private message to someone in a room, double-click on the person's screen name in the upper-right corner of the chat-room window. This will open a small dialog box with the person's screen name in the title bar, like the one in Figure 7.22.

Click on the Message button to open a Send Instant Message window like the one shown in Figure 7.23. AOL does the work of putting the person's screen name into the To box, so all you have to do is fill in the message box. If you want the person to join you in a private room, you might phrase it something like: "Would you care to join me in a private room?" When your message is ready, click on Send.

You will probably get a response rather quickly, whether yes or no. If it's no, then lay off. Don't bug people if they don't want to be alone with you. If the answer is yes, then you should let the person know what you're going to name the room. Reply with something like, "Great! See you in a few minutes in the private room called *The Casbah*." Try to think of a somewhat off-the-wall name to ensure it isn't taken.

FIGURE 7.23: You can send private messages to other members in a room using instant messages.

How to Create Your Own Private Room

Once another member has agreed to chat with you privately, you've got to create a private room in which to hold the conversation. To do so, click on the Private Room button in the chatting dialog box.

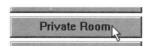

The Enter a Private Room dialog box will appear, as shown in Figure 7.24. Type in the name of the room you wish to create.

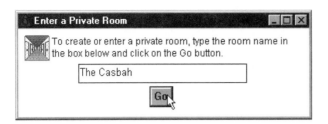

FIGURE 7.24:
You create a private room in the Enter a Private Room dialog box.

If the name you chose for your room is already taken, you will be informed of this and asked to choose another. Keep trying until you hit upon something original. When you are successful, the OnlineHost will simply say, "You are in *The Casbah*" (or whatever your room name was), as shown below.

OnlineHost: *** You are in "The Casbah". ***

> **NOTE**
>
> **If you are forced to choose a different name for your private room, be sure to send *another* instant message to the person you have asked to join you, telling them the *new* name of the private room.**

Once in your own private room, you can chat as usual, typing what you want your friend to see and pressing Enter to send it. You might have to wait a moment or two for the person to join you, though.

If You Are Invited into a Private Room

If you are invited to join someone in a private room, be sure you get the correct name of the room (you might even wish to copy it to the clipboard using Ctrl+C). Then click on the Private Room button to open the Enter a Private Room dialog box. Type in the name of the private room you wish to join (or use the paste command—Ctrl+V), and click on Go. The OnlineHost will inform you and the person who invited you that you have arrived in the private room.

Ending a Private Chat

To end a private chat, or any chat for that matter, just click on the People Connection icon in the flashbar.

Advanced Chatting

Once you've mastered the basics of chatting, you might want to make things a little more interesting by bouncing sounds to the people you're chatting with, or you may want to keep a record of everything that's said by keeping a chat log. Let's look at both of these options now.

Bouncing Sounds

One way to personalize chatting a bit more is to *bounce* sounds into the chat room. The way this works is that you send a command from your computer to someone else's computer that says, essentially, "play this sound file." There are several things to know before you try to bounce sounds:

- You must have a sound-capable computer to hear sounds.
- The people to whom you are bouncing the sounds must have sound-capable computers to hear them.
- The people to whom you are bouncing the sounds must have the sound files you are bouncing to them in the Aol30 folder on their hard disk (sound files have the extension *wav*).
- In order for you to hear chat sounds, you must have the option enabled in Chat Preferences.
- In order for people to hear chat sounds, they must have the option enabled in Chat Preferences.

If all these criteria are met, then you can bounce sounds and receive sounds.

Let's say you are in a chat room and you want to welcome a new member who has just entered the room (it might be someone you know, or maybe you're just being friendly). In the text box at the bottom of your chatting screen, type the following:

```
{S filename
```

where *filename* is the name of the wav file you want to play. For instance, you might want to type **{S Welcome** to play the "Welcome" greeting you hear when you sign on to AOL. When you have typed the command correctly, click on the Send button to send it to everyone in the room.

To bounce a sound to only one person, you would type the text shown above in an instant message addressed to the desired screen name.

Keeping a Chat Log

If you like, you can keep a record of all that is said during a chat session. You use the *Chat Log* feature to do so. There are lots of good reasons for keeping a chat log: there may be information you need, ideas you want to reread, or exchanges you found particularly amusing or interesting.

To keep a log of your chatting, first choose File ➤ Log Manager to bring up the Logging dialog box, as shown in Figure 7.25. Click on Open Log, and in the Open dialog box, click on OK to create a new file called *chat.log.* (All of these steps can be done offline.)

If you are not still online, sign on now in the usual way. Then go to the chat room where you want to keep track of things. As long as you leave the log window open, the chat log you have started will keep track of everything that is said.

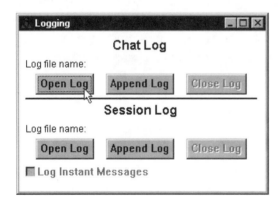

FIGURE 7.25:
You start and stop your chat logs here in the Logging dialog box.

When you are finished logging, choose File ➤ Log Manager again to bring up the Logging dialog box. This time, click on the Close Log button and then close the dialog box. You can then peruse the chatting log offline by opening the file with the command File ➤ Open.

> **TIP**
>
> One of the really great features of chat logs is that you don't even have to stay in the chat room for them to keep track of the conversation. They will run in the background while you do other things in AOL, and then you can go offline to read them at your leisure.

Part 3

Finding Cool Stuff on AOL

Chapter 8

AOL RESOURCES

- **The ABCs of browsing**
- **News and other information**
- **Stock quotes and personal finance**
- **The AOL software libraries**
- **AOL bulletin boards**
- **For Kids Only**
- **Travel**
- **Sports, movies, and other entertainment**
- **The International Channel**

In Part II, you learned about meeting people and communicating with them online. But that's really only one side of AOL. There is also the *information* side. Not only is AOL great for keeping in touch, it's also an excellent way to stay abreast of news, entertainment, trends, and finances. Furthermore, there is an incredible amount of reference material available online, including a huge software library. Chances are, if there's something you want to know about, it's out there on AOL.

Before we continue, though, it is important that you understand the distinction between what's available on AOL and what's available on the Internet. AOL offers a large amount of information directly from its service. This means that you can hook up to AOL and probably find what you need there. The Internet is a much larger storehouse of information than AOL, but to see what's there, you need a special program called a *browser*. But let's not get ahead of ourselves. We'll look at the Internet in all its glory in Chapters 10 and 11. In Chapters 8 and 9, we'll just focus on AOL; there's more than enough there to keep us busy!

There is a further distinction to be made with respect to information that's available on AOL. Some of the news, entertainment, bulletin boards, and so on that you find on AOL is created by and is unique to AOL; we will look at these areas in this chapter. Other areas, although part of the AOL service, are created by outside companies who then place the information on AOL; these we will cover in Chapter 9.

As you might imagine, the line between these two types of areas is somewhat blurred. For instance, AOL has its own news area; yet within this news area is the Reuters wire service. Reuters is a separate company from AOL, so the news that comes over the wire is generated from outside AOL. Maybe the best way to think of it is to realize that the *form* of the news area (how it looks and how you interact with it) is created by and belongs to AOL, while the *content* of the news area is derived from outside sources.

> **NOTE** The term *wire* refers to a constant newsfeed, such as that offered by Reuters and the Associated Press. Most newspapers subscribe to the AP wire and rely on it for news stories outside their local coverage area.

The ABCs of Browsing

One of the most daunting aspects of any online service is the amount of information available. If you're new, you probably don't know where to start. Well, my hope is that in this chapter, you'll develop a sense of what's out there and what you think you might find interesting. Since you'll be interacting with AOL in a more sophisticated way than you have up to now, let's go over a few of the rudiments of *browsing*, the official term for clicking around from area to area to find interesting stuff.

AOL has several areas designed specifically to introduce newcomers to the service. You've already seen the Channels feature, as well as the Welcome menu and the AOL Live! area. There are several other commands on the Go To menu that you may wish to include in your exploring. If there is a keyboard shortcut to the command, I will give it in parentheses.

NOTE Since all of these features are found online, I'm not going to always remind you to go online. I'll just assume you know how to do so and are already there.

First, there is the Go To ➤ Discover America Online command (or use the Ctrl+2 keyboard shortcut). When the Guided Tour window appears, you can click on any of the buttons to learn about different aspects of AOL. The Guided Tour is a great way to get acquainted with AOL and get an idea of the services offered. In fact, before moving on, it may be well worth your time to take a few minutes now to click around in Discover America Online, just to get a better sense of the breadth of the service.

Next, there is Go To ➤ New Services (Ctrl+1). This command brings up the New Features & Services dialog box, shown in Figure 8.1. As you might imagine, AOL adds new services and features every day. This dialog box is a good place to keep abreast of what's new. More than once, you will find yourself wishing AOL did this or offered that, only to discover that they've just added it to the roster.

Similar to the New Services feature is the What's Hot feature. If you click on the What's Hot button in the Welcome menu or on the What's Hot icon in the flashbar, the What's Hot dialog box appears, as shown in Figure 8.2. Here you can keep up with the latest trends, including news and AOL services. The What's Hot feature differs from the What's New feature in that a service does not necessarily have to be new to AOL to be of current interest. For example, there is always an Olympics area available for you to visit; but during an Olympic year, when it is, naturally, of much greater interest, you're likely to find that area in What's Hot.

Arranging Windows

As you browse in AOL, you might find yourself opening a great many windows; the reason is that as you click in each window to find a new area or to explore an area more deeply, AOL leaves each preceding window open for you as a reference. You already know that you can revisit any open window, even if it's not showing, by

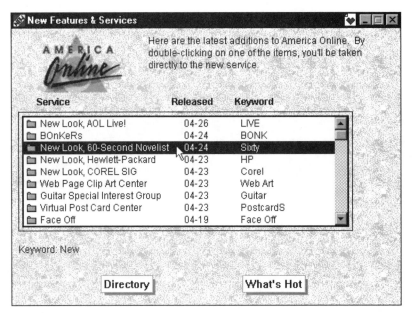

FIGURE 8.1: The New Features & Services dialog box highlights new features that AOL has added.

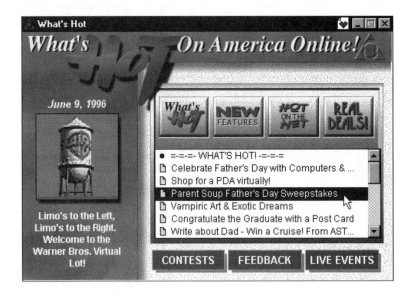

FIGURE 8.2: Keep current with new trends in the What's Hot dialog box.

choosing its name from the Window menu. Where you might run into trouble is when you have so many windows open that they either cover each other up or you can't remember which was which. Fortunately, there are several commands to help you manage windows.

 The most obvious thing to do with open windows is to close them. You close a window by clicking on the close button in its title bar, as shown at left.

This can be tedious, especially if you have lots of open windows. In such a case, you can close all open windows by choosing Window ➤ Close All.

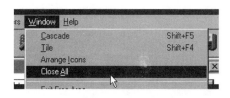 If you want arrange your windows, rather than close them, AOL offers several options. First, you can *tile* all open windows. Choosing Window ➤ Tile arranges all of your open windows in the AOL screen in a grid; you see a little bit of each window, with its title for reference, as shown in Figure 8.3. You can click in any window to make it active, and you can maximize the window to see its contents.

WARNING The Window ➤ Tile command is useful only if you have a limited number of windows open. If you have more than, say, ten windows open, your tiled windows will be so small as to not be of much use.

Tiled windows do not overlap. They are deliberately kept small so that you can see a little bit of the contents of each window. Conversely, the Window ➤ Cascade command places each window in front of its predecessor, with only the title bar showing. When you *cascade* windows, they all overlap, but they retain their original size. This command is useful when you want to see which windows you have open and then click from one to the next without having to zoom each screen to see its contents. Figure 8.4 shows cascaded windows.

There are several other commands on the Window menu that you might find useful. The Remember Window Size and Position command tells AOL that the next time it opens a particular window, you want it to appear in the same size and place as it appears now. The Remember Window Size Only is a similar command. You might use this for large windows that you don't want to open up to full size. To cancel any such settings, choose Window ➤ Forget Window Size and Position.

FIGURE 8.3: These windows were tiled with the Window ➤ Tile command.

Graphics-Viewing Preferences

As you explore more and more places in AOL, you will no doubt download a lot of art to your hard disk. This is perfectly normal and expected. However, art downloads can become problematic when they start to fill up your hard disk. Fortunately, you can control just how much art is stored on your hard disk, as well as several other aspects of graphics.

Choose Members ➤ Preferences to bring up the Preferences dialog box. Then click on the Graphics button. This will bring up the Graphics Viewing Preferences dialog box, shown in Figure 8.5.

FIGURE 8.4: These windows were cascaded with the Window ➤ Cascade command.

Graphics Viewing Preferences

While you are online AOL will save online art to your PC's hard drive, this saves time when you enter the area again as you already have the necessary online art. You can control how much art is stored on your PC by changing the number below. If you increase the disk space AOL will run faster but take more space on your hard drive.

Maximum disk space to use for online art: 10 megabyte(s)

☑ **Display image files on download**

JPEG compression quality: 100

    Set Color Mode   OK   Cancel

FIGURE 8.5:
You specify your graphics-viewing preferences in this dialog box.

The first option allows you to specify how much art can be downloaded to your hard disk. If you have a small hard disk, you might want to set this number lower to preserve space. Conversely, if you have a large hard disk, setting this number higher will make AOL run faster, as it will have fewer art downloads. When the size of your collective art downloads reaches the maximum, AOL purges the earliest files to make room for new ones.

The other options tell AOL whether to show you image files when they are downloaded, and how good the quality of compression should be with downloaded images. If you decrease the percentage in the compression quality box, either by clicking or by typing in a number, the images AOL brings over will be of lesser quality.

Now that we've gotten the preliminaries out of the way, let's start browsing AOL.

News and Other Information

What makes AOL (and other online services) more accurate than newspapers or magazines is that news is *constantly* updated. If you're following a rapidly breaking story in the newspaper, it can be hours or even days before you get the complete picture. Not so with AOL's news. Whenever you enter AOL's News Services area, you will likely see something new.

News

To enter the Top News area, choose Go To ➤ Top News, click on the News icon on the flashbar, or use the Ctrl+4 command on your keyboard. Any of these commands bring up the Today's News dialog box, shown in Figure 8.6. Clicking on the Today's News option in the Channels window will also bring you here.

As you can see, there are several ways to navigate this area. You can double-click one of the stories in the list to read it immediately. Or, if the story you are interested in has been deemed a hot news item, you can click on the icon for that story located at the bottom of the screen. If you want to search for articles on specific topics, click on one of the boxes running down the left and right sides of the screen; these cover the major news areas (politics, weather, business, sports, and so forth). There are even photos of major news events that you can view online or download to your computer for later viewing.

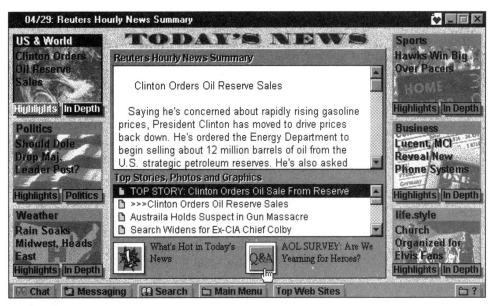

FIGURE 8.6: You can get all your news in the Today's News area.

Weather

As you saw in the previous section, you can find weather information in the News Services area. You can also go directly to the Weather Service area (shown in Figure 8.7) by choosing Go To ➤ Keyword, typing in **Weather**, and clicking on Go.

Like News Services, the Weather Service area contains articles about the latest movements of storm fronts. But there is also more general weather information, such as current (and expected) temperatures and conditions for all parts of the United States and the world. For example, if you wanted to find out what the weather was like in Boston, you would click on U.S. Cities to bring up the U.S. Cities Travel Forecast Table window. Then you would double-click on Massachusetts to see a summary of the forecast, as shown in Figure 8.8. (You might have to click on List More to find Massachusetts.) Since these forecasts are updated continually, you will always be seeing the most current available weather conditions.

All the News that's Fit to Print...

If you stop to think about it, getting your news through AOL (or other online service) gives you much more complete coverage of events. Putting aside all issues of censorship, the sheer volume of news information that is produced on a daily basis is staggering. No newspaper, however comprehensive, could hope to cover all the stories that unfold.

For online services, on the other hand, there is no practical limitation to the number of different stories that can be run. What's more, there are no limitations on the number of articles that can be made available on the *same topic*. What this means to you is that you will always find different viewpoints on the same issue or event. Furthermore, you will probably find articles in the AOL news service that might not run in your local newspaper, either due to space constraints or censorship.

This great strength (variety and comprehensiveness of news) can also be a detriment, however. There *are* practical limitations on the amount of time you can spend reading the infinite number of news stories. So it's a good idea to develop a fluency with the AOL news area to optimize your use of it.

And AOL is just the tip of the news iceberg, when compared to what's available on the Internet (which we'll cover in Part IV). As you'll soon realize, it's now possible to be very well informed on issues that, several years ago, you could not have even found articles on. As always, when you find an interesting article, you can download it to your hard disk and read it later offline to save yourself valuable connect time.

Reference Material

The amount of reference material available online is positively overwhelming. Not only can you find dictionaries and encyclopedias, but there are many areas set up by companies and by periodicals (such as *Consumer Reports*) where you can find even more articles. AOL calls their reference area the Reference Desk. In a sense, it is much like a reference desk in a library, but like everything else in AOL, it's always being updated and improved.

FIGURE 8.7:
The Weather
Area dialog box
is your window
on the world of
meteorology.

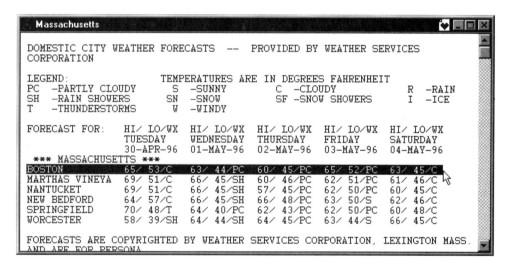

FIGURE 8.8: You can find out what the weather is like in Boston, even if you live in Los Angeles.

If you click on the Reference Desk button in the Channels window or use the Keyword **Reference**, you will bring up the Reference Desk window, as shown in Figure 8.9.

Here you can scroll the window on the right-hand side to find what you need, or you can click on one of the icons on the left-hand side to go directly to a reference source. Even the Encyclopedia Britannica is online. The advantage to having the EB

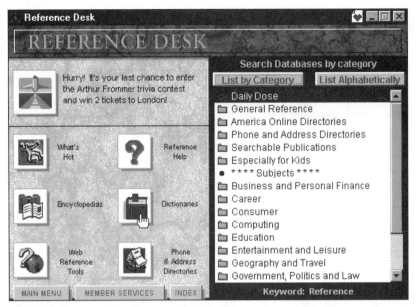

FIGURE 8.9: The Reference Desk is your warehouse for any kind of reference information.

online is that, as facts change (populations of countries, national boundaries, etc.), the electronic version of the EB can keep up in a way that the published reference never could dream of doing. It also saves you from having to buy a new set of $1,500 encyclopedias every few months!

Let's just see what we can find in the dictionary. Click on the Dictionaries icon to get to the Dictionaries window, shown in Figure 8.10. Then click on the Merriam-Webster's Collegiate Dictionary icon in this window to bring up the main dictionary.

What word shall we look up? How about one of my favorites: *codswallop*. Type the word **codswallop** and click on the Look Up button. You'll soon see the definition. Needless to say, this is something writers want to avoid.

> **NOTE**
>
> As you've no doubt noticed, one common thread running through all AOL's services is currentness of information. In almost every area, the advantage to getting your information online, as opposed to getting it from printed matter, television, or radio, is that everything you see online is right up-to-date.

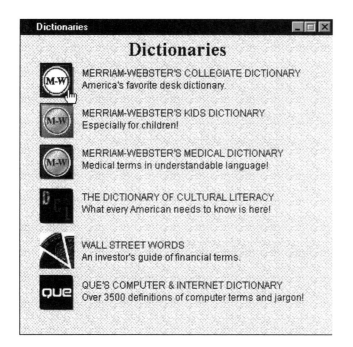

FIGURE 8.10:
You can look up words in this online version of the Merriam-Webster dictionary.

Stock Quotes and Personal Finance

Perhaps no piece of news is more volatile—and more crucial to business—than the stock ticker. The Dow Jones Industrial Average, along with the values of individual stocks, bonds, and commodities, changes constantly. Thousands of businesses, (including yours perhaps), investors, bankers, and stockbrokers depend upon accurate reports of stock values in making their business decisions. While you could get your information from radio reports, AOL makes it easy to check stock quotes and to access hundreds of other personal finance services.

NOTE AOL updates stock and other commodities information every 15 minutes.

To enter the world of high finance, click on the Personal Finance button in the Channels window to bring up the window shown in Figure 8.11.

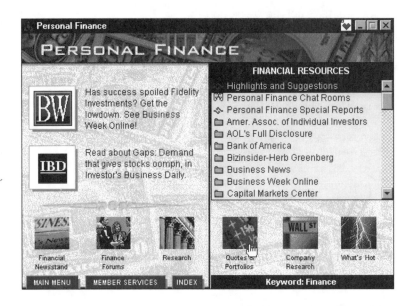

FIGURE 8.11:
The Personal Finance area plugs you into the financial world.

There are lots of places to visit here, including Business Week Online, finance chat rooms (where you can chat with people about business and investments), a financial newsstand, and an area where you can check up on stock quotes and follow the performance of your portfolio. There are dozens more places in the scrolling window on the right-hand side of the screen.

Let's look up a stock value, just so you can see how this command works. Click on the Stock Quotes icon in the flashbar to bring up the Quotes & Portfolios window, shown in Figure 8.12. Next, double-click on any stock to see an up-to-the-minute quote of its trading value.

If you know the four-letter symbol for the stock you're interested in, you can type it into the Enter Symbol box to go directly to it. Otherwise, you can choose your stock from the alphabetical list.

TIP You can also reach the Quotes & Portfolios window by choosing Go To ➤ Quotes or by using the Ctrl+5 keyboard shortcut.

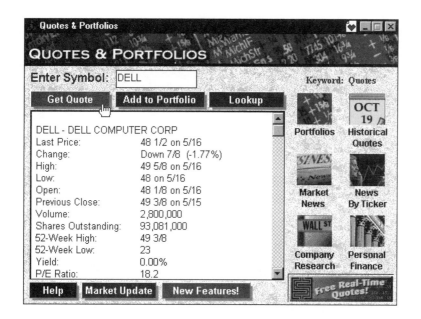

FIGURE 8.12:
You can get up-to-the-minute stock quotes in the Quotes & Portfolios window.

Computer and Software Information

Planning to buy a new computer? Looking for software? Want to find interesting sites on the Internet? If the answer to any of these questions is yes, then you'll want to check out the Computers and Software area on AOL. To visit this area, click on the Computers & Software button in the Channels window. Alternatively, you can bring up the Keyword dialog box, type **Computers**, and click on the Go button. However you do it, the Computers and Software dialog box shown in Figure 8.13 will appear.

There are many different paths you can take from this window. We'll discuss the software libraries next, so for now, let's just see if we can find a review of new consumer electronics products. Click on the Consumer Electronics button to reach the Consumer Electronics window. To read any article that catches your interest, just double-click on it.

The AOL Software Libraries

If you've ever wanted to try out a piece of software before buying it, or if you've ever come up with a specific need only to find that there is no existing software to fill

FIGURE 8.13: Your gateway to the world of computers and software is the Computers and Software window.

it, then you will love the AOL Software Libraries. While some of the programs you find here will be demo versions of popular programs, many others will be fully operational.

> **NOTE**　A *demo* version of a piece of software is one that has had certain features disabled (such as the print or save functions). The idea is that the software manufacturer wants to tempt you into buying the fully functional program by showing you its features through the disabled program.

The software libraries are not limited to programs. There are also images, sound files, multimedia files, utilities, film clips, etc. The only real limitation is your patience! First let's see how to browse the libraries, and then we'll look at how to update AOL online and how to find virus-scanning software.

To reach the software libraries, click on the Computers & Software button to bring up the window shown in Figure 8.13. This time, click on the Software Center button to bring up the Software Center dialog box, shown in Figure 8.14.

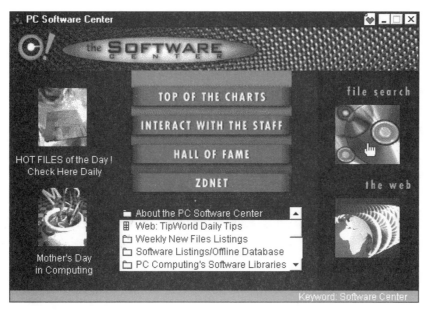

FIGURE 8.14: You can browse for software in the Software Center.

To search for software, click on the File Search button. This will bring up the Files Found window. The biggest problem you will encounter in searching for software is limiting your search. This is the downside to having such large software libraries. However, there are a number of ways to limit your searches. Let's examine them.

The first option is to limit by *date*. For example, you can choose to look for software which has been added to the libraries only within the past week or the past month. This way, you not only limit the number of programs you'll find, you also ensure that you're bringing up the most recent offerings. The next option is to limit by *type* of software. AOL's library includes many types of software: communications programs, word processors, databases, sound and graphics files, utilities, and so forth. Click on any of these to confine the search to just the specified libraries.

> **TIP**
> You can click on more than one type of software in the Software Center. If you select more than one category, AOL will find software in all of them.

Finally, you can specify by keyword. For example, you might want a utility for a certain version of Microsoft Word or Aldus PageMaker. Or you might want only certain types of image files.

Let's look at an example that finds a very specific kind of software. First, click to specify that you want to find software added in the past month. Then choose Music & Sound files. Finally, type the words **Monty Python** in the keyword box, and click on Find Matching Files; after a few moments, a list will appear that looks similar to the one below.

```
Category          Subject                          File Name
Speaker Music     QBASIC: Improved Monty Python Mus MONTYP.BAS
Music Progs       JASON: Jason Linett's Music Menu  MONTYP.BAS
Speaker Music     QBASIC: Eric The Half-a-Bee       ERICBEE.BAS
```

Select any item, and click on View description to see a short blurb on it. If you like what you see, you can download it to your hard disk by clicking on Download. If your computer has a sound card installed, you can also listen to the sound clip by double-clicking on its icon.

> **TIP** You can listen to just about any sound clip, watch any movie clip, or see any image in AOL if your computer is multimedia-ready. Just click or double-click, as specified.

In similar fashion, you can browse other types of software, or simply check out what's new. Speaking of new, you might be wondering how to get the new version of AOL if you're using an old one. Read on to find out.

Updating the AOL Software Online

One of the slicker aspects of online software is that you can upgrade to new versions of your software without having to go find it at your local store or wait for it to arrive in the mail. You can actually use an older version of AOL to go online and get a newer version, then download it to your computer and use the newer version instead. And it's all so painless.

In fact, you don't even need to search through the software libraries to find new versions of AOL. Rather, bring up the Keyword dialog box and type in **Upgrade**. Then click on Go, and before you know it, you'll be in the upgrade window, shown in Figure 8.15.

FIGURE 8.15: You can quickly and easily upgrade your AOL software in the upgrade window.

Click on Download Now; you will be given the choice of going into a free area while the software is downloaded. Click on Yes. After several minutes (the exact time depends upon the speed of your modem), you will get a message telling you that the download is finished. Click on OK and sign off. To set up the new version of the software you've just downloaded, turn to Chapter 1 and follow the steps outlined in the section "Installing the AOL Software."

AOL will then work as before, but you will have access to new features that weren't available with the previous version. If you haven't done it yet, the first thing you might want to do with your newfound bounty is to find yourself some good virus-scanning software. Read on to find out how.

Finding Good Anti-Virus Software

As mentioned in Chapter 2, viruses are not something to panic about. They are, however, something to think about. One way to set your mind at ease with respect to possible virus infection is to find yourself some good virus-scanning software. It's easy in the AOL software libraries.

If you're not already browsing in the software libraries, go there now by clicking on the Computers & Software button in the Channels window. Then click on the Software Center button to bring up the Software Center window, and from there click on the File Search button. Since you'll want a program that's up-to-date, click to see just those programs added in the last month. Then click on the Utilities option and type **Virus** in the keyword box. When you are finished, click on the Find Matching Files button.

AOL will bring up a window similar to the one shown in Figure 8.16. Yours will differ from mine, of course, since we will be searching at different times.

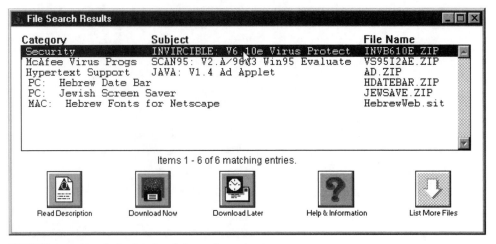

FIGURE 8.16: Here is the list of anti-virus software I got.

If the window is full, you might want to scroll around a bit just to see what's there. If there are more than 20 programs, click on the More button to see them. To find more files, you can do another search, only this time specifying "all dates."

You can click on any item in the list and then click on the View Description button to see a short description about the software, who makes it, what it does, and what it costs, if anything. (If you don't understand the distinction between software that you must pay for, shareware, and freeware, please see the section called "Paying the Piper.")

One very good piece of anti-virus software is Disinfectant. First of all, it's free! Also, it's been around a long time; the people who wrote and continue to rewrite this software know what they are doing. Finally, its interface is quite easy to use. However, you might want to experiment with different types of anti-virus software to find what works best for you.

When you have found the anti-virus program (or programs) you wish to use, click on Download to download it to your computer. Once you have the software on your hard drive, you still need to install it. Since programs differ as to how they are installed, read the instructions carefully (the instructions are always downloaded along with the software).

Paying the Piper

What's the difference between regular commercial software, shareware, and freeware?

First, there is commercial software, the kind you are probably used to, which you see offered in stores and advertised in magazines and which you have to pay for. It is illegal to use such software by copying it from a friend's hard disk to your own hard disk. The distinguishing features of such software are that you pay for it up front and that it's usually distributed through retail outlets. You may not legally sell or resell such software to someone.

Next, there is *shareware*. Shareware is software that costs you nothing to obtain but that you are expected to pay for if you use it a lot. Much of the software you find online is shareware. You might wonder how the folks who offer shareware make any money. The answer is, shareware payments depend on the *honor system*. You are trusted to pay for shareware if you find it useful. You may distribute such software to anyone you like, but you may not legally sell it.

Finally, there is *freeware*. This is software written by good souls who expect no remuneration. We can only assume that for them, virtue is its own reward. Like shareware, you can obtain freeware without paying for it. What's even nicer, though, is that you *never* have to pay for freeware. And you can distribute it to anyone you like. You may not, however, charge people for freeware.

There are a few other variations, such as *postcardware* and *groupware*, but these pretty much cover the basics. In case you're wondering, postcardware is software that you can use for free but if you do, the author asks you to send him or her a postcard. Groupware is commercial software that is sold with the explicit understanding that it will be loaded on to a (usually specific) number of computers. Sometimes this is called a *site license*.

> **WARNING** Be sure to update your virus software on a regular basis (about every three to six months). Since the bad guys are always writing new viruses, you'll need up-to-date anti-virus software to avoid the machinations of the villains of the software world.

AOL Bulletin Boards

A bulletin board in AOL isn't much different from the bulletin boards you're used to seeing in your office or in other public places. People post messages, whether specific or general, and other people read these messages and answer them if they wish. AOL has bulletin boards all over the place. There is hardly any area of AOL that you'll visit where you won't find a bulletin board.

The purpose of bulletin boards is to give all members who visit an area a chance to ask questions, make suggestions, or leave messages for other members who will visit. For instance, you might want to find individuals who share a particular interest of yours, or you might want to voice your opinion about a new AOL feature.

Let's look at how to post and read messages on AOL bulletin boards. For this example, use the keywords **Member Services** to reach the Member Services dialog box. Scroll to the bottom of the screen; notice that the Members Helping Members item has a bulletin board icon next to it, as shown at left.

Anytime you see this icon, you know you've found a bulletin board. Double-click on the Members Helping Members item, and then click on the Members Helping Members button to bring up the window shown in Figure 8.17.

Reading Messages

Figure 8.17 is typical of the bulletin boards you'll see in AOL. There are several options in the scrolling window, any of which you can double-click to see other windows. For now, double-click on the General AOL Questions item to bring up the window shown in Figure 8.18.

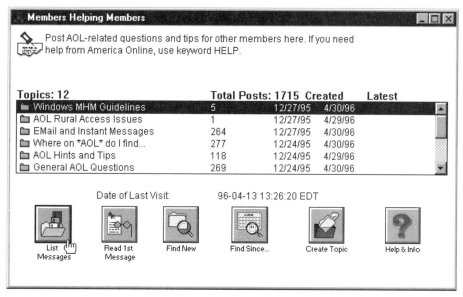

FIGURE 8.17: Here is the Members Helping Members bulletin board.

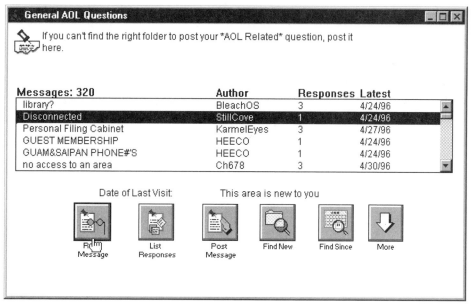

FIGURE 8.18: You can read any of these messages by double-clicking.

To read a message, double-click on it, or select it and click on Read Message. You can answer a message if you wish by clicking on Post Response and typing your reply.

(You can also read other people's responses by clicking on the Read 1st Response and List Responses buttons, if they are there.) When you have finished typing your reply, click on Post, and AOL will inform you that your message has been sent.

Then you can close the window for that message and continue browsing and reading other messages. If you wish to go back to the previous window (the one that contains other categories), either click to close the window containing the messages you were browsing, or choose Previous Screen from your Window menu.

Posting Messages

The steps for posting messages are similar to those you followed to read them. Let's assume that you wish to post a message on the bulletin board you were just looking at in the previous section. Use the keyword **Member Services** to reach the Member Services dialog box. Scroll to the bottom of the screen, double-click on the Members Helping Members item, and click on the button of the same name to bring up the window shown back in Figure 8.17. Then double-click on the General AOL Questions item to bring up the window shown back in Figure 8.18. This time, though, don't double-click any of the existing messages. Instead, click on the Post Message button. This will bring up the Add A Message window shown in Figure 8.19.

Type the subject and text of your message. When you are finished, click on Post. You will be advised that your message is on its way, and soon it will be added to the other messages on the bulletin board.

TIP

If you post messages to bulletin boards, it is a good idea to regularly visit those bulletin boards to see if anyone has responded to your messages. You can follow the steps outlined in the section "Reading Messages" to see what people have written to you.

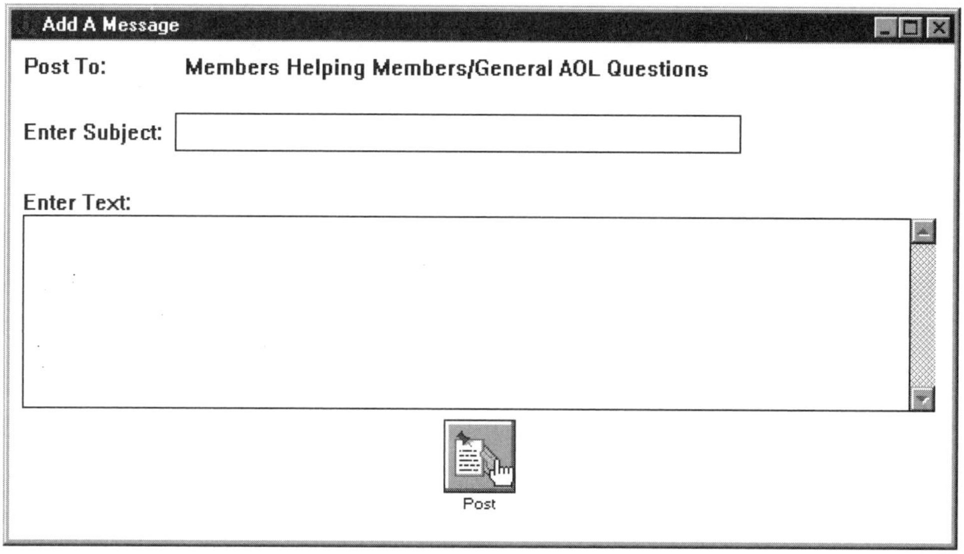

![Add A Message window with Post To: Members Helping Members/General AOL Questions, Enter Subject field, Enter Text field, and Post button]

FIGURE 8.19: You can post messages to the bulletin board in this window.

The Find Command

Another useful command to know when you want to locate bulletin boards is the Find command. When you click the Find icon in the Flashbar

you will see this dialog box:

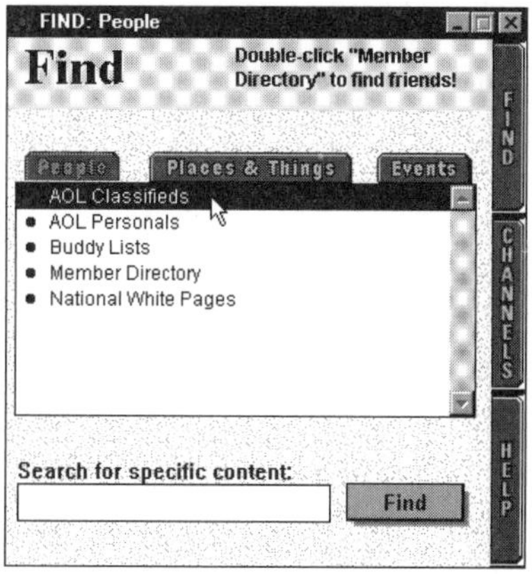

![FIND: People dialog box with Find title, "Double-click 'Member Directory' to find friends!" text, tabs for People, Places & Things, Events, listing AOL Classifieds, AOL Personals, Buddy Lists, Member Directory, National White Pages, and Search for specific content field with Find button]

where you can click around to find interesting bulletin boards. Just click on AOL Classifieds to see a list of items and services or AOL Personals to see a list of personal ads. As you can see, you can also search the member directory from this dialog box.

For Kids Only

Way back in Chapter 3 we looked at Parental Controls, the feature of AOL that lets you block parts of AOL and the Internet from certain screen names on your account. The most common use of this feature is for parents to block parts of the service that they don't want their children to access. If you spend any amount of time browsing, especially in the chatting areas, you'll see that the conversation can get pretty steamy or, at other times, rather vindictive. So if you'd prefer to have your kids learn about sex and cusswords from the usual sources (i.e., television and their classmates at school), you can block their access to chat areas and other places you feel might be risky. The problem is, it would be quite tedious to find every area on AOL that offers features you might not want them to use. That's where Kids Only comes in.

Kids Only is a special area in AOL that is closely monitored by AOL guides. They ensure that nothing X-rated (lewd chatting, etc.) goes on in there. But Kids Only isn't boring; AOL has done a nice job of adding lots of features that youngsters (and some oldsters) will enjoy and places for them to visit. And unless you turn off *all* chatting privileges, kids can exchange ideas, viewpoints, opinions, and gripes ("Mom turned off my other chatting privileges") in Kids Only.

You can reach Kids Only from the Channels dialog box by clicking on the Kids Only button. This brings up the Kids Only dialog box, shown in Figure 8.20.

There are dozens of places for kids to explore and have fun, including a cartoon area, a study break area, a Disney area, and a Kids Biz area. Just to get an idea of what's there, click on Kids Biz. This will bring up the Kids Biz dialog box where kids (or you!) can see what's going on in AOL this week.

Travel

You may not realize this, but when you installed AOL, you also opened up a travel agency. Anything you used to rely on travel agents for you can now do yourself. Find out where are the popular spots to visit, and whether you want to be part of the action or go off the beaten path. Look up flights and find the best airfares, then book the

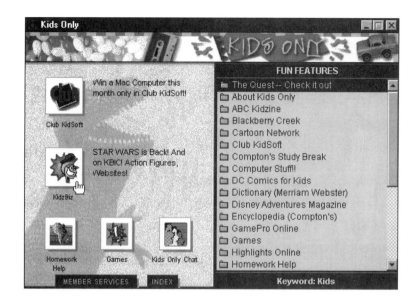

FIGURE 8.20:
Youngsters will find lots of things to do in the Kids Only area.

seats yourself. Choose a nice hotel or other accommodations. Make arrangements for a rental car and for leisure activities such as golf, tennis, or skiing. All of these are possible in AOL's Travel area.

To reach it, click on the Travel button in the Channels window. The Travel window will appear, as shown in Figure 8.21.

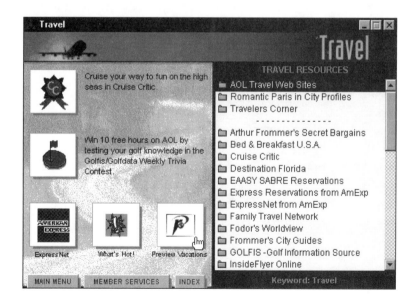

FIGURE 8.21:
The Travel window allows you to find and book airline tickets, accommodations, and leisure activities.

Let's take a quick peek to see what the travel tip of the day is. Double-click on Arthur Frommer's Secret Bargains in the list on the right-hand side of the window.

This will bring up the Arthur Frommer window. Here you have lots of choices, but for now, just double-click on the Bargain Cruises item to bring up the Bargain Cruises window. See, you've already started planning your next vacation!

Sports, Movies, and Other Entertainment

Just in case you're not having fun yet, AOL offers a wide array of features that are either entertainment themselves, such as the Games area, or that tell you all about entertainment events that you can attend, such as movies, sporting events, and concerts. You can also find reviews of the latest books and CDs, or do a little armchair traveling with Digital City. Plus there are features on general trends, lifestyles, and fashion.

> **NOTE** Since all of these areas are reached from the Channels window, I will assume that you are in this window. If you aren't, just click on the Channels icon on the flashbar.

Sports

Click on the Sports button in the Channels window to bring up the Sports window, shown in Figure 8.22.

The Sports area in turn leads to other areas on specific subjects such as baseball, basketball, football, golf, hockey, tennis, collegiate sports, individual sports, the Olympics, the Special Olympics, etc. There are also paths to magazines and newspapers devoted to various sports. Since I've foisted the baseball area on you in other parts of the book, let's look at the World Wrestling Federation area. Click on the Pro Wrestling button in the Sports window to bring up the window shown in Figure 8.23.

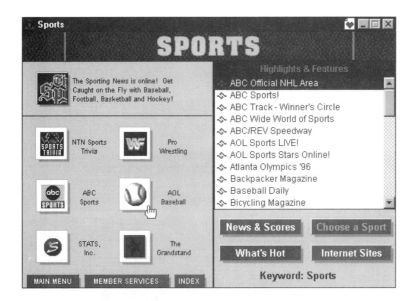

FIGURE 8.22:
If you're a sports nut, you could *live* in AOL's Sports area.

FIGURE 8.23:
You can find out everything you always wanted to know about the world of pro-wrestling here.

This area contains a wealth of information about the World Wrestling Federation—the sport of kings! Well, sort of. You can find out who's doing well and who's slumping, dates of upcoming matches, and lots of other cool stuff. There's even "Mat Rap," where you can go to the mat with other WWF fans. When you're on your feet again, meet me at the movies!

Movies

Click on the Entertainment button in the Channels window to bring up the Entertainment window, and then click on Movies to bring up the Movies window, shown in Figure 8.24.

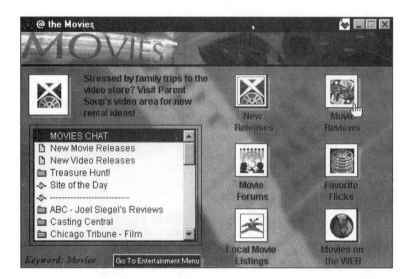

FIGURE 8.24: You can read reviews of the latest movies here, as well as find out where they are playing.

In this area, you can read about new films to decide what to go see, as well as find out where they are playing in your neighborhood. You'll also find interviews with the stars and other interesting gossip about the film industry. Be the first person on your block to know who is going to win *next* year's Academy Award for Best Supporting Actress. There are also clips of films. Often, individual films will have their own areas, giving you the opportunity to offer feedback on movies you loved or hated. In short, if it's about movies, you'll find it here.

Music

Click on the MusicSpace button in the Channels window to bring up the MusicSpace window, shown in Figure 8.25.

Similar to the Movies area, MusicSpace is your ticket to the music industry. Find out about new CDs by your favorite recording artists, as well as their upcoming tour dates. You'll also find interviews, pictures, awards, and so forth. One distinctive aspect of MusicSpace is that there are many areas devoted to individual bands. For example, if

FIGURE 8.25:
Visit the Music-Space area to find out about new releases, tours, and other events in the music world.

you double-click on Music Message Center, you'll see a list of music genres. Double-click on one of these, and you'll see another dialog box that allows you to view certain ranges of recording artists (A–F, for instance). Double-click on A–F, and you'll see this scrolling list:

Topics: 36	Total Posts: 10317	Created	Latest
Alice in Chains!!!!	409	10/20/94	4/29/96
AMC	106	5/25/95	4/29/96
Tori Amos	413	11/27/93	4/30/96
B-52's	405	7/8/94	4/29/96
Babes in Toyland	402	9/25/95	4/29/96
Bad Religion	230	5/25/95	4/29/96

Double-click on an artist or group to visit that area. It is said that members of musical groups sometimes read and answer messages posted here; certainly other fans read and respond to messages.

Games

Click on the Games button in the Channels window to bring up the Games window, shown in Figure 8.26.

There are all kinds of games available here. As you might expect, there are the usual sorts of games you can play by yourself or against a computer opponent, such as chess, poker, or Trivial Pursuit. What's really nifty, though, are the interactive games,

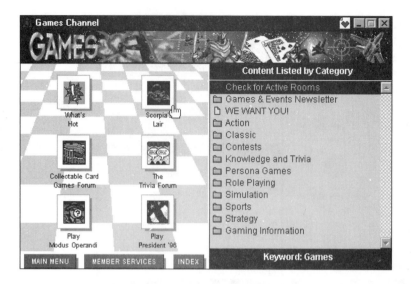

FIGURE 8.26:
You'll never get bored in the Games area, where there are always dozens of things to do.

in which you play against other AOL members. These include role-playing games such as the Federation Space Fantasy Game, trivia games such as the Trivia Forum, and adventure games such as Scorpia's Lair. Figure 8.27 shows the opening screen to Scorpia's Lair.

Digital City

Click on the Digital City button in the Channels window to bring up the Digital City window, shown in Figure 8.28.

Digital City is a gateway through which you can travel to other cities in the United States, or even abroad. Click on a region of the country you'd like to know more about to see a list of cities in that region. Click on one of the cities, and you'll see another screen like the one below that lists all kinds of interesting aspects of that city.

FIGURE 8.27: You'll find adventure games like Scorpia's Lair in the Games area.

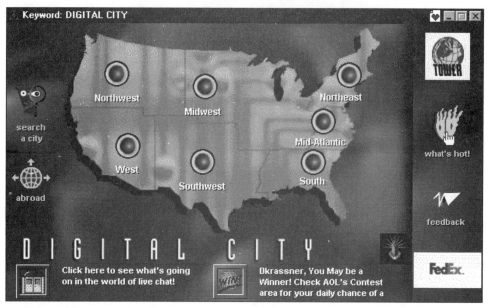

FIGURE 8.28: You can zoom in on places you'd like to know more about in the Digital City window.

From this window, you'll find inroads to entertainment, people, the community, the marketplace, and other aspects of life in whatever city you're "visiting."

Life, Styles & Interests

Click on the Life, Styles & Interests button in the Channels window to bring up the Life, Styles & Interests window, shown in Figure 8.29.

The Life, Styles & Interests area is a catch-all for fashion, architecture, hobbies, home improvement, etc. Here you'll see what to wear and how to wear it, what to eat and where to get it, where to live, where to work, where to play, where to hang out, where to vacation... You get the idea. If you want to be "in the loop," this is the place to go.

FIGURE 8.29:
No matter what your interests, you'll find something that speaks to you in the Life, Styles & Interests area.

Learning & Culture

Click on the Learning & Culture button in the Channels window to bring up the Learning & Culture window, shown in Figure 8.30.

The Learning & Culture area is a another catch-all, in this case for all things highbrow. Cuisine, careers, science, art—you name it. If George Will likes it, you'll find it here. Book reviews and essays are just a few of the things you can read to enrich yourself. There are also interviews and pictures of authors, educators, and other cultural figures.

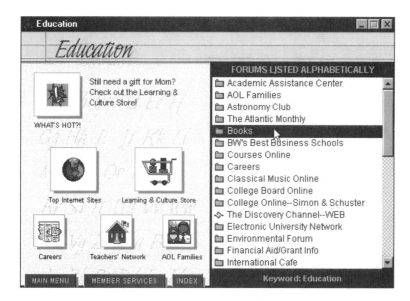

FIGURE 8.30:
You can broaden your mind in AOL's Learning & Culture area.

The French (and Brazilian, and Japanese, and…) Connection

Last but not least, there is the International Channel. This is the AOL equivalent to traveling abroad and seeing the sites, or to reading foreign magazines and journals. Click on the International button in the Channels window to bring up the window shown in Figure 8.31.

As you can see, this window is a gateway to many foreign countries. You can enter foreign-language chat rooms, a boon if you're a foreign national visiting or living in the United States. If you click on one of the country buttons—say, France—you will open a window for that country, as shown in Figure 8.32. Here you can browse French journals, check up on the French stock market, or plan your next trip to Paris.

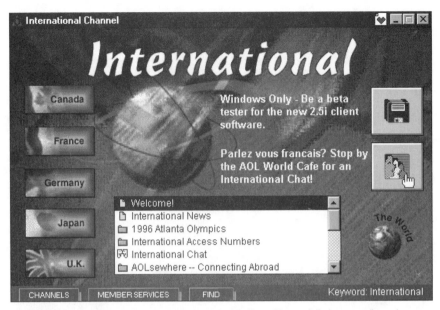

FIGURE 8.31: Visiting the International window is like taking a daily journey abroad.

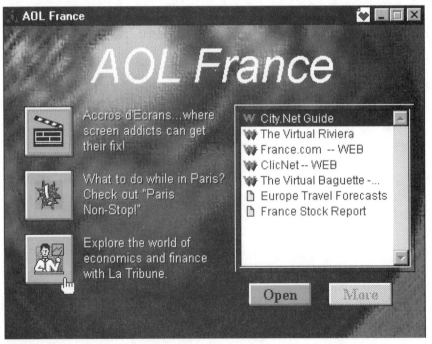

FIGURE 8.32: *Parlez-vous français?* work on your French in this window of the International Channel.

Health and Fitness

For all those fitness buffs out there, there's a place in AOL just for you! If you click on the Health & Fitness button in the Channels window, the Health and Fitness window will appear, as shown in Figure 8.33.

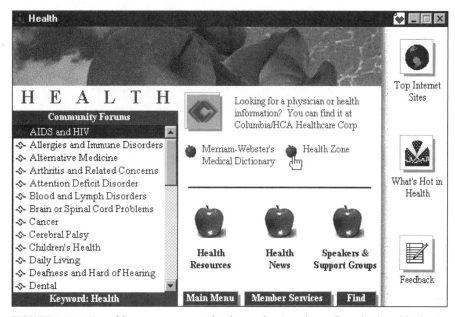

FIGURE 8.33: Everything you ever wanted to know about staying well can be found in the Health and Fitness area.

Here you can get information about all sorts of health issues, and even find a physician. For the hypochondriac in all of us, there's a medical dictionary. Then there's the Health Zone, shown in Figure 8.34, a sort of bazaar for folks interested in health issues. It includes a "spa," a fitness area, and even a link to Web health sites.

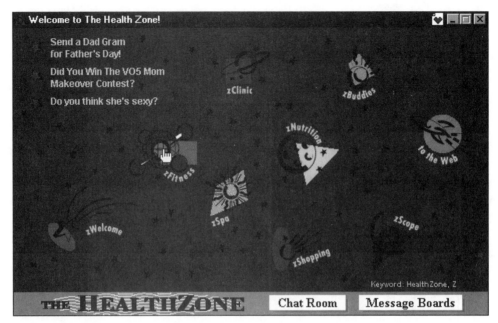

FIGURE 8.34: The Health Zone is the place to work out on AOL.

The Style Channel

The contents of the Style channel somewhat overlap with those of the Life, Styles & Interests channel. The difference is that the Style channel tries to stay on top of what's trendy (i.e., what's going in and out of style), whereas the Life, Styles & Interests channel focuses more on lifestyles and pastimes. If you click on the Style Channel button in the Channels window, you'll reach the Style area, shown in Figure 8.35.

This area may look a little like *People* magazine to you, only not quite as sophisticated or classy. But it's a fun place to browse around, especially if you're really interested in Joan Collins's custom-made brassieres. Click on The A-List to get a voyeuristic glimpse into the lives of the rich and famous; as shown in Figure 8.36, at least they named the window accurately!

FIGURE 8.35: Stay abreast of the latest trends in the Style area.

FIGURE 8.36: On slow news days, you can always check out The A-List.

> **NOTE**
>
> You might be wondering why AOL has both a Life, Styles & Interests area and a Styles area. This is just one example of how the AOL interface is always in a state of flux. Areas *will* overlap, and the reason is twofold. First, AOL wants you to be able to find what you're looking for easily; hence, some things can be accessed from more than one place. Second, AOL is always trying to find better ways of presenting material; hence, you will sometimes see older areas in the process of being phased out even as new ones spring up to take their place.

The Hub

The Hub is an evolving area that's under construction, even as you read these words. I've visited it, and can't quite figure out what it is! I think it's a place where you can find chatting that's a little more controversial than in other places in AOL and topics that are a little weirder than you're used to. My guess is that the Hub is an attempt on the part of AOL to shed its puritanical image and to give notice that AOL is just as hip and shocking as the next online service.

At any rate, when you click on The Hub button in the Channels window, you'll enter the Hub (no doubt with mild trepidation), as shown in Figure 8.37.

Here you can find out what to think, get your dreams analyzed, read blustering criticism of cultural icons by people who don't know what they're talking about, and so forth. If it sounds as though I'm not enamored of the Hub, you're right. It can be mildly diverting, though. For instance, if you click on The Hot Button, the window shown in Figure 8.38 appears.

How The Hot Button area differs from other parts of the Hub is not clear to me. They call it staying abreast of the latest trends and thinking right. Sounds like fascism to me, but, hey, I'm a different breed of cat…

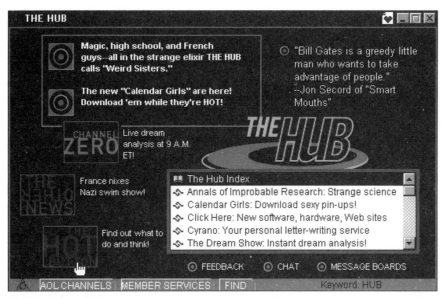

FIGURE 8.37: The Hub is an evolving area where cool people hang out and, er, evolve.

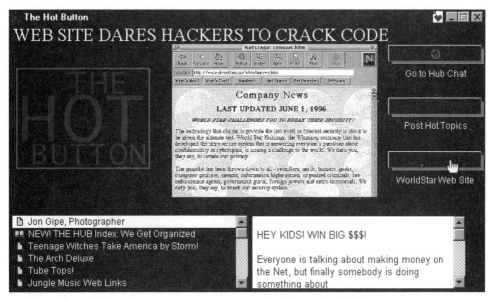

FIGURE 8.38: Click on The Hot Button to enter a world of alternative thinking.

What's Behind the Curtain?

A *chestnut* is a nifty little idea, place, or discovery that may or may not be of great importance, but that is fun to know about anyway. One such chestnut in AOL is the Curtain (as in, "what's behind the…"). If you click on the AOL icon in the Welcome window,

the Curtain parts, so to speak, revealing a virtual inner sanctum, as shown in Figure 8.39.

FIGURE 8.39: The Curtain is a work in progress, but you can discover new and interesting AOL features here.

This seems to be a place where you'll alternately find jokes, cartoons, weird stuff, interesting stuff, bizarre stuff, and just, well, stuff. Clicking on The Vault, Anticipation, and The Curtain all reveal various things that change constantly. Clicking on Rate-O-Rama allows you to register an opinion about something. This brings up the Rate-O-Rama dialog box, shown in Figure 8.40, where you can tell AOL what you think of the daily fare. To indicate your opinion, just click on the face that best expresses your own feelings.

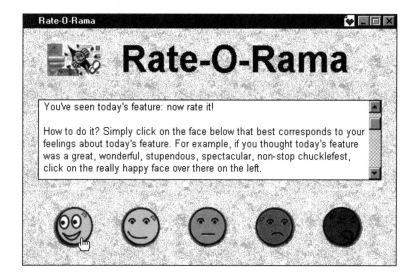

FIGURE 8.40:
In the Rate-O-Rama area, you have a chance to vent your spleen.

Just keep in mind that all of these areas that can be reached by clicking on the AOL icon in the Welcome window will be different all the time. But that's okay, because change is a good thing.

Chapter 9

COMPANY AREAS ON AOL

- **How to find company areas**
- **Shopping in the Marketplace**
- **The best company areas**
- *Consumer Reports*
- **The Newsstand**
- **Entertainment**

As you saw in Chapter 8, AOL has many of its own areas to inform, entertain, and enlighten you. Along the way, though, you probably saw a few corporate names that you recognized, like American Express, Disney, Eddie Bauer, Fedex, and Hallmark, as well as some familiar periodicals, such as *The Atlantic Monthly, Business Week, Consumer Reports, The Sporting News,* and *U.S. News & World Report.* These might seem like mere advertisements to you, but in fact they are much more. Often, a company area on AOL gives you access to the products and services which that company provides, just as if you were visiting their offices or buying from their stores. What's more, if companies have areas in AOL, you can frequently get online customer service and support for many products that you buy.

As discussed in Chapter 8, we are now casting the nets just a bit farther. Granted, we are still within the friendly confines of AOL, but we are now broadening our horizons to include corporations that advertise on but which are not a part of AOL. Rather than seeing this chapter as a giant advertisement, though, I hope you'll view it instead as a springboard to the Internet, which we'll be covering in Part IV. *Everyone* is on the Internet. There is hardly a Fortune 500 company (not to mention many smaller ones) that doesn't have a site on the Internet. This chapter will ease you into the overwhelming amount of company information available on the Net by introducing a slightly less overwhelming number of company areas in AOL.

> **NOTE**
> Many of the company names you see in this chapter you'll see again when we look at the World Wide Web in Chapter 10 and the Internet as a whole in Chapter 11. Don't let this confuse you. A company does not have to choose between AOL and the Internet; it can have sites in *both* places. All the places you see in this chapter, however, will be those contained within AOL.

The notion of buying stuff online might seem a bit futuristic to you, but it really is not much different from ordering items in catalogs by phone or purchasing something from the Home Shopping Network. In some respects, it's better than either of those methods, since in those cases the only feedback you get comes from the company you're buying from. With AOL, you can shop before you buy, asking other AOL members if they've purchased the item you are interested in and how they liked it. You can even visit *Consumer Reports* magazine online to check out what they have to say. Before you dig in, though, let's look at a few ways to find the sorts of places you might be looking for.

As in the previous chapter, I will assume throughout this chapter that you are online. If you are not online, either sign on now in the usual way, or, if you prefer, you can peruse this chapter first, thereby conserving your online time.

How to Find Company Areas on AOL

To my mind, there are four ways of finding companies on AOL: the Marketplace, specific searching, calculated serendipity, and lucky accident. Since the Marketplace deserves a section all its own, let's look at the other three first.

> **TIP**
>
> **When you find an interesting company area to which you think you might want to return, add it to your Favorite Places list. Then you can quickly reach it from anywhere in AOL at any time.**

Specific Searching

If you know the product or service you are looking for and know the company you want to get it from, your task is straightforward. Using the Keyword command, you can search for just about any company that advertises on AOL. This is a good way to find corporate areas, because one company may have bits and pieces all over AOL, especially if it's involved in more than one kind of business. Furthermore, the general area that houses the company may not be intuitively apparent to you. Using Keyword, you bypass screens you might not want to see. (As a byproduct, you also save time, which as you know, equals money.) For fun, let's see how you might use the Keyword command to find the area for Disney.

Bring up the Keyword dialog box by choosing Go To ➤ Keyword, clicking on the Keyword button on the flashbar, or using the Ctrl+K keyboard shortcut. Type the word **Disney** (capitalization doesn't matter for keywords) and click on Go, as shown in Figure 9.1.

The Disney Services window will appear, as shown in Figure 9.2. As you might have expected, it is in the Entertainment area. The advantage of using Keyword, though, is that you didn't have to know exactly where it was to find it, and you bypassed all the windows you would have otherwise had to click through.

Now that you're here, browse around a little. You can read up on the latest movies and products, see a history of the company, find out about job openings, plan a trip to Disney World, and much more. And if you do decide to take the family to Disney World, you're probably going to need to finance the trip, so let's turn next to finding some lending institutions using another searching method: calculated serendipity.

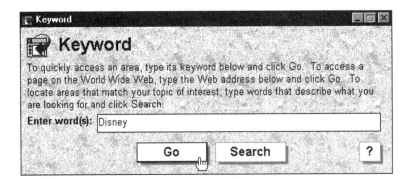

FIGURE 9.1:
To find the Disney area in AOL, type the word **Disney** and click on Go.

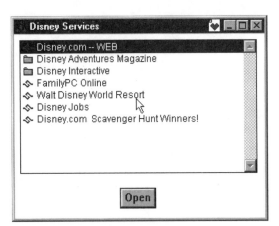

FIGURE 9.2:
It's easy to find company areas such as Disney Services by searching with the Keyword command.

Calculated Serendipity

If you've been following along with this chapter, you've seen how to find a specific company using the Keyword command. Sometimes, though, you will not know what particular company you are looking for. You may not even know exactly *what* it is you are looking for. This is where the strategy of *calculated serendipity* comes in handy. The word *serendipity* refers to a happy but unintentional discovery. With a little fore-thought, you can tip the scales your way such that all your searches lead to happy, if unintended, discoveries.

This method of searching is a bit more tricky than using the Keyword command because it requires a bit more thinking, but not too much. To pick up the thread from the previous section, let's see if we can't find some lending institution to help us get that coveted Disney World trip.

Now, when I said "lending institution," you probably thought to yourself, "Hey, that's just a big word for *bank*. Why doesn't he say *bank* if he means *bank*?" The answer to that question is, I'm pompous! More important, though, you quickly and intuitively went from the notion of needing money, to somewhere to borrow it from, to finding a

bank. If you were going to search AOL for banks, where would you look? If you said in the Personal Finance area in the Channels window, go to the head of the class. If you go to that area now, you'll see that Bank of America is listed right there in the scrolling window.

Furthermore, there are other banks and savings & loans farther down in the list. Double-click on any of these to bring up that lending institution's individual area. As shown in Figure 9.3, Bank of America even has a Personal Finance button you can click on.

See how easy that was? With a few mouse-clicks and a little common sense, you found exactly what you were looking for. And if you aren't satisfied with what you find at Bank of America, you can try another bank or, instead, enter one of the chat rooms to find out what other people do on their vacations.

FIGURE 9.3: Here in the Bank of America window, you can click on Personal Finance to see more about their personal loans.

Lucky Accident

As you browse in AOL, you will continually come across corporate areas because, as you might have noticed in Chapter 8, *every* major area in AOL features at least one corporate sponsor right there in the main window. You'll find *The Sporting News* and ABC Sports in the Sports area; *Business Week* in the Personal Finance area; MTV in the music area; and so on. So no matter where you browse, you're sure to come across lots of advertisements, some of which may surprise you.

If you happen upon a company area you think you might want to visit again (but you don't want to have to remember where it is), you can add it to your Favorite Places list. To do this, open the company area window, and then just click on the icon with the little heart in it, located on the right side of the window's title bar. From then on, you can visit this area no matter where you are in AOL by double-clicking on it in your Favorite Places list.

Of course, you might want to save some space on your Favorite Places list for a few areas in the Marketplace. More than any other place in AOL, this is where you go to buy stuff. Let's check it out.

Shopping in the Marketplace

Even bigger than the SuperMall in Edmonton, Alberta, the Marketplace in AOL houses hundreds upon hundreds of companies, retail outlets, and stores within its virtual walls. The advantages of virtual shopping are probably obvious: no traffic or parking problems, no dragging the kids with you, no jostling up against the rest of humanity, no hassling with surly clerks, and, maybe not so obvious, you can shop any time of the day or night. The disadvantages are probably equally obvious: you can't try stuff on, you can't pick up an object and heft its weight, and you can't hear how a stereo system sounds or see how good that VCR's picture really is. So it's a trade-off. Ultimately, it comes down to sacrificing the certainty of hands-on shopping for the conveniences of online shopping.

To reach the Marketplace, click on the Marketplace button in the Channels window. The Marketplace window will appear, as shown in Figure 9.4. What you see here will be seasonal. For instance, I was looking around just before Mother's Day.

No doubt as you browse around in the Marketplace, you'll find favorite areas to visit; these may be set up more intuitively than others, or you just might find their stuff

FIGURE 9.4: You can find virtually anything in the Marketplace, including great gifts for Mother's Day, Father's Day, or any day.

more interesting and appealing. For whatever reasons, some company areas just seem better than others. I have my own preferences, both within the Marketplace and elsewhere in AOL. Let's talk about those next.

The Best Company Areas

Naturally, my "best company areas" list is going to differ from yours or anyone else's. But there are a few areas that are set up especially well. I'll explain what I mean by that as we go. So feel free to click and browse along with me, or just read along if you don't want to spend the online time.

Windham Hill

An old favorite of mine is the Windham Hill label. It's grown quite a bit since the days when William Ackerman was running it out of his basement! At any rate, you can check out their area by using the keyword **Windham**. This brings up the window shown in Figure 9.5.

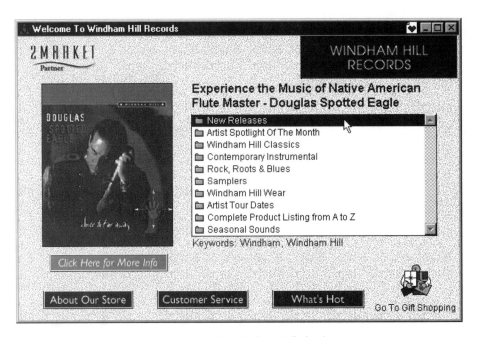

FIGURE 9.5: Find out what's new on the Hill—Windham HIll, that is.

Turn here for information on musical offerings and other products, artist profiles, and even sound samples if you have a sound-ready computer. Double-click on New Releases to bring up a window listing the most recent albums that have come out on Windham Hill. Then double-click on a title to read more about it. As you can see in Figure 9.6, guitarist Steve Morse is still alive and kicking. You can even order this latest album by clicking on the Click Here To Order button. On AOL, music shopping is really just as simple as that.

Get Wired

If you want to know what's going on in the world of cyberspace, *Wired* magazine is a must. Use the keyword **Wired** to reach the screen shown in Figure 9.7.

You can read articles, see back issues of the magazine, visit the *Wired* auditorium, and even chat with other *Wired* readers. You can preview the current issue by double-clicking on Wired *X.OX* at a Glance. In my screen, the issue number is 4.04 (see Figure 9.8); yours will doubtless be different. Interestingly, the magazine gives the volume and issue numbers in the form of a software release number, indicative of *Wired*'s close alliance with the digital world. In fact, *Wired* probably makes more use of the interactive format available to online magazines than does any other publication.

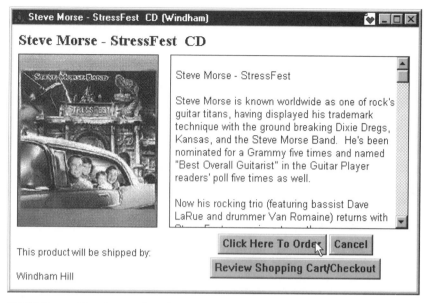

FIGURE 9.6:   Here is a preview of Steve Morse's newest release.

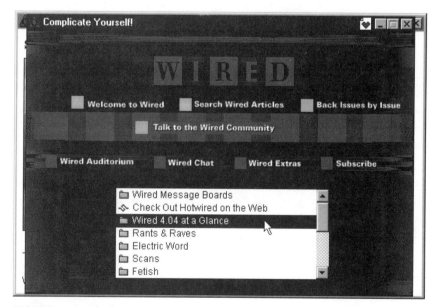

FIGURE 9.7:   *Wired* magazine is on the cutting edge of just about everything.

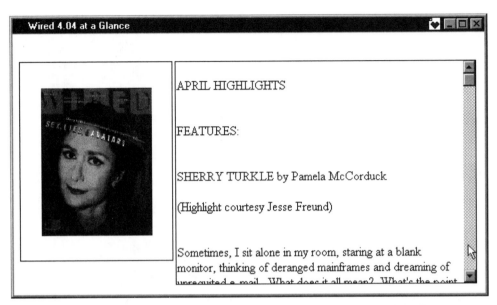

FIGURE 9.8: You can preview the latest issue of *Wired* and even read feature articles online.

Eddie Bauer

If you're the outdoor type—or you just want to dress like one—the Eddie Bauer area may be exactly what you're looking for. The keywords **Eddie Bauer** will bring up the window shown in Figure 9.9.

Here you can get online customer service, see what's hot, or just browse the catalog online. Double-click on items in the scrolling box to see more. My interest in *gear* has led me to the window shown in Figure 9.10, which includes a picture and a thorough description of the product offered—an all-weather windshield cover.

If you see an item you want, you can order it online—no need to mail an order form or even make a phone call. And since Eddie Bauer guarantees everything it sells, you can always return that windshield cover if you suddenly remember you don't own a car.

The Kaufmann Fund

How can you resist the avuncular gaze of those two guys on the Kaufmann Fund screen? I'd trust them with *my* money. You can reach the window shown in Figure 9.11 by using the Keyword **Kaufmann**.

FIGURE 9.9: The Eddie Bauer area is a great place to find all sorts of outdoor gear, from beach chairs to snowboots.

FIGURE 9.10: You can find useful items like an all-weather windshield cover in the Eddie Bauer online catalog.

FIGURE 9.11:
You can get all kinds of investment advice in the Kaufmann Fund window.

Here you can learn about the Fund and how to invest in it, or just see what is new in the world of high finance. Clicking on What's New at Kaufmann? brings up the window shown in Figure 9.12.

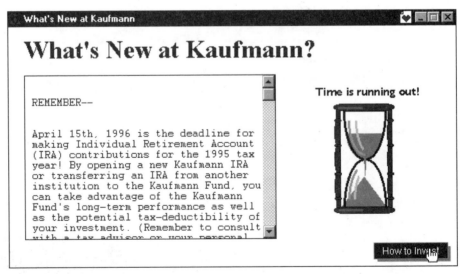

FIGURE 9.12: This window tells you what's new in the Kaufmann Fund.

Consumer Reports

No discussion of consumer services and online purchasing would be complete without at least a nod to *Consumer Reports* (*CR*) magazine. This magazine accepts no corporate sponsorship (i.e., no ads) and makes a valiant effort to remain free of corporate influence, which means there's never a conflict of interest between the magazine's bottom line and a product it is reviewing. Also, the magazine's writers are brutally honest about the products they review. If something stinks, they'll tell you it stinks.

> **TIP**
>
> It is an *excellent* idea to turn to *Consumer Reports* before buying any new product. Chances are, they've reviewed most of the brands you're considering and can tell you both what's a good deal and what's a rip-off. You'll make a lot fewer dumb purchases and probably save yourself some money. Never buy on name alone until you've read a review in *CR*.

In fact, if everyone read *Consumer Reports* and followed their cues, many of the companies that brag of their "top-selling" products wouldn't be able to do so, because no one would buy them. The reason is, many people buy on brand name alone. *Consumer Reports,* however, has tested many familiar brand names and found some of them wanting. On the other hand, *CR* frequently tests not-so-well-known brands and finds them to be excellent deals.

Let's see an example of this by looking up *CR*'s reviews of the newest television sets. To do so, bring up the Keyword dialog box and type **Consumer Reports**. When you click on the Go button, AOL will display the window shown in Figure 9.13.

Click on Electronics to bring up the list of articles shown below.

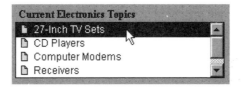

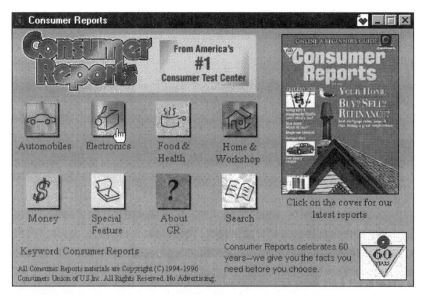

FIGURE 9.13: Turn to *Consumer Reports* for reviews of all kinds of different products.

Double-click on 27-Inch TV Sets to bring up the article shown in Figure 9.14. As you can see, *CR* is matter-of-fact when it finds flaws in a product.

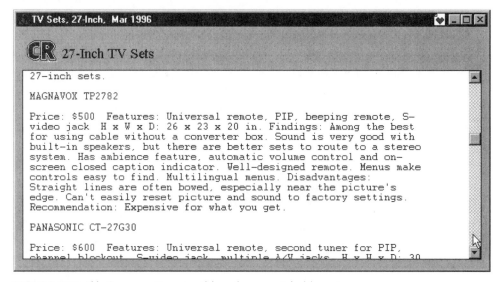

FIGURE 9.14: This *Consumer Reports* article reviews new television sets.

Note that when you look in the electronics section of *CR,* you might see stuff that's totally different from what we're looking at here. In any case, *CR* is just one magazine among hundreds on AOL. Let's take a look at how you can find many, many more.

The Newsstand

One place in AOL that's completely devoted to company-created areas is the Newsstand. As mentioned in other parts of this book, one of the truly outstanding advantages to reading publications online, as opposed to in print form, is the current-ness of the information. It's very easy for a newspaper or periodical to correct an error, update a story, or run a much lengthier analysis online, because there are none of the production and distribution limitations endemic to disseminating printed matter.

There are additional advantages to online news. For instance, a magazine can be much more interactive online than it can be in its printed form. *Wired* magazine, which we looked at earlier in this chapter, is an excellent example of this, with its chatting, polls, sound and video clips, and so on.

Let's take a quick look now at how you can mine this wealth of online information. In the Channels window, click on the Newsstand button. You will arrive at the Newsstand window, shown in Figure 9.15, where you will find dozens of dailies, weeklies, and other periodicals and newspapers.

In Chapter 2, we looked at the *Arizona Republic/Phoenix Gazette* area. This time, let's explore a different area. Scroll down to find *Flying* magazine and then double-click to bring up its window, shown in Figure 9.16.

Here you can click to read articles, post messages to other flying buffs, and even join chat rooms to talk about flying and airplanes.

Entertainment

Although we visited the Entertainment area in Chapter 8, we'll give it a second look here, since many entertainment companies maintain their own areas on AOL. The category with the most such areas is probably music, but there are also areas for books, magazines (as we saw in the previous section), films, theatre shows, sporting events, television shows, and so on.

FIGURE 9.15:
You can find hundreds of newspapers and magazines at the Newsstand.

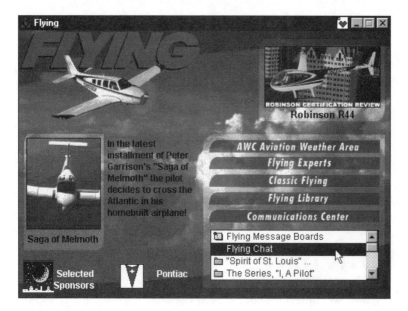

FIGURE 9.16:
Flying magazine is a favorite of pilots and nonpilots alike, with great photos and articles about current and vintage aircraft.

To find these areas, click on the Entertainment button in the Channels window.

This will bring up the Entertainment window, shown in Figure 9.17.

If you're wondering what to do on Saturday night, browse through the Entertainment area a little bit. Try clicking on Movies to bring up the Movies window, where you can go to home pages for lots of different films. Notice that most of these say *WEB*, indicating that you must journey out onto the Internet to see them. We'll do that in the next chapter. For now, just double-click on Joel Siegal's reviews and double-click again on a film. I chose *Jane Eyre*, the review of which is shown in Figure 9.18.

Your patience is your only practical limitation in browsing this and the many other corporate-sponsored areas in AOL. So go ahead, indulge yourself!

FIGURE 9.17:
The Entertainment window is home to dozens of entertainment-oriented companies.

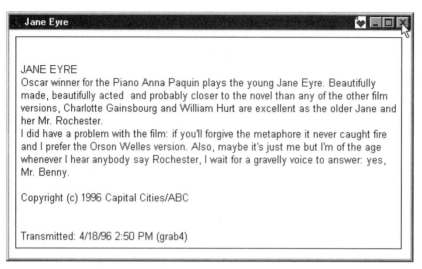

FIGURE 9.18: This is Joel Siegal's review of the movie *Jane Eyre*.

Part 4

Finding Cool Stuff on the Internet

Chapter 10

NAVIGATING THE WORLD WIDE WEB

FEATURING

- **Starting the AOL Browser**
- **The AOL home page**
- **URLs and HTTP**
- **Multimedia files**
- **Using Netscape Navigator**
- **Visiting other Web sites**
- **Downloading stuff you like**
- **Search engines**
- **Great Web sites**

Continuing the branching out we started way back in Part II, where you learned to send messages, here in Part IV we will take a final, quantum leap into the dynamic chaos of the Internet. We'll explore the Internet as a whole, its origins, its future, and what it means to you in a lot more detail in Chapter 11. In this chapter, you will learn how to navigate the Internet via the *World Wide Web*.

As its name implies, the Web is an attempt to weave some continuity and to forge some links among all the far-flung elements that compose the Internet. The

World Wide Web (or just the *Web*) is part of the Internet, but it's also an information organization imposed upon the Internet. We speak of it as if it were something tangible, even though it's really just a set of protocols that stipulate how Internet sites are to be set up to best link up with other Internet sites. (Keep in mind that the Web is not the only means of linking Internet sites, nor are all Internet sites Web sites.) And it is also lots and lots of linked documents. In short, the Web is a somewhat shape-shifting entity that defies easy description. For now, just think of it this way: imagine a dew-covered spider web; if the dew drops are individual Internet sites, then the spider web is the Web.

What distinguishes the Web from other protocols and methods of cruising the Internet is *hypertext*. Hypertext refers to pieces of information that are linked to other pieces of information. If you've ever used Help in Windows, you've encountered hypertext. You know how sometimes you see words that are either underlined or presented in a different color? You might have noticed that when you click on them, you go to related topics. Web documents work the same way, only you might go to a completely different document at a completely different site on the Web.

> **NOTE**
>
> I will refer to places on the Internet as *sites* to distinguish them from places on AOL, which I call *areas*. You can reach Internet sites and AOL areas with equal facility, as AOL integrates the Web rather seamlessly into the flow of information.

Perhaps the best way to get a sense of the Web is to use it, as we will do in this chapter. We can browse the Web just as we browsed areas of AOL, but to do so, we will need a special program called a *browser*.

A browser is simply a program that understands the language of the Web. As such, a browser can help you navigate the Web the same way Windows Explorer helps you get around and see what's stored on your hard disk. There are lots of different browsers from which to choose, and they come in all shapes and styles. There are *text-based* browsers, such as *lynx* and *www* that show you only the text of the sites you visit. There are also *graphical* browsers, such as *Mosaic,* Netscape's *Navigator,* AOL's own browser, and many others. Since Mosaic was the first graphical browser, other browsers that emulate its interface are often called *Mosaic clones*. AOL comes with just such a browser, which it simply calls the Browser.

Starting the AOL Browser

Use of the AOL Browser is more or less seamlessly integrated into your prowling around in AOL. You probably recall in earlier chapters that we sometimes saw the word *Web* next to certain items in the areas where we were browsing. Had you clicked on any of those items at the time, the Browser would have launched, and you would have been cast upon the seas of the Internet to fend for yourself. In this chapter, we actually will click on a lot of those buttons and double-click on a lot of those items to see what's caught in the Web.

Even though America Online comes with its own browser, AOL and Netscape have an agreement whereby AOL members can elect to use Netscape's Navigator instead of the AOL Browser. There are a number of advantages to using Navigator over the Browser. However, setting up Navigator can be a little tricky. I cannot assume that all AOL users will download and install Navigator; therefore, throughout this chapter and Chapter 11, I will assume that you are using the AOL Browser, since *all* AOL members have access to that program. If you do want to use Navigator, though, please see the section called "Using Netscape Navigator Instead of the AOL Browser" later in this chapter.

You can actually start the AOL Browser manually, if you wish, by clicking on the Internet Connection button in the Channels window; then, in the Internet Connection window, click on the World Wide Web button.

This launches the AOL Browser and, by default, takes you to the AOL *home page,* shown in Figure 10.1. (For a full discussion of home pages, please see the section "What's a Home Page?" later in this chapter.)

We will explore the AOL home page in a few moments, using it as a springboard to cruise the Web and see what's out there. First, though, there are a few terms you need to understand.

| TIP | There's also an Internet button in the Welcome window, as well as in many other AOL windows. |

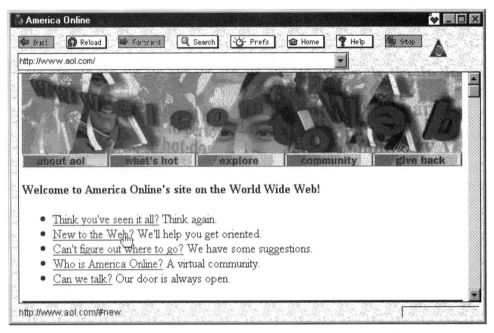

FIGURE 10.1: When you start the AOL Browser program, you will find yourself at AOL's home page.

Webspeak

To a newcomer, the world of Web browsing often seems to be a bit of an alphabet soup. There are so many acronyms tossed around, you'd think you were at a political convention. Therefore, I want to define certain terms for you, such as *URL* and *HTTP*, as well as *home page,* so that you have some idea of what all that jargon means. Although you can navigate the Web without reading the following explanations, things always seem easier when you understand the terminology.

The other thing to know is that, like most browsers, the AOL Browser works by your clicking on *hypertext* items in documents. As discussed earlier, hypertext is text that has hidden codes incorporated into it. When you click on a hypertext item, it is the same as clicking a button; the programming code associated with the hypertext item takes you to another place within the site, or can even take you to a completely different site.

There are a few other ways to get around, which we'll see in a moment.

What's a URL?

The acronym *URL* stands for *uniform resource locator*. This mouthful really refers to something quite simple. As we discussed in Chapter 1, every AOL screen name must be unique. If there were identical screen names, AOL would be unable to distinguish between them, and would thus not know where to deliver mail, newsgroup messages, and so forth. What a screen name is to an AOL member, a URL is to a Web site. It is the *address,* so to speak, of the site. Therefore it too must be unique, and it must follow certain rules that govern its appearance. The general form for a URL Web address is as follows:

http://*service.site-locator.type*

The *http* part of the address stands for *hypertext transfer protocol,* which is discussed in detail in the next section. The colon and the double foreslash tell the browser (or whatever program is reading the address) that what's coming up next is the unique part of the address.

The *service* part is actually optional. Some addresses have the site-locator part right after the double foreslash. However, when the service part is included, most often this will be *www,* which stands for World Wide Web. If you see that *www,* you know that the address you are reading is found on the World Wide Web. Other service names you might see are *ftp* and *gopher.*

The *site-locator* portion of the address identifies the site itself (as opposed to what service it's found on). For businesses and corporations, the site-locator quite often is the name of the business. For example, the site-locator for Fedex is simply *Fedex.* The site-locator for AOL is just *aol.* For Yahoo! (a search engine, covered later in this chapter), it's *yahoo.* The site-locator might have several words separated by periods (called *dots*). An example of this is the Lycos home page, which is *lycos.cs.cmu.* Lycos is another search engine, based at Carnegie-Mellon University in Pittsburgh. This illustrates nicely how you can often get some idea of where the site is geographically by looking at the site-locator (*upenn* for the University of Pennsylvania, etc.).

Finally, the *type* refers to what kind of site it is. Business addresses will most frequently end in *.com* or *.net.* University addresses usually end in *.edu,* and other organizations' addresses end in *.org.* There are no hard-and-fast rules about this, but most sites try to follow these accepted standards to avoid confusion.

One caveat: URLs are case-sensitive. To a browser, the word *Lycos* is not the same as the word *lycos.* So be sure to type addresses *exactly* as they appear. If you get it wrong, the browser will scold you, saying there is no such URL.

What Does HTTP Mean?

The acronym *HTTP* stands for *hypertext transfer protocol*. A protocol, generally speaking, is a set of rules governing how data communication and transfer take place. When you type *http,* you are actually giving a command. You are telling your browser to set up a link with the site you have specified using the rules of hypertext transfer protocol.

These rules tell the browser where to find the site, what to do when it reaches it, how to load text, how to show graphics, how to highlight hypertext items, and so forth. In fact, you may occasionally hear someone say "HTTP to that site." The person is using "HTTP" as a verb, synonymous to "go" or "jump." Since all of the browsing we'll be doing will involve HTTP'ing, you really don't have to give this command too much thought; usually the HTTP part of the address is already filled in.

What's a Home Page?

You can hardly listen to a radio ad or see a TV commercial these days that doesn't include some reference to the advertiser's "home page." Pretty much every major institution and large company (and many small businesses), as well as many individuals, has a *home page*. What is this thing?

For businesses, at least, you can think of the home page as a giant Yellow Pages ad. In the phone book, companies that do a particular type of business often run half- or full-page ads to tell you who they are. They include their name, logo, goods or services offered, and location. An Internet home page usually shows these things too, but because of hypertext, this is just the beginning. Hypertext allows a business to have buttons in the home page that lead to other pages, which may include lists of new products or services, prices, and perhaps even a history of the company. Furthermore, clicking on a product might take you to another page with a profile of that product. Clicking from *that* page, in turn, might take you to related products. You're probably starting to get the idea. For a business, a home page is really like a catalog with the various pages linked to each other electronically so that you can easily jump from one page to another with a simple mouse-click.

For individuals, the home page is something a little bit different. It can serve as a bulletin board displaying a person's interests, perhaps a photo or two, and often a list of favorite Web sites. If the person has set it up properly, you can click one of their listed Web sites and go directly there, again through the miracle of hypertext. If the person has published articles—or even if they haven't—you might find things they've written as part of the home page. There are no conceptual limitations to what sort of information you can include in your home page, although there are some practical limitations, mostly centering around the size of the home page.

For institutions, a home page will be set up yet another way. For instance, a college's home page might include its seal and motto and a photo of the campus, along with hypertext links to major aspects of the college, such as admissions, athletics, financial aid, housing, individual departments or schools, and so on. Clicking on any of these might take you to another page filled with hypertext links. Clicking on the departments link would probably show you a list of departments at the college; you could then click on a specific department, such as biology, to learn more about the program. Some schools' Web sites even offer opportunities for incoming students to get to know each other *before* they get to the school. The University of Pittsburgh Medical School, for example, has a bulletin board set up for incoming students to communicate with each other about housing, personal interests, and other subjects.

Suffice to say, you never know what you'll find on someone's home page, which is what makes home pages such interesting browsing bait. In Chapter 11, I'll even give you a few tips about creating your own home page.

A Primer on Multimedia File Formats

In the course of your browsing, you will no doubt come upon many files you wish to download to your computer. These will include not only documents but also *multimedia* files. Multimedia is a catch-all word used to describe graphics files, sound files, and video files, and there are many different formats for each kind. My hope in this section is to acquaint you with these formats and how they differ, how to view or play them on your computer, how to send them to other AOL users, and even how to create them yourself.

As for finding such multimedia files, almost any software library will have plenty of them in any format you might desire. The best approach for finding multimedia files is to decide what you want before you go searching. Then turn to the section "My Favorite Web Sites" later in this chapter for examples of where to look. If you have no idea where to begin looking, but you know that you want, say, images of tigers, then your best bet is to search software libraries, specifying the file formats you wish to find and perhaps adding the keyword **animals** to your search string. See Chapter 8 for full details on searching AOL's software libraries and Chapter 11 for details on searching for software on the Internet.

Oh Those Formats!

At first, the variety of formats may seem a bit daunting, but it needn't be. You might already know, for instance, that Microsoft Word files all have the extension **.doc**. Or that Excel files all have the extension **.xls**. Similarly, multimedia file formats have unique extensions that identify them. What this means to you on a practical level is that, if you want to download a file, you must pay attention to the format to make sure you're getting something that your PC can work with.

Following is a list of multimedia formats and what they mean:

File Name	Type of File	Distinguishing Features
.BMP	graphics	common, lesser-quality image file format
.GIF	graphics	common, large, high-quality image file format
.JPG	graphics	common, small, high-quality image file format
.TIF	graphics	common, large, high-quality image file format
.AU	sound	the Basic audio format
.WAV	sound	the Windows audio format
.AVI	video	the Microsoft video format
.MOV	video	the QuickTime video format (Macintosh)
.MPEG	video	a compression standard for video

In the above list, the terms *large* and *small* refer to the size of the graphics file. Naturally, a larger file will take longer to download than a smaller one. AOL supports all of these file formats. To understand what this means, please go on to the next section.

How to View or Play Multimedia Files

Generally speaking, you will not have to worry too much about how you are going to view or play any files you have downloaded, because AOL supports most of the common multimedia file formats (including all of those listed above). The word *supports* in this context means that AOL can display or play the files for you without any help. In fact, in most cases, you can see or hear files right in AOL, without having to download them to your own computer. Just double-click on the file. It's that simple.

There are cases, however, where you might want to use an application other than AOL to view or play a multimedia file. In such cases, you can assign what are called *helper applications* to certain formats. This is easy to set up. Choose Members ➤ Preferences to bring up the Preferences dialog box, then click on the WWW button to bring up the WWW Preferences dialog box. Click on the Helper Applications button, shown here,

Helper
Applications

to bring up the Helper Applications dialog box.

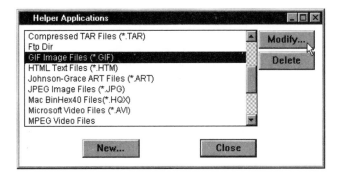

Next, choose the file format (for example, .GIF) that you wish to assign to a helper application, and then click on the Modify button. This will bring up the Modify Helper Application dialog box. Click on the Use a Separate Application radio button, and then click on the Browse button. This will open the Choose Application box, which may remind you of the standard Open dialog box. Find the application you wish to use, select it, and click on OK.

You're home free! From now on, whenever you double-click on a .GIF file, instead of AOL showing it, the application you have chosen as the helper will start up and display the .GIF file.

NOTE   One reason for using helper applications to view and play files is that you cannot edit image, sound, or video files in AOL. If you want to manipulate the files you are downloading, you're better off using a helper application.

Sending Files to Other AOL Members

There are two ways you can send files to other AOL members.

The first way is to attach the file to an e-mail message. Please see "Attaching Documents to Messages" in Chapter 5 for details on attaching files to e-mail messages.

The second way is to actually "bounce" the sound to the other AOL member in an instant message. Please see the section "Bouncing Sounds" in Chapter 7 for full details.

How to Create Multimedia Files

There are lots of programs out there that you can use to create image, sound, and video files of your very own. One common one that is included with Windows is called Paint (or, for Windows 3.x users, Paintbrush). You can use this program to create .BMP files, which you can then send to friends via e-mail by attaching the file. There are many other more sophisticated programs as well, such as CorelDraw and PhotoShop, which you can use to make high-quality images, even if you don't know how to draw. There are also applications that let you record sounds and turn them into formats that your computer can use. The best way to keep up with these is to look through one of the computer weeklies (such as *PC Week*) to see what's new.

Another way to create images is to actually take photographs to a copy shop or to a service bureau (a shop that specializes in digital images) and have them *scan* the photograph for you. To scan a photo is to take a digital picture of it that can be stored on a computer disk. This is surprisingly inexpensive and is a great way to get photos into your computer. Once you have a scan file of your photograph, you can send it just as you would any other by attaching it to an e-mail message.

> **TIP**
>
> **Don't forget, you are not limited to just sending files to others. You can use sound files as your Windows start-up sound, or use image files as your Windows background. The possibilities are endless.**

Using Netscape Navigator Instead of the AOL Browser

The Web browser called Navigator (by Netscape) is generally regarded to be one of the best and easiest to use. In March 1996, AOL licensed Navigator for use with all of its products. So even though AOL comes with a browser program of its own, you can opt to use Navigator if you so desire.

I'll take you through the download and installation step-by-step, and then we'll see what Navigator looks like when you've got it up and running. Before we do, though, I just want to give you a few tips on why you might want to use Navigator instead of the Browser:

- Netscape has good, fast servers, meaning you will get the most out of your online browsing time. Since the Netscape servers are different from the AOL servers, and since they are specifically designed to handle huge amounts of network traffic, with Netscape you will spend more time browsing sites and less time waiting for them to appear.

- Navigator is a very stable browser. It doesn't crash or hang very often.

- Navigator has an excellent user interface. It has buttons for things you will find yourself wanting to do a lot, and it has preference options for preferences you will find yourself wanting to specify. It also has a number of built-in features that make finding and returning to sites very easy.

- If you're so inclined, Navigator has a refined set of tools (called *publishing tools*) for designing your home page as well as for other applications. This is a bit more advanced, but it's nice to know.

- Although the Netscape home page has many sites, it is very easy to use, with a lot of well-designed hypertext links that make it easy to find what you're looking for. This home page also has comprehensive Web directories to help you get around the Web.

- Netscape has very good customer support.

- Since browsers are what Netscape is about, you will be using the premier browser, designed and refined by folks who know what they're doing. It's not that the AOL Browser is bad; but because AOL does not specialize in browsers, it's not their strong point.

Downloading and Installing the Software

If you've decided to take the plunge and at least play with Netscape Navigator, you will need to download and install it first. Follow along here with me. The procedure for installing Navigator is somewhat complicated, so if you're not computer savvy, you might want to have a knowledgeable friend help you.

To obtain the software, use the Keyword **Netscape** to reach the Netscape area in AOL, shown in Figure 10.2. Here you will find several files to download as well as installation instructions. Be prepared to spend quite a bit of time (40 minutes to 1½ hours) downloading the files to your computer.

FIGURE 10.2: You download the Navigator software from this window.

First, read the document called *Installing Navigator*. Do this *before* you attempt to download the software, since there are several caveats. The best way to read the instructions is to save them to your hard disk and then read them offline. When you're done reading the instructions, sign back on and return to the Netscape window.

Be especially careful to follow the instructions exactly in the section that deals with backing up winsock.dll. If you blithely download winsock.dll, you will *overwrite* your existing winsock.dll. As Netscape warns, the winsock.dll that you will be downloading can cause other communications software to malfunction. If this happens, you might have to reinstall the old winsock.dll. To ensure that you can do this, copy the old winsock.dll to a floppy disk before you download the new one.

Once you have copied your old winsock.dll to a floppy disk, double-click on the item called *Download Winsock.dll* to download the new winsock.dll file that you will need to your hard disk. You should be able to just click on OK for the location suggested for the download (your Aol30 directory). This download will only take a few moments.

Next, you're going to want to download the Navigator software. Before you do this, prepare a new folder called **Netscape** for the download. You'll want to download Navigator into its own folder, since the file is actually several different files and programs that have been compressed to make the transfer faster. These will expand to their full size and number in the directory, and it's best to keep the Netscape files separate from files of other programs.

Then double-click on the *Download Netscape!* button to bring up a download destination window. Click until you've opened the Netscape folder you just created, and then click on OK. This download will take about 40 minutes if you have a fast modem. While this might seem like an inordinately long time to wait for a program, consider this: you are spending only a small percentage of your online time to download for free a program that costs fifty bucks in computer software stores. If you like, you can click on the "Sign off when download is complete" option and leave the room.

Do check your download periodically, especially if you leave your computer to go do something else. It is not uncommon for your modem to lose its connection during a long download. This is no problem, since the Download Manager keeps track of where the download stopped. If this happens, just sign on and try again. You will have to go through only the portion of the download that still remains.

When the download is complete, you will see a file called *n16e201* in your Netscape folder. Double-click on this file, and a small window will open up, showing you the progress of the decompression program as it returns the compressed programs and files to their full and usable sizes.

Now double-click on the application called Setup. You will be taken to a setup screen that will remind you of the one you saw when you installed AOL for the first time. Follow the prompts (they are quite straightforward) to set up your copy of Navigator. When you are finished, close all open programs and restart your computer. You will see the window shown in Figure 10.3 on your desktop.

FIGURE 10.3:
You should find these files in your Netscape folder.

Incidentally, as this book was going to press, Microsoft announced that they were going toe-to-toe with Netscape Navigator by introducing the new version of *their* browser, Internet Explorer. For more information, see the section titled "Microsoft Makes Its Move."

Browsing with Navigator

Once you've got Navigator up and running, you can use it to cruise the Internet, since it integrates as smoothly with AOL as AOL's own browser does.

> **NOTE**
> You could write an entire book about Navigator. In fact, someone has. Brenda Kienan and Dan Tauber have written an excellent book called *Surfing the Internet with Netscape Navigator*, available from Sybex. If you decide to use Navigator as your browser, I strongly encourage you to peruse this book to learn the full potential of Navigator's many features and tools.

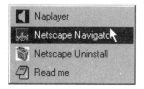

Although there's a lot to know about Navigator, for now, let's just see how to get it up and running and learn the basics of using it to browse the Web. Sign on to AOL in the usual way. When you are online, click on Start to bring up the Start menu. Move the highlight to Programs, and then, on the submenu, highlight Netscape 2.0. On this submenu, choose Netscape Navigator.

The window shown in Figure 10.4 will appear.

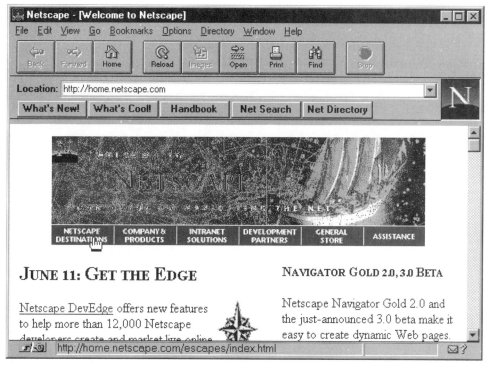

FIGURE 10.4: The Netscape Navigator window.

Notice that Navigator immediately goes to the Netscape home page, rather than the AOL home page (discussed next). From here, you can browse the Internet and the Web by clicking on hypertext items that pique your interest. You also have access to several search engines from this page, including Lycos, Yahoo!, and Excite. (We'll discuss search engines a little later in this chapter.)

Visiting Other Web Sites

As mentioned earlier, if you use the AOL Browser, you will go first to the AOL *home page,* shown back in Figure 10.1. This is your gateway to the World Wide Web. There are lots of things you can do in the AOL home page itself, but what you're probably itching to do is explore the Web, so let's get started.

There are two basic ways to leave the AOL home page and dive headlong into the Web. First, there is enlightened searching, which involves clicking on sites that sound interesting or using a search engine (discussed later) to find interesting sites. The other is specific searching, whereby you type in a specific URL that you want the AOL Browser to find. (Refer back to the section "What's a URL?" for more details on URLs.) Let's look at both, beginning with enlightened searching.

> **TIP**   When you position the cursor over a hypertext link, the URL for the link will appear at the bottom of the page.

As you scroll through and click around the AOL home page, you'll see frequent references to other sites on the Web. Clicking on any of these will take you directly to the site. Let's try one now. In the AOL home page window, scroll down and click on Auto-By-Tel. This will take you to the Auto-By-Tel site, shown in Figure 10.5.

Here you can click around and visit the various parts of the Auto-By-Tel site. For instance, try clicking on Make a Purchase/Lease Request. This will take you to the Make a Purchase/Lease Request dialog box, part of which is shown at left.

You can continue to navigate the Web in this manner, clicking on hypertext items to see where they go. In a way, it is like finding your way through the world's most complicated labyrinth.

The other way to go to places on the Web is to type in specific URLs. To do this, you simply highlight the current URL, type in the new one, and press Enter.

> **TIP**   If you put a foreslash (/) at the end of a URL, you will see an index of topics at the specified site.

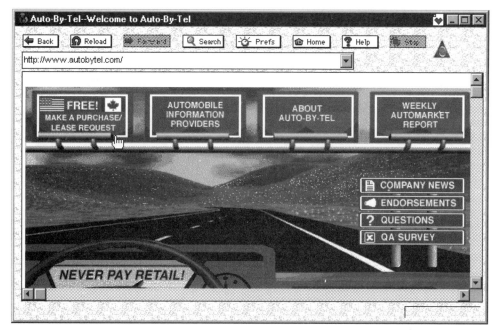

FIGURE 10.5: You can purchase or lease your next car from the Auto-By-Tel Web site.

Adding Sites to Your Favorite Places

As you browse around the Web, you will doubtless find many sites of particular interest to you. You will probably also notice that many of these sites have complicated names that are difficult to remember. Other sites might require going through dozens of windows just to get there. That's why AOL offers the Favorite Places feature, which you learned about in Chapter 2. To add a Web site to your Favorite Places list, just click on the little folder icon with the heart in it, located in the upper-right corner of the site's window (in the title bar).

From then on, whenever you want to visit that site again, just open up the Favorite Places list by clicking on the Favorite Places icon in the flashbar (again, the folder with the heart in it) and double-clicking on the name of the site. AOL will go directly to the site, bypassing any intermediate steps you might have otherwise taken.

Microsoft Makes Its Move

Stop the presses! A late development in the writing of this book is that Microsoft, never to miss out on a trend, has fired another salvo in the browser fray. Microsoft recently announced that the newest version of their browser software (called Internet Explorer) is due out in late summer 1996, and the reviews are pretty good. The criticisms of the software seem leveled more at Microsoft than at the program itself, as competitors try to weaken the software giant's latest attempt to corner the browser market. How this affects you is that AOL is planning to make Internet Explorer the default browser for AOL, replacing the proprietary browser you've been used to seeing up to now.

Also of interest is an impending struggle between Microsoft and Netscape. The latter controls the market; however, when Microsoft digs in for a pitched battle, they usually prevail. For example, WordPerfect used to have the lion's share of the PC word-processing market; now Microsoft Word is firmly entrenched as the front-runner. And one could point to their many entries into various markets that were, at the time, new for them, and Microsoft's track record is remarkably good. So Internet Explorer may eventually unseat Navigator as the browser of choice, especially in light of one important fact.

Microsoft is *giving* away Internet Explorer. That's right. It's free. Navigator has a list price of fifty bucks, and it's hard to justify spending that much dough on a program when you can get the competition *gratis*. Of course, this argument is somewhat academic for AOL users, since you can download Navigator for free. AOL seems to be hedging its bets, setting up both Internet Explorer and Navigator. Not only have they licensed Navigator from Netscape, but they recently inked deal with Microsoft will make Internet Explorer AOL's default browser in the reasonably near future. So you cannot use Internet Explorer with AOL yet, but you will be able to do so soon. The upshot is that you, the AOL user, have a choice right now between the AOL Browser and Netscape Navigator. By the end of 1996, you will have a choice between Navigator and Microsoft's Internet Explorer.

To use the specific searching method, you need to know the exact name of the URL. There are some excellent programs, called *search engines,* which are specifically designed to be used with your browser to find Web sites. We'll discuss these shortly. But first, let's take a quick detour to downloading, since that's something you might want to do straight away.

Downloading

You will often find files on the Internet that you want to download to your computer. These files fall into two broad categories: software and documents. By software, I mean programs that you can run on your computer. These can range from word processors to utilities to device drivers to dictionaries. Documents can include just about anything written down that you want to read: articles, messages, jokes, even home pages.

> **TIP** If you come across a long document—or any document, for that matter—on the Internet, you're better off downloading it to your computer to read later. That way you don't waste valuable browsing time.

Later in the chapter, we'll take a look at a few dozen great sites where you might find especially worthwhile documents. Right now, though, we'll take a look at a site that contains software libraries of truly staggering proportions.

Some Terrific Software Libraries

As discussed in Chapter 8, *shareware* is software that is distributed for free. You *are* expected to pay for shareware if you make use of it, and are on the honor system to do so, but you may try out shareware programs at no cost. There are many sites on the Internet where you can get shareware, but none is larger than the site called Shareware.com.

Claiming to have more than 180,000 pieces of shareware in their archives, Shareware.com makes it surprisingly easy to find what you are looking for. To reach it from the AOL browser, type the following, exactly as it appears, into the Location box where you can enter a specific URL:

`http://www.shareware.com`

This will take you to the Shareware.com Web page, shown in Figure 10.6. Shareware.com is, in a sense, a big brother of the AOL software libraries that you visited in Chapter 8.

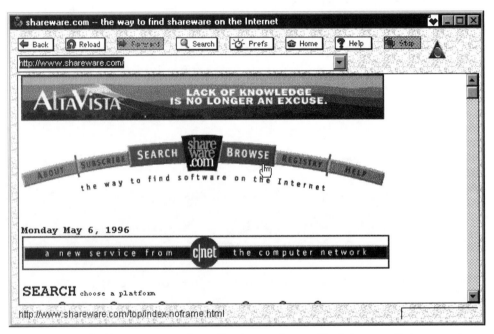

FIGURE 10.6: The Shareware.com software libraries contain a wealth of shareware that you can download to your computer.

Type in the kind of software you are looking for (such as *browsers, utilities, video clips, sound, spreadsheets,* and so on), and click on Search and to see a list of programs. Shareware.com will tell you how many files it has found.

SEARCH RESULTS

```
File Platform: MS-Windows95
Description or file matches: Browsers
Files per page: 25
```

TIP Another good shareware site is ZDNet, which you can reach from the AOL Software Center.

As you begin to comprehend how immense the World Wide Web is, you may also be growing more and more anxious about how on earth you'll ever find your way around or find things of interest. This is where search engines come in.

Search Engines

A *search engine* for the Web is very much analogous to the "Find" command found in many popular software programs. You issue the "Find" command, type in the text you want to search for, and you're off. Or, if you've ever used a database program, using a query to find information on the database is very similar to using a search engine to find stuff on the Web. Most search engines work more or less the same way. They usually have some kind of box that might remind you of the Keyword box in AOL. All you have to do is type in what you're looking for and then let the search engine do its thing. It will come up with a list of sites that include the keyword (or words) you have typed. Try to choose as specific a keyword as possible; otherwise, you'll get huge lists that you cannot possibly even browse. It's not unusual to have a vague search return three or four *thousand* sites. For example, if you just type the word *literature,* the response will be overwhelming. And if you are really vague, the search engine may come up with nothing at all.

Most search engines also offer a list of "hot" or new sites that you might want to visit. Usually the name of the site is hypertext, and you can just click on it to go there.

Let's look at some of the more popular search engines, which will give you a better idea of how they actually work.

Lycos

Lycos is a sentimental favorite of mine, because it was the first search engine I discovered. You reach it by typing the URL

```
http://lycos.cs.cmu.edu
```

which brings up the window shown in Figure 10.7.

FIGURE 10.7: The Lycos home page.

WebCrawler

WebCrawler is one of the older search engines. It's still a good choice, though, and it sometimes works faster than Lycos. You reach it by typing the URL

```
http://webcrawler.com
```

which brings up the window shown in Figure 10.8.

Yahoo!

Yahoo! is another venerable search engine, with the added benefit of a funny name. But there's nothing bush-league about its searching capabilities, and it too works very quickly. You reach it by typing the URL

```
http://www.yahoo.com
```

which brings up the window shown in Figure 10.9.

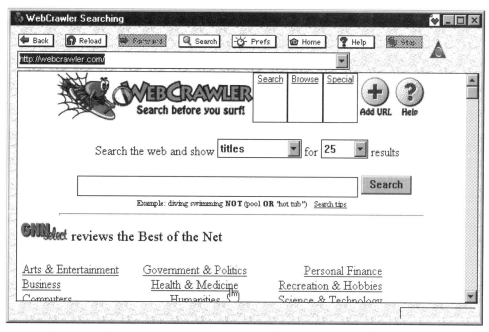

FIGURE 10.8: The WebCrawler home page

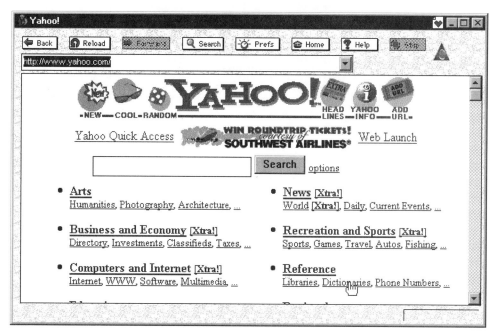

FIGURE 10.9: The Yahoo! home page

Magellan

Magellan is a recent entry in the search engine stable. You reach it by typing the URL

```
http://www.mckinley.com
```

which brings up the window shown in Figure 10.10.

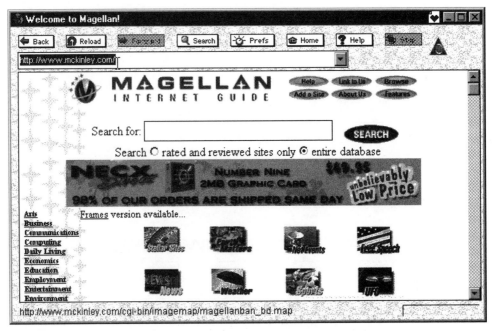

FIGURE 10.10: The Magellan home page

Excite

Excite is a new search engine that offers special features not found in other search engines. You reach it by typing the URL

```
http://www.excite.com
```

which brings up the window shown in Figure 10.11.

FIGURE 10.11: The Excite home page

Gopher

Gopher is an entirely different kind of software from the rest of this group; strictly speaking, it isn't a search engine, but it can function as one. I'll cover Gopher more fully in Chapter 11. For now, just know that if you want to reach it from AOL, use the Keyword feature and type in **Gopher**.

My Favorite Web Sites

It seems that in every Internet book, the author feels compelled to include a "my favorite Web sites" section. Yours truly is no exception. Since there is no way I can possibly anticipate all of your interests, though, I'm going to direct you primarily to general sites and let you explore on your own. My goal is to show you a number of sites that you could visit all in one AOL session, arranged by category. My hope is that they whet your appetite and that you return to these sites many more times to explore them fully. But enough of my yakking! Let's start browsing.

The Arts

Each of these sites somehow relates to the fine arts, drama, and literature. Often they will have hypertext links to other sites with similar content. Many search engines have categories such as "arts" as a separate hypertext item. You can click on these and be taken to general sites concerning the arts.

Amazon Books: http://www.amazon.com

With over a million volumes in their database, Amazon books claims to be the world's largest online bookseller. They may be right. Here I found four different editions of *The Magic Mountain* in English alone!

For Bibliophiles: http://www.clark.net

Another must-see for book lovers, this site lists thousands of rare and out-of-print books available for downloading. You could spend hours just browsing the titles! A real treat.

Images of Fine Art: http://www.rahul.net/iamfree

This URL takes you to a page where you can search for sound, art, and writing. There are beautiful images that you can download to your computer to use as Windows background. You can also download the sounds for use in Windows Startup.

MTV: http://www.mtv.com

You'll never have to miss another episode of "Beavis and Butthead."

Shakespeare: http://www.nova.edu

All of the Bard's works online? "'Tis a consummation devoutly to be wished for!" And you can find them at this site. Now you can resolve all those office arguments about what the three witches say in *MacBeth*.

Song Lyrics: http://vivarin.res.cmu.edu:80/cgi-bin/search

This is a great site. It allows you to search both by artist and by song (or album) title to see just what they're really saying in those lyrics. For instance, in the R.E.M. song "Driver 8" (on *Fables of the Reconstruction*), there is a line that reads "Power lines have floaters so the airplanes won't get snagged." Now what does that mean?

Business Sites

Each of these sites somehow relates to business. Often they will have hypertext links to other sites with similar content. Many search engines have business-type categories as separate hypertext items. Clicking on such items will take you to general sites concerning business issues.

Classified Ads: http://www.newsclassifieds.com

This site is like a huge classified section for just about any service or commodity that you might want to buy or sell. If you post classifieds here, you can be sure that they'll be seen by many thousands of people.

DejaNews: http://www.dejanews.com

This site is a news outlet, which you can use to follow current events.

Exchange Rates: http://www.olsen.ch/cgi-bin/w3ex-form

This handy site tells you up-to-the-minute exchange rates on over 100 different currencies. And you are not just limited to U.S. dollar exchanges. You can actually convert from, say, Swiss Francs to Austrian Sterling. The simple interface asks you for the amount you want to convert, then asks for the "from" currency and the "to" currency and calculates the exchange. Very slick!

Fedex: http://www.fedex.com

This site lets you track packages online, provided you know the shipment's tracking number.

Mac Prices: http://www.crl.com/~amcoex/acemo.html

Wanna know how much a used Quadra 450 goes for on the open market? Or the street price of a new PowerBook 190cs? This site has the answers, and more.

UPS: http://www.ups.com

Similar to the Fedex site, this site offers some really great services from United Parcel Service. You can even track packages you've sent, provided you have the package tracking number.

Science and Knowledge

Each of these sites somehow relates to science and knowledge. Often they will have hypertext links to other sites with similar content. Many search engines have science categories as separate hypertext items. You can click on these items and be taken to general sites.

Community Safety: http://www.cancer.com

If you are concerned about the environmental health of your community—and who isn't?—you can find out how safe your drinking water and air quality really are by visiting this site.

Encyclopedia Britannica: http://www.eb.com

This site houses the complete online version of the Encyclopedia Britannica.

Mapping with Scary Accuracy: http://www.mapquest.com

This site contains an amazing city map database that lets you pinpoint addresses exactly. I had a friend coming to visit me from back East, and even though I'd told him my address, I hadn't given him directions to my house. Yet with this program, he was able to obtain perfect directions, including what side of the street I lived on and how many houses down from the corner! Needless to say, I moved the next day…

Medicine: http://www.medaccess.com

A must for doctors and other health professionals, this site is a clearinghouse for hundreds of articles and papers on all aspects of health and medicine.

NASA: http://www.nasa.com

As you might guess, this is the NASA (National Aeronautics and Space Administration) program's Web site. If you have even the slightest interest in astronomy and space travel, this site is for you. As you would expect, it has a wonderful history of the space program in all its pageantry. It also has a nifty feature that lets you track the space shuttle during flights, as well as listen in on the radio communications!

Radar Images: www.intellicast.com

This site provides up-to-the-minute radar images from all over the world. So if you want to track the progress of a storm, you can follow it in real time.

The University of Pennsylvania: http://www.upenn.edu

This URL takes you to the University of Pennsylvania's home page, which is an excellent example of an educational institution's Web page. Most major colleges and universities have similar home pages, which you can find using one of the search engines. The UPenn home page has lots of great hypertext links to other pages. And, of course, there's tons of information on the university itself. Interestingly, one of the hypertext links is to Lycos. So you could use Lycos to find UPenn, and then use UPenn to return to Lycos. This is a good example of how interrelated the sites are on the Web.

Sports and Leisure

Each of these sites somehow relates to sports or leisure activities. Often they will have hypertext links to other sites with similar content. Many search engines have categories such as "sports" as a separate hypertext item. You can click on such items and be taken to general sports-related sites.

Chess: http://www.tcc.net

If you are a chess buff, this is a wonderful site for chess news and events. In March 1996, they "broadcast" live the match between Garry Kasparov, the world chess champion, and the chess-playing computer Deep Blue. Kasparov won, by the way.

More Chess: http://www.ibm.park.org

IBM, the creators of the chess-playing computer Deep Blue, designed this site for enthusiasts who are interested in keeping up with developments on the cyber-chess front.

Dodgers Home Page: http://www.dodgers.com

This URL takes you to a full-color Los Angeles Dodgers home page. It has all sorts of great images, along with schedules, player profiles, accounts of games, and box scores; it even gives you a place to shop for Dodgers merchandise. As you might imagine, all other major sports teams have similar home pages.

Instant Baseball Updates: http://www.InstantSports.com/baseball/sn96/gamedetails

This interesting site gets updated every minute or so, meaning you can actually follow along, pitch by pitch, to see what's happening in any Major League Baseball game.

The clear, easy-to-follow format tells you who's batting, how many outs, the count, who's pitching, and who's on base (if anyone). A real treat for the baseball junkie.

Sports News: http://www.sportsline.com

This is a great site for catching up on the latest sports scores.

Web Information

Each of these sites somehow relates to using the Web, including navigational aids. Often they will have hypertext links to other sites with similar content. Many search engines have a category such as "Web navigation" as a separate hypertext item. You can click on such items and be taken to general sites.

Alta Vista: http://altavista.digital.com

Realizing that search engines have their limitations, Digital Corporation has come up with Alta Vista. The words *alta vista* mean "the high view" in Spanish, and that is precisely what this site is for: to give you an overview of the World Wide Web. Alta Vista is a *Web-mapping utility*, which means you can use it to keep track of what's out there on the Web.

Charles Hymes' "Don't Spread that Hoax!" page: http://www.crew.umich.edu/~chymes/newusers/Think.html

This site lets you in on the latest computer-related hoaxes and how to avoid them.

Electronic Frontier Foundation: http://www.eff.org

The EFF is the unofficial guardian of the Web. You might have heard about the recent laws passed by Congress that effectively censor what you can see on the Web. The EFF fought hard to defeat the legislation, and will no doubt continue to do so. The organization also tries to keep on top of Internet issues that all onliners should know about.

NetCarta: http://www.netcarta.com

Like Alta Vista, NetCarta is a Web-mapping utility, which helps you keep track of what's out there on the Web.

U.S. Dept. of Energy Computer Incident Advisory Capability: http://ciac.llnl.gov/ciac/CIACHome.html

This site is a good place to turn for the latest on computer viruses.

Odds and Ends

These sites fall into no particular category, and as such tend to be more difficult to find than most. They include some very funny and interesting information, though, and are well worth a look.

The Fish Tank: http://www2.netscape.com/fishcam/fishcam.html

This amusing and peculiar site refreshes (redraws the screen) every few seconds, as it shows the goings-on in an ordinary fish tank. A great stress reliever!

Handey's Deep Thoughts: http://cruciform.cid.com

If you like Al Franken's books that lean toward the bizarre side of homespun philosophy, you'll love this site; it contains many of Jack Handey's famous "Deep Thoughts," which originated on the TV show "Saturday Night Live." Included are such gems as "The face of a child can say a lot. Especially the mouth part."

Harry Shearer's Spinal Tap Address: http://www.pobox.com/harry/tap.html

This hilarious site is the brainchild of Harry Shearer, co-writer of and musician in the cult classic *This Is Spinal Tap*. Harry lampoons the band members at every turn, drawing threads from the film and weaving entertaining and outrageous stories about their exploits. This site goes to 11.

Mirsky's Worst of the Net: http://www.mirsky.com

A lot of places claim to have "hot" Web sites or "best of the Web" sites, but who else claims to have the *worst* of the Internet? Only Mirsky! (Mirsky is a person, by the way.) Visit this site daily to see what Mirsky has come up with this time. Always entertaining, the "Worst of the Net" entries are examples of what the Internet can be in the hands of morons.

Why the Internet Is Better than Television

I hate television. There, I've said it. Not to be iconoclastic, but TV really is a brain drain. The Internet may not be perfect, but it serves a similar purpose to that of TV, and it's a heckuva lot better at it. First and foremost, the Internet is *interactive*. You can't just sit back and watch. You have to *go* places to see things and to meet people. Furthermore, when you do meet people and chat with them, exchange e-mail, or respond to newsgroup postings, you are interacting with real people, not imaginary characters. And you are called upon to express your opinions in writing.

I once had a teacher in college who insisted that you do not have a thought until you have written it down. There's something to this; an unformed thought is a pretty thing, but it is essentially useless. You may recall times when you had a great idea but couldn't explain it to someone, either verbally or in writing. If you cannot express your thoughts, they die within you. If you explicitly state a thought, however, all of a sudden, it becomes a dynamic entity that others can stretch, bend, and otherwise reshape to codify it. It's no coincidence that two individuals developed calculus simultaneously, or that it took a team of scientists to discover the aesthetic perfection of the double helix.

We must share our thoughts in order for them to attain viability. The Internet allows for this more than any other medium that has ever existed. Oddly, though the quality of writing on the Internet is quite mediocre, the overall quality of the written word has improved in the last few years. Some credit for this must be given to the Internet and its essentially text-only interface. You cannot communicate with other people on the Internet without writing, so many people are forced to develop at least an uneasy acquaintance with the written word and its strictures.

Television offers none of these challenges. It is an enervating medium that discourages analytical thinking, offering only discordant imagery as a substitute. The limitation is one of time and continuity. Shows must be short to hold a viewer's attention, and the demands of advertising dictate that they be interrupted constantly for commercials. Under such restrictions, in-depth treatment of any subject is impossible.

Monty Python Songs:
gopher://ocf.berkeley.edu:70/00/Library/MontyPython/rock

You can't sing along to "Knights of the Round Table" or "Every Sperm Is Sacred" if you don't know the words! This site lists many of the more popular songs of Monty Python.

More Spinal Tap: http://www.voyagerco.com/spinaltap

For those of you who simply can't get enough Spinal Tap, this site contains additional Tapobilia.

No Nukes: http://www.iijnet.or.jp/nuke

Catch up on the latest nuclear testing, regardless of who's doing it. This is a good site for all human beings who are alive and wish to remain that way.

100 Hot Sites: http://www.100hot.com/

If you are not satisfied with the sites I've directed you to here, try visiting this place. It lists the 100 "hottest" sites on the Web, with the criterion for hot being the number of people who visit the site. This list is a great way to find out what people are doing on the Web and why.

NOTE

When a user visits a site, it is called a *hit*. You will probably hear people talking about the number of hits on their home page. This simply means the number of people who have visited the site.

Chapter 11

EXPLORING THE INTERNET

FEATURING

- **What is the Internet?**
- **Mailing lists**
- **Usenet newsgroups**
- **FTP sites**
- **Gopher**
- **Netfind**
- **Building your own home page**

In Chapter 10, you delved into the Internet via the World Wide Web, an organization imposed upon some of the Internet's data via protocols and documents linked by hypertext. But the Web is hardly the entire Internet; it is one of the largest and most conspicuous parts of the Internet, but there are many other pieces that contribute to the Internet picture.

In this chapter, we'll explore many of those other pieces that compose the Internet. These include mailing lists and their more sophisticated successors, Usenet newsgroups, as well as FTP and Gopher. I'll even give you a few hints on creating your own home page. But before we get started, a brief history of the Internet is in order.

What Is the Internet?

Like computers and many of the other neat inventions we now take for granted, the Internet was originally a military project. The problem military communications experts faced was one of disruption of the lines of communication. A military campaign is only as effective as the communication between the commanders and their armies. The solution to this knotty problem was to design a system that *does not rely on specific lines of communication*. Instead, the message could be sent from a command post with certain specifications about where it was supposed to end up (i.e., the address); since such messages (or *message packets,* as they were originally called) don't rely on specific routes, they can easily reroute when they come across a communications relay that is "down."

You probably didn't realize it, but many of the messages you've sent in the course of reading this book took circuitous routes to reach their final destinations. In fact, if you look at the headers for different messages going to the same address, you'll often find that the messages have taken different routes. If this is still a somewhat nebulous concept to you, think about how you get to work in the morning. If you come across a traffic jam or a detour, you don't go home and take the day off; you find another way to get to work. This is what the messages you've been sending do when they come across an Internet "roadblock."

As the Internet community has expanded, interest in the business applications of the Internet has grown as well. After all, it's a great way to get up-to-the-minute information to potential customers, an advantage not lost to those in the business world. This is why you see so many ads all over the place: in AOL, in Lycos, in Yahoo!, and in home pages for businesses themselves. No matter where you look on the Internet, you see advertising.

NOTE   Much of the information in this chapter was adapted from Christian Crumlish's excellent book *The ABCs of the Internet,* available from Sybex. If you'd like to read about the Internet in much more detail, Crumlish's book is a cogent, enjoyable, and above all, accessible introduction to the world of the Internet. While many of the ideas in this chapter are his, any errors you come across are my own.

But there's much more to explore on the Internet than mere advertisements, including Usenet newsgroups and mailing lists, which we'll explore in a moment. The more I get into the Internet, the more amazed I am, not so much by the wealth of information that's out there (although that *is* mind-boggling), but rather by the variety of *applications* that folks have thought up for the Internet. I mean, who would have ever thought that a real-time page that just shows a fish tank would be of interest to anyone? And yet the fish-tank site (mentioned in Chapter 10) is very popular.

> **NOTE** AOL supports most kinds of multimedia you'll find on the Internet, including images, movies, sound, and a variety of other multimedia. In most cases you can play files right in AOL by simply double-clicking.

In thinking about the Internet, I can't help recalling Marc Antony's famous speech near the end of Shakespeare's *Julius Caesar,* the one he begins with "Friends, Romans, countrymen, lend me your ears." Later in the speech, he speaks of a "tide in the affairs of men." To me, the Internet and its potential represent a tide in the affairs of humanity. Certainly anyone in business who ignores the possibilities of the Internet is destined to be left in the wake of those who are more prescient. For the full text of the passage to which I allude, please see the following section, "Marc Antony's Famous Speech." For a more in-depth discussion of the same themes, please see James Burke's book, *Axemaker's Gift.*

But enough lofty analysis. Let's turn to mailing lists and their practical applications.

Mailing Lists

Mailing lists were the original Internet bulletin boards. Although mailing lists have been largely replaced by Usenet newsgroups (discussed later) and other kinds of bulletin boards (such as those found in AOL), they are still worth knowing about, since mailing lists are the most democratic way to communicate ideas. Why? Because anyone who has an e-mail address can subscribe to a mailing list. While you need a Usenet newsreader to read Usenet messages, and you need to be an AOL member to use the AOL bulletin boards, mailing lists require only an e-mail address. Consequently, you might receive messages through a mailing list that you would not see otherwise;

Marc Antony's Famous Speech

Near the end of *Julius Caesar,* there is speech by Marc Antony that resonates with me in terms of the importance of the Internet, both to business and to personal communications. The passage of which I'm thinking goes like this:

"There is a tide in the affairs of men / Which taken at the flood, leads on to fortune. / Omitted, and all the voyages of their lives / Are bound in shallows and in miseries. / It is upon such a full sea that we are now afloat, / And we must take the current as it serves / Or lose our ventures."

The above passage articulates what many people believe but perhaps have never expressed: that there are events and inventions that change the very face of society, both in terms of its organization and structure and in the way individuals relate to one another. Such periods of change are called *paradigm shifts.*

The Internet seems to herald a paradigm shift, and yet I can't help but laugh when I read things like the Harper's Index claim that the entire world will have Internet access by the year 2004. When I read something like that, the image that springs to my mind is that of a starving Bangladeshi child sending the following message to the West from his ThinkPad: "I'm hungry…"

In other words, this stuff is interesting, but try to keep things in perspective.

---

conversely, messages you send to mailing lists might be seen even by people who have limited (e-mail only) technology.

To understand these claims, let's look at how mailing lists work. A mailing list is essentially an automatic program that takes any messages sent to it and reroutes them to all e-mail addressees that have subscribed to the list. So, for example, if you were a scuba-diving enthusiast, you might subscribe to a scuba-diving mailing list to keep up with the latest news about good places to dive, advances made in equipment, and so forth. Because mailing lists are interactive, you can also offer advice to others, drawing from your own experience.

In most mailing lists, there are dialogs (called *threads*) between individuals that all members of the mailing list can actually see. Therefore, you can either watch threads to gain new information, join in the discussion, or start your own threads. Threads can be amusing or tedious, informative or controversial, depending upon the tone. Some mailing lists encourage inflammatory discussion, while others are more information-oriented.

> **TIP** When you subscribe to a new mailing list, it is an excellent idea (and is usually expected) to *lurk* for awhile. Lurking means reading mailing list messages without responding to them. The advantage to this approach is that you get a good sense of what people are talking about before putting in your two cents' worth.

There are two types of mailing lists: moderated and unmoderated. In *moderated lists,* each message that arrives at the mailing list hub (the program that routes messages to mailing list subscribers) is read by a live human being, who decides whether or not to send it on to all subscribers. The advantage of this is that fewer "off-topic" messages get through (these range from the merely tangential to the insulting and inflammatory). The disadvantage is that your own messages might be censored. It's up to you what you can put up with.

In *unmoderated lists,* all messages that arrive at the mailing list hub are routed to the subscribers, irrespective of content. The pros and cons of such a mailing list are mirror opposites to those of moderated lists. Even in unmoderated lists, though, other mailing list subscribers often conspire to keep obstreperous subscribers in line. Chances are, for whatever topic you are interested in, you'll find both kinds of lists.

Let's now take a look at how you can find interesting mailing lists.

How to Find Mailing Lists

There are lots of ways to find mailing lists on the Internet; we'll look at two of the most straightforward.

First, there are several e-mail addresses to which you can send a request for a list of mailing lists. One such address is

```
mail-server@rtfm.mit.edu
```

When you write your e-mail request to this address, you can type anything you want in the subject box, but be sure to type the following in the message area:

```
send usenet/news.answers/mail/mailing-lists/partn
```

where *n* can be any number from 1 to 8. You will receive, as an e-mail message, a list of mailing lists, which you can save to your hard disk for reference. Each part (1–8) contains a different selection of mailing lists, which should give you some idea of how many mailing lists there are.

TIP

If you attempt to send a message with a blank subject line, AOL will tell you to fill out the rest of the form. The best way to get around this in the examples we're doing in this section is to just make the subject text and the message text the same.

Another good address for getting lists of mailing lists is

`bbslist@aug3.augsburg.edu`

For this address, you don't need to type anything in particular in the message area (although you must type something), and you can type anything you like into the subject area as well. You will again receive a response in the form of e-mail, similar to the one shown in Figure 11.1.

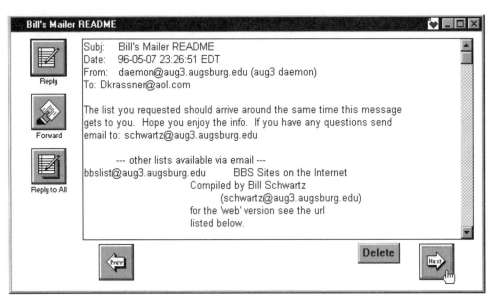

FIGURE 11.1: Here is a response to my message requesting mailing lists.

A second way to find mailing lists is to look for lists on specific subjects. To do this, send an e-mail message to this address:

```
listserv@bitnic.educom.edu
```

Type something simple into the subject area, and in the message area type the following:

```
list global/topic
```

The *topic* can be whatever you are interested in. Returning to our earlier example, if you were to type **list global/scuba diving** as the message, you would soon receive a selection of mailing lists that deal with scuba diving, as shown in Figure 11.2.

TIP Another obvious way to find mailing lists is to find addresses in magazines or have friends tell you about their favorite lists.

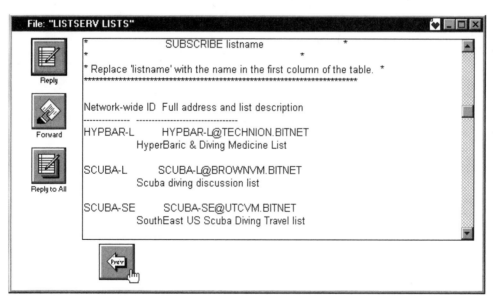

FIGURE 11.2: Here are the results of my scuba-diving mailing list search.

How to Subscribe to a Mailing List

Once you've found a few interesting mailing lists, you'll probably want to subscribe to them and see what's shakin'. How you subscribe depends upon whether the mailing list is handled by a live human being or an automated program. If the name of the mailing list is something like

`list-request@address`

where *list* is the name of the list and *address* is its address, then you are dealing with a real person. If, on the other hand, the address starts with either

`listserv@`

or

`majordomo@`

then you are dealing with an automated program.

 **WARNING** The address to which you send your subscription request is *not*, repeat, *not* the same address as that of the mailing list itself. If you send your request to the mailing list, everyone subscribed will receive your message and you'll look like an amateur. So be sure you send your request to the correct address.

To subscribe to a mailing list handled by a person, send an e-mail message to this address:

`list-request@address`

where *list* is the name of the list and *address* is its Internet address. Type whatever you like in the subject line, and type a normal message in English saying that you'd like to subscribe.

To subscribe to a mailing list handled by an automated program, send an e-mail message to this address:

`listserv@address`

where *address* is the list's Internet address. Type whatever you like in the subject line, and type the following in the message area:

subscribe *list yourname*

Again, *list* is the name of the list and *your name* is your name (not your e-mail address).

> **TIP**
>
> **Many mailing lists have files called *FAQs*. The acronym FAQ stands for *frequently asked questions,* and the file will contain answers to obvious questions that others before you have asked. It's a good idea to read the FAQs before you enter the fray, not only to learn how the list works but also to give you a sense of the tenor of the mailing list.**

Once you subscribe to a mailing list, you will start receiving messages posted by other subscribers. As discussed earlier, it's advisable to lurk a bit before responding to any messages. (Lurking is reading messages and threads without entering the conversation.)

> **TIP**
>
> **You can unsubscribe from an automated mailing list by following the same steps you used to subscribe; this time, however, send a message that reads unsubscribe *list yourname*, rather than typing *subscribe*.**

A somewhat more sophisticated form of mailing lists are Usenet newsgroups. Let's turn to those now.

Usenet Newsgroups

The first point to be made about *Usenet newsgroups* is to distinguish them from mailing lists. Whereas messages sent to mailing lists are then routed on to you as e-mail, messages posted to newsgroups usually are not. (We'll see how you read newsgroup articles in the section "Sending and Receiving Newsgroup Messages with

FlashSessions.") Also, Usenet is a specific network, while mailing lists are scattered about the Internet with little or no organization to them, apart from their protocols.

Usenet newsgroups can be thought of as the direct descendants of mailing lists. As discussed earlier, mailing lists are more democratic; but newsgroups are in many ways more useful because of their organization. While you *can* get newsgroup messages sent to your e-mail account, similar to mailing list messages, another (some would say better) way is to use a program called a *newsreader* (a sort of Usenet browser) to see what newsgroups there are and which ones interest you. The interactions between people in newsgroups are much more rapid, since you can browse messages with your newsreader and respond immediately, without having to wait for e-mail to arrive.

Using Usenet

News Groups
Internet Message
Boards

AOL has its own Usenet interface. You can find this by clicking on the Internet Connection button in the Channels window and then clicking on the News Groups icon in the Internet Connection window. This will bring up the Newsgroups window, shown in Figure 11.3.

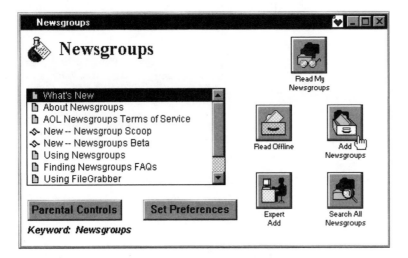

FIGURE 11.3:
The Newsgroups window is your starting point for finding newsgroups that match your interests.

Add
Newsgroups

From here you can delve through the layers of incredibly diverse choices to find newsgroups. Generally, you'll begin by clicking on the Add Newsgroups button.

This will bring up another window that lists the general topics for newsgroups. From here, you continue to get more and more specific in your searching until you reach actual newsgroup messages themselves.

Usenet Tips

Keep the following in mind when reading and responding to newsgroup messages:
- Don't be surprised if you see information that is blatantly wrong. People sometimes deliberately post erroneous information to see if they can make other people look silly by responding to it. This practice is called *trolling*.
- Another behavior intended to bait you is the practice of *flaming*. You read about this in Chapter 7 in the context of chatting, and it occurs in newsgroups as well—people will sometimes say outrageous or nasty things just to provoke a response.
- Don't be fooled into thinking that Usenet is part of AOL, or any other service for that matter. Usenet afficionados get very unhappy when they are seen simply as a small part of a large service provider.
- As always, watch what you say. Your words are the only thing a recipient sees. With no tone of voice, eye contact, or any of the other nonverbal forms of communication we take for granted, it's very easy for a newsgroup message to be misconstrued.

Sending and Receiving Newsgroup Messages with FlashSessions

Throughout this book I've encouraged you to perform as many tasks as possible offline, and newsgroup tasks are no exception. You can have AOL retrieve unread newsgroup messages and send your responses to earlier messages during Flash-Sessions, thereby allowing you to read and respond to newsgroup messages offline. Setting up your FlashSessions to include newsgroup messages is explained in detail in Chapter 6 in the section called "Setting Your Offline Newsreader." When you go through the procedure, you will notice that the list on the left-hand side of the Choose Newsgroups window will include newsgroups you added in the section "Using Usenet" earlier in this chapter.

After you've specified which newsgroups to read offline, again refer to Chapter 6; the section called "Setting Up FlashSessions" explains how to specify that you want newsgroup messages downloaded and uploaded during FlashSessions. Once you do this, you can read newsgroup messages just as you read e-mail messages: double-click to open a message, or select it and click on the Open button.

FTP

FTP (which stands for *file transfer protocol*) is another aspect of the Internet that is usually accessed with programs that now come standard with almost any Internet service provider. AOL has an FTP application of its own that gives FTP a straightforward, user-friendly interface.

FTP has been around for years. The original use of FTP was to transfer large or heavily formatted files from one computer to another. You might recall from Chapter 4 that formatting often gets lost in e-mail messages. FTP was invented to solve the problems involved in sending such files intact. Although files are now routinely attached to e-mail without incident, FTP still has its place. Poke around the Internet and you'll find an enormous number of interesting FTP sites filled with useful and entertaining files. In particular, many universities and software companies depend on FTP for reliable, trouble-free file distribution.

One of the key differences between using FTP and accessing the World Wide Web is that many FTP sites allow you to not only retrieve their files, but also to send them files of your own. This two-way traffic makes FTP ideal as an in-box where friends, relatives, and business partners can drop off and pick up all sorts of programs and documents. For this reason, AOL's Member FTPspace will be of particular interest to some—it lets you maintain your own FTP site on AOL's hard drives. Although AOL limits your FTP hard-drive space, this is a great way to get a good feel for how FTP can make your life a little easier if you spend a fair amount of time exchanging files with other people on the Internet.

Let's take a brief look at AOL's FTP interface. You can find it by clicking on the Internet Connection button in the Channels window and then clicking on the FTP icon in the Internet Connection window. This will bring up the File Transfer Protocol (FTP) dialog box, where you click on the Go To FTP icon.

Now you've arrived at the window shown in Figure 11.4. Here you can make your way through a series of screens to eventually reach information (files, applications, images, sound files, etc.). In many cases, you'll find that you need to click on an OK button to get past a page or so of text that welcomes you to a particular FTP site. Compared to Web sites, FTP sites are decidedly plain-looking—all you see are text, directories, and files.

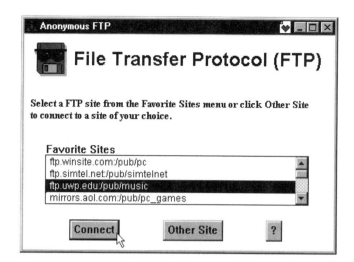

FIGURE 11.4:
When you click on the Go FTP icon in the File Transfer Protocol (FTP) dialog box, you will see this window.

Take a few minutes to check out some of AOL's recommended FTP sites. If you're interested in learning more, the time you spend reading About FTP, Using FTP, Searching FTP, and Member FTPspace (all found in AOL's FTP window) will be well rewarded.

Gopher

Gopher is yet another "elderly" program that you can use to browse the Internet. Gopher is not exactly a search engine (the search engine that you use to find Gopher sites is called *Veronica*); rather it is a way of organizing information. However, as is the case with the search engines you've seen, you can browse Gopher by typing in keywords to find specific information. Gopher is somewhat outmoded now that the Web has gained ascendancy, but there are still a few advantages to it.

The primary advantage of Gopher is that it is a *nongraphical interface*. Gopher is text-driven (menu-driven, actually), which means it's fast. Images take up a lot more disk space than text, so your modem can download Gopher "pages" much more quickly than Web pages.

Another advantage is that the hierarchy of files in a Gopher site is often much more logical than in Web pages. As a result, it's often easier to find stuff at Gopher sites, because you're just making choices from menu lists to get from one topic to the next or to refine your search. Let's see how this works.

Using Gopher

AOL has its own Gopher interface, shown in Figure 11.5. You can find this by clicking on the Internet Connection button in the Channels window and then clicking on the Gopher & WAIS icon in the Internet Connection window.

FIGURE 11.5: The world of Gopher is similar to that of the Web, only totally text-driven.

From the Gopher window, you can click on one of the icons to either search, learn more about Gopher, get help, or visit Gopher Treasures. The Treasures are sites considered to be particularly interesting. For example, there is a terrific University of Minnesota site that contains lists of all known Gopher sites. (Gopher was invented at the University of Minnesota.) If you know a Gopher URL, all you have to do is click on the Quick Go button and enter the address. That's one way to access a neat Gopher site called Netfind, described below.

Finding People with Netfind

Ever wonder if someone you know might be on the Internet? Well, now you've got a way to find out. There is a Gopher site called Netfind at the following URL:

```
gopher://ds.internic.net:4320/1netfind
```

If you type this into your browser, you will see a site with an option called "Search Netfind for E-mail addresses."

- 🔭 Search Netfind for E-mail addresses
- 📄 How to Use the Gopher to Netfind Gateway

Click on this item to bring up a small search box. Then type in the name of the person you are looking for. Just for fun, I typed in **Bill Gates**. Figure 11.6 shows the results of my search.

NOTE Another way to find someone on the Internet is to enter their name into a World Wide Web search engine such as Alta Vista (http://altavista.digital.com). If the person you're searching for is associated with a Web site, their name may be in the database. Of course, if they're not on the Web, your search will probably come up empty. If you have time and interest, search for your last name and see what you find.

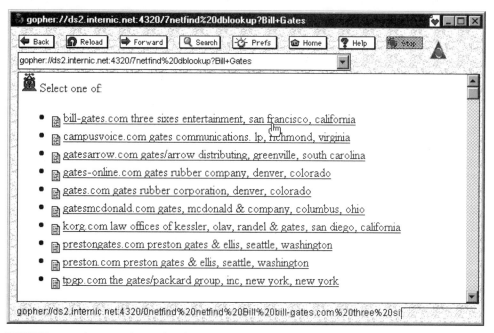

FIGURE 11.6: These are the results of my Netfind search for Bill Gates.

Building Your Own Home Page

As we discussed in Chapter 10, a *home page* is your own site on the Web, where you can place information about yourself, paste in photographs that you've scanned, and add hypertext links to your favorite Web sites. There are lots of good programs out there for creating your own Web page—including a nice tutorial in AOL called Personal Publisher (keyword: **Personal Publisher**)—but what about some sound advice? Well, I was browsing around the other day and found a site that offers just that, both on the technical aspects of home page design and on content issues. The URL is

`http://www.cc.ubc.ca/ccandc/sep95/design.html`

and I'd encourage you to visit it when you muster up the courage to start creating your own home page. Although the nuts and bolts of designing your own Web page are beyond the scope of this chapter, I'd like to leave you with a few terms you should understand if you've decided to make your own home page.

> **NOTE** It's a good idea to keep your home page fairly small, especially the opening screen. The reason being, folks often won't be patient to wait for your opening screen to load into memory and might just skip your page. One way to keep the size of the opening screen down is to avoid using really complicated or fancy graphics.

HTML

The acronym *HTML* stands for *hypertext markup language*. HTML is a way of writing code so that the browsers, search engines, etc. that people use to find stuff on the Web work properly. Lets look at an example. Figure 11.7 shows a home page created by a couple of guys who, for a nominal fee, will create an attractive home page for *your* business.

But what's behind all those icons and hypertext links? As you might imagine, it's a language. You can probably already see where I'm heading. The language is HTML— really nothing more than a standard code that tells your computer "If the user clicks here, go to this site," or "Show the user a box where he or she can type in some search

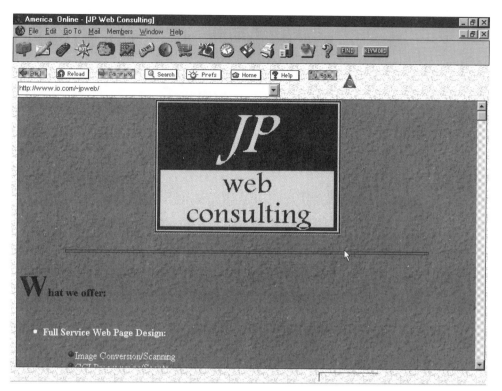

FIGURE 11.7: This home page was created by guys who design Web pages for a living.

string." Figure 11.8 shows the same home page you just saw, only with its slip showing, so to speak. All of that coding tells the home page what to do.

That's all there is to understand about HTML. Many of the Web page design programs automate icons and other hypertext links, so you probably won't ever have to write this stuff from scratch.

> **TIP**
>
> One way to get hypertext links just the way you want them is to find a home page that has links you like. Study how they have been done, and follow their example when you create your own home page.

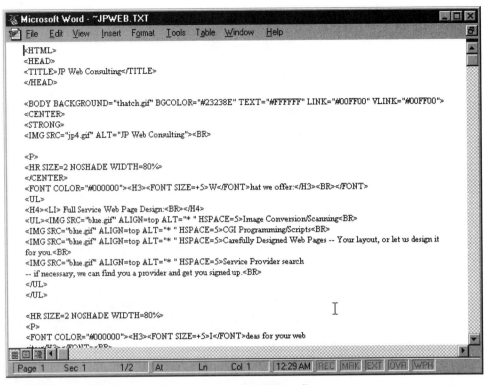

FIGURE 11.8: Here is the guts of the home page–the HTML coding.

> **TIP**
>
> If you find the 2MB limit on the size of your home page to be constraining, you can use the space designated for your other screen names—up to 10MB for the five screens names—as well.

Java Applets

Since Java is such a popular buzzword lately, you should probably at least know what it is. Java is a programming language that allows designers of Web pages to add little applications, or *applets,* to their pages. These applets then allow people who visit the site to actually interact with the site and make it more useful; for example, you can design your own buttons and hypertext links to make getting around the site easier. But because Java is a programming language, unless you're pretty knowledgeable about programming, you will spend most of your time as a user of Java rather than a designer.

Closing Thoughts

Well, it's been my pleasure to be your tour guide for AOL and the Internet. I hope you feel a bit less daunted by the buzzwords and concepts you've probably been hearing, and a whole lot more empowered about using these technologies.

The ways people use the Internet and AOL vary. There are as many different approaches as there are users! My advice to you is, don't be afraid to browse around and see what's out there. The Internet is a vast and almost infinitely rich source of information about anything under the sun. If you name a topic, chances are there is a newsgroup, a home page, or a Gopher site dedicated to it.

In this, the so-called information age, they who control the information control the world. So take control, be bold, and above all, have fun.

Happy landings!

Appendix A

911 FOR AOL

FEATURING

- **Getting help**
- **The One Stop Infoshop**
- **Other online help**
- **Reporting problems**
- **Member Services**
- **Community updates**
- **Canceling your account**

AOL has an extensive array of features designed to help you out when you get stuck and answer your questions when you're curious to know more about various aspects of the service. In this appendix, we'll look at the ways to get help in AOL, as well as take a look at the Member Services area. This is a large interactive area in AOL where you can go for help, exchange messages with other AOL members and AOL staff, search for information, or check on your bill. Let's begin by delving right in to the Help features.

Getting Help

If you've taken any time to browse through the Help feature of AOL when you are offline (reached by choosing one of the options on the Help menu), you might have felt that the information was rather lean. This is deliberate. If you look closely, you'll see that most of the topics in the *local* help (the help information stored with the software on your hard disk) deal with signing on. The rationale is that, if you are having trouble signing on, it is best to have information on sign-on problems right there on your local computer disk drive. Once you sign on, however, there is a huge Help database on AOL that you can access for free at any time.

> **TIP**
>
> If you're really having problems signing on and you are fairly computer savvy, try AOL's Technical Support BBS (bulletin board service). The number to call is (800) 827-5808. You'll need to configure your communications software as follows: 14,400 bps; 8 data bits; 1 stop bit; no parity.

Having most of the Help features online makes a lot of sense, because online help can be updated and expanded continually to reflect new features and cover new topics without your having to repeatedly download the new material to your computer. Since time you spend searching the Help features online is free, you can take your time and browse around as much as you like. Our first stop is the One Stop Infoshop (it's starting to sound like Dr. Seuss, isn't it?).

The One Stop Infoshop

The One Stop Infoshop is one of dozens of different ways to get help in the Member Services area. To reach it, go to Member Services (choose Member ➤ Member Services or click on the Member Services icon in the flashbar), and then double-click on the All About AOL folder; this reveals the One Stop Infoshop, which contains advice on e-mail, the Internet, FlashSessions, billing, connecting, downloading, and many other topics, as illustrated in Figure A.1.

> **TIP**
>
> You can also use the keyword **Questions** to get to the One Stop Infoshop.

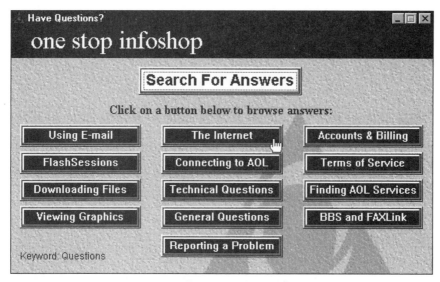

FIGURE A.1: You'll find help on a variety of topics in the One Stop Infoshop.

Furthermore, if you click on the Search For Answers button, the Member Services Search dialog box appears, as shown in Figure A.2. This is a keyword-driven feature that lets you search for help on just about any AOL service you can think of.

Just type in the subject you want AOL to search for help on, and click on the List Articles button. A selection of articles will appear, any of which you can read by simply double-clicking on it.

Once you have finished reading an article, you can close it up and double-click on other articles to read them. Remember, you can always save any information you might want to reread later to your hard disk by clicking on the Save icon in the flashbar.

FIGURE A.2: The Member Services Search dialog box is a keyword-driven feature that lets you find help and advice on just about any AOL topic.

Other Ways to Find Help

Back in the Member Services window, there are many more routes to finding help. If you double-click on any of the other folders (Accessing America Online, Download 101, GPF Help, High Speed Access/Modem Help, etc.), you will see help on those topics. For example, if you double-click on Download 101, the Download 101 dialog box appears, as shown in Figure A.3. Here you can click on any of the lessons to learn more about downloading.

| TIP | You can even get help via fax with AOL's FAXLink Service. Call (800) 827-5551 and follow the instructions to have FAXLink send your fax machine a list of available topics. Then call the toll-free number again to request the faxes you wish. This service is free of charge. |

FIGURE A.3:
You can find lots of help on downloading in the Download 101 dialog box.

Members Helping Members

At the bottom of the list of topics in the Member Services window is an item called Members Helping Members; this is a bulletin board where you can post questions to be answered by other members. You can recognize this topic as a bulletin board by the icon that appears next to its name, as shown above. Double-clicking on this topic brings up a Members Helping Members dialog box.

Click on the Search button to see a database of questions already asked and answered. Chances are, you'll find the answers to your questions here. If not, you can click on the Members Helping Members button to go to yet another Members Helping Members dialog box, shown in Figure A.4.

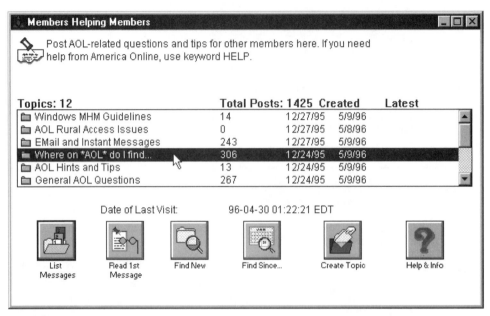

FIGURE A.4: This Members Helping Members dialog box is where you do your in-depth questioning and browsing.

Here you can browse for answers to messages you've left previously or leave new messages in the folders shown. If you have a new topic, you can even create a new folder in which to file questions and answers on that topic.

> **TIP** There is a special option on the Help menu called New Member Info. This area is specially designed to help AOL neophytes find their way around in what might at first seem a big, scary place.

Online Help Chat Rooms

Last but not least, there are online chat rooms. These are areas staffed with live AOL techies during usual business hours, where you can ask your questions in real time and get immediate answers. These chat rooms work just like those described in Chapter 7.

> **TIP** You can also get help from an actual human being by using AOL's toll-free help line. The number is (800) 827-3338. Be forewarned, however, that you may have to wait quite a while on hold.

To use online chat help, click on the Tech Support Live button in the Member Services window, which will bring up a Tech Support Live dialog box. Click on the Enter Tech Support Live button in this dialog box to bring up another Tech Support Live dialog box, shown in Figure A.5.

If you want to know more about Tech Support Live, click on one of the buttons (such as Overview of Tech Live) to read about protocol. When you are ready to chat, click on Enter Live Tech Lobby. Here a real person will help you with your problems. Pretty slick, eh?

> **NOTE** If you go to Tech Support Live during nonbusiness hours (3:45 a.m. to 8 a.m. eastern time), you can usually find hackers who are willing to try helping you out.

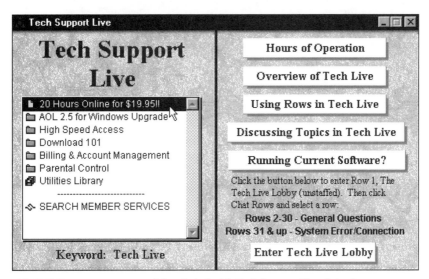

FIGURE A.5: You can get real-time help in this Tech Support Live dialog box.

Reporting Problems

AOL tries to keep on top of any problems with the service, but with over two million members worldwide and with as many different services as they offer, it's just about impossible. However, they always like to know if something goes wrong, such as if you having trouble signing on. And they will pay very strict attention to reports of online threats or harassment.

TIP	Most of the error messages you will receive can be found in AOL's offline help. Try browsing there before reporting a problem, since you might be able to solve it on your own.

In general, the service you can expect from AOL depends upon the importance of the problem you have to report. If you have a problem and would like to report it, you can do so in one of four ways:

- By phone
- By e-mail
- From a chat room
- From the System Response Report area (for service response problems)

We'll look at all four, but before we do, keep in mind that the more information you can provide, the better AOL will be able to assist you. Therefore, before reporting any problem, be sure you know at least the following:

- What kind (make and model) of computer you have
- What microchip your computer has (Pentium, 486, etc.)
- What kind of modem you have, and how fast it runs
- Any error messages you saw
- For obscene or threatening messages, the offending user's screen name or Internet address, along with the text of the message (if possible)

Reporting Problems by Phone

To report a problem by phone, call (800) 827-3338 and follow the prompts. That's really all there is to it.

Reporting Problems by E-mail

It's best to reserve the e-mail method for problems that violate the Terms of Service agreement, such as harassment, threats, or other impeachable behavior. To report a violation of the Terms of Service, choose Go To ➤ Keyword, click on the Keyword icon in the flashbar, use the Ctrl+K keyboard shortcut to bring up the Keyword dialog box. Type in **Terms of Service** (or just **TOS**), and the Terms of Service dialog box will appear, as shown in Figure A.6.

Click on the Write to Community Action Team button in the lower-right corner of the window. This will bring up the Write to Terms of Service Staff dialog box, shown in Figure A.7.

Click on any of the buttons, choosing the one that best describes the violation (chat, instant message, e-mail, etc.), and a message dialog box will appear. Type in your complaint, describing the problem in as much detail as possible and giving any information you think will be useful (including the offending message, if possible). When you click on Send, your message will be sent to the powers that be at AOL, who will try to ensure that the problem doesn't happen again.

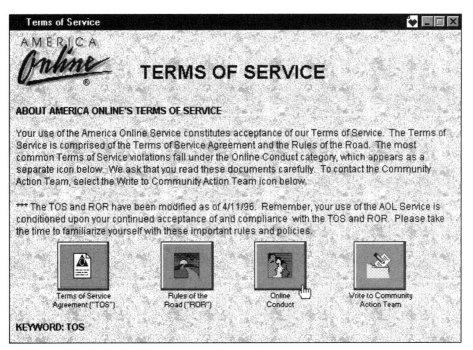

FIGURE A.6: Report violations of the Terms of Service in this dialog box.

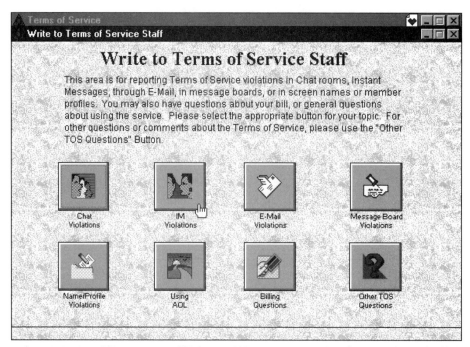

FIGURE A.7: Click on the appropriate button to send a message regarding violations of the Terms of Service.

Within a day, you should receive a response to your message apprising you of what has been done. If you don't, you might try resending your original message.

Reporting Problems in Chat Rooms

E-mail is a good way to report problems, but what if you want to report a problem right away? From a chat room, there are two different ways to report problems and get immediate help, depending on what type of problem it is. For general problems, you can access Tech Support Live. For help with chatting violations, AOL has a handy feature called *Guidepager*.

Using Guidepager

If there is a violation in a chat room, an AOL *guide* (sort of an online police officer) will sometimes jump in to restore order. If there is no guide in your chat room, you can summon one using the Guidepager feature. This works similarly to those pocket pagers that everyone seems to tote these days. When you page for a guide, one will be "sent" to your area immediately to try to resolve any problems.

To page a guide, choose Go To ➤ Keyword, click on the Keyword icon in the flash-bar, or use the Ctrl+K keyboard shortcut to bring up the Keyword dialog box. Type in **Guidepager** and click on Go; the Guidepager dialog box will appear, as shown in Figure A.8.

To report a problem, click on one of the six buttons. The buttons are more or less self-explanatory: click on Report Password Solicitation if someone has asked you for your password, click on Report Room Name Violation if someone has created a chat room with a vulgar or racist name, and so on.

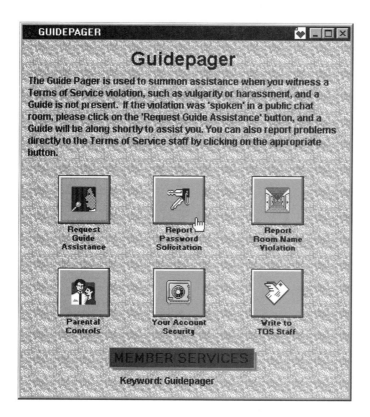

FIGURE A.8:
You can use the Guidepager dialog box to report serious Terms of Service violations in chat rooms.

TIP You can also send e-mail complaints from the Guidepager window by clicking on the Write to TOS Staff button.

Each button brings up a dialog box where you can fill in information about the violation. For example, if you click on Request Guide Assistance, another Guidepager dialog box appears, as shown in Figure A.9. Here you can type in the screen name of the individual causing problems and the room in which the violation occurred, along with a description of the violation. When you have filled in the boxes, click on Send to page a guide to come to your aid.

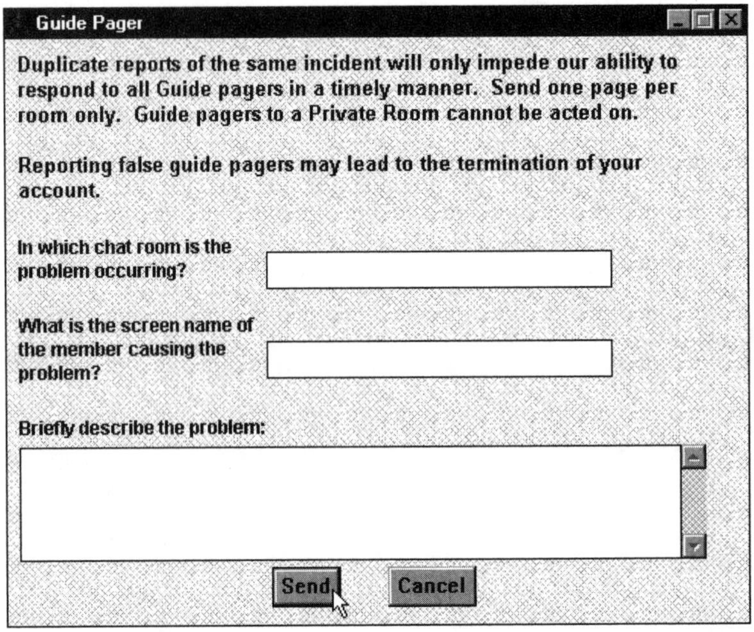

FIGURE A.9: You can summon help to a chat room from this Guidepager dialog box.

Using Tech Support Live

Just as you can get technical help from Tech Support Live, you can also go there to report chat-room problems. To do so, click on the Tech Support Live button in the Member Services window, which will bring up a Tech Support Live window. Click on the Enter Tech Support Live button in this dialog box to bring up the Tech Support Live dialog box shown back in Figure A.5. Finally, click on Enter Tech Live Lobby to report your problem to a person who can help you.

Reporting Service Response Problems

You can report service response problems automatically. A service response problem is one in which AOL didn't do what you asked it to do; that is, these are hard-ware/software problems as opposed to problems with other members who are harassing or annoying you. In the Member Services window, double-click on All About AOL to bring up the One Stop Infoshop window. Then click on the Reporting a Problem button.

This will bring up the System Response Report dialog box. As always, AOL tries to divert you to a list of frequently asked questions (FAQs) or to a list of things to check before reporting your problem. This is actually a good thing, since it means that technicians will not be spending time on problems that have already been reported and solved.

After you have examined all the FAQs and other things to check, if your problem persists, click on the Report a Problem button at the bottom of the dialog box; the System Response Problem Report window will appear, as shown in Figure A.10.

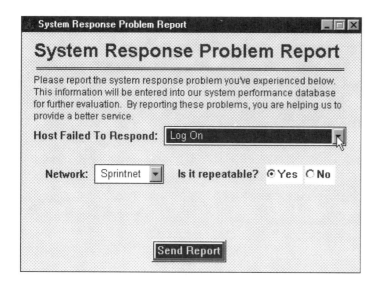

FIGURE A.10:
You report problems with your service in the System Response Problem Report window.

In this dialog box, you can choose from a drop-down list the area in which the host (the AOL computer) failed to respond to your command. Click on the down arrow on the right-hand side of the Host Failed To Respond box to see more options, and choose the option that best fits your problem area (logging on, e-mail, etc.).

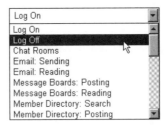

Be sure to indicate which network it was you had problems with (this will usually be selected for you automatically). Also indicate whether you were able to repeat the error. Then click on the Send Report button to dispatch your report on its way.

Member Services

The first thing to know about the Member Services area of AOL is that it's free. Yes, *free,* as in you don't get docked online time while you're here. This area of AOL is a bit of a catch-all for a variety of services. Most of them have to do with your account status and billing, online help, technical problems, and so forth. As mentioned earlier in this chapter, this is also the place where you can access the Members Helping Members bulletin boards.

To access any and all of these features, you must be online. If you aren't online, go online now by running a FlashSession and clicking on the "Stay online when finished" checkbox. When you are ready to explore, choose Members ➤ Member Services, use the Keywords **Member Services**, or click on the Member Services icon in the flash-bar, as shown below.

You will see a dialog box that asks you if you wish to enter a free area.

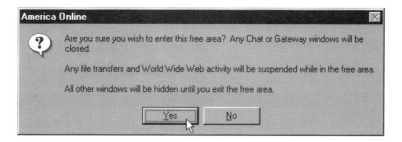

The reason this box appears is that all activities (downloads, Internet browsing, etc.) are suspended while you are in the free area. AOL wants to be sure that you know that all such windows will be hidden or closed. Click on Yes or press Enter to bring up the window shown in Figure A.11, which is the gateway to all member services.

Since member services are free, there isn't the usual online time pressure. Feel free to browse around for as long as you like. You can download (save) any documents you find in the Member Services areas by choosing File ➤ Save, clicking on the Save icon in the flashbar, or using the Ctrl+S keyboard shortcut. A Save dialog box will appear, where you can give the document a meaningful name and then save it to your local hard disk. This way, you have it for reference anytime you need it, even when you are offline.

FIGURE A.11:
You can access all of AOL's member services from this window.

Community Updates

Periodically, the president of AOL, Steve Case, sends out newsletters to bring you and other AOL members up to speed on what's going on with AOL. These *community updates,* as they are called, often contain useful or interesting information about the service. To find the latest community update, go to the Member Services dialog box and double-click on the folder called Community Updates. A dialog box will appear with all the recent community updates. Double-click on one to open it up, as shown in Figure A.12.

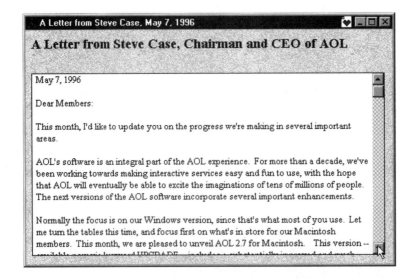

FIGURE A.12: Peruse the community update files from AOL president Steve Case to catch up on what's new in the AOL service.

As always, you can save the file to disk if you wish to read it later.

> **TIP** If you want to find out what else is new in AOL, click on the What's New icon in the flashbar.

Canceling Your Account

AOL recognizes that their service may not be for everyone. You might get to the end of your trial period and decide that you don't need or want the features AOL offers. If this is the case, you can cancel your account.

WARNING

You must cancel your account *before* the 30-day trial period is up. If you go past the 30 days, even by just one day, you will be charged the usual monthly fee ($9.95).

To cancel your account, use the Keyword feature (either press Ctrl+K or click on the Keyword icon in the flashbar) and type **Cancel** in the Keyword box.

You will then be visited by three ghosts…no, wait a minute, that was Ebenezer Scrooge. You will be visited by several dialog boxes that entreat you not to cancel. If you are firm in your resolve, you will eventually reach a dialog box where you can terminate your relationship with AOL. There's no avoiding the intermediate dialog boxes, though, including one that asks you why you have chosen to cancel. You can probably choose the item that says "My free trial period is over."

Appendix B

TIPS FOR RUNNING WINDOWS 3.X

FEATURING

- **Program Manager and File Manager**
- **Installing AOL under Windows 3.*x***
- **Task Switching under Windows 3.*x***

If you decided not to make the jump to Windows 95, never fear. All of the great AOL features covered in this book are still available to you. In fact, the functionality and look of AOL will remain virtually identical, irrespective of which version of Windows you are using. There will be a few minor differences between what you see throughout this book and what you see on your screen, although these differences are mostly cosmetic.

The only major differences you'll see will arise in Chapter 1, when you go to install the AOL software on your computer. In this appendix, we will therefore cover the installation of the software for users of Windows 3.*x*, as well as look at the cosmetic differences between Windows 3.*x* and Windows 95, at least those germane to our topic.

The first things to look at, though, are the Program Manager and the File Manager, two features in Windows 3.*x* that were replaced by the Start menu and Explorer in Windows 95.

The Program Manager and File Manager in Windows 3.*x*

In Windows 3.*x*, the tasks of running programs and managing your files are accomplished in the Program Manager and the File Manager, respectively. Since you have to start the File Manager from the Program Manager, let's look at the Program Manager first.

When you start Windows, the first thing you will probably see after the copyright screen is the Program Manager, as shown in Figure B.1. Yours will, of course, look different than mine. Unlike in Windows 95, where most programs are found on the Start

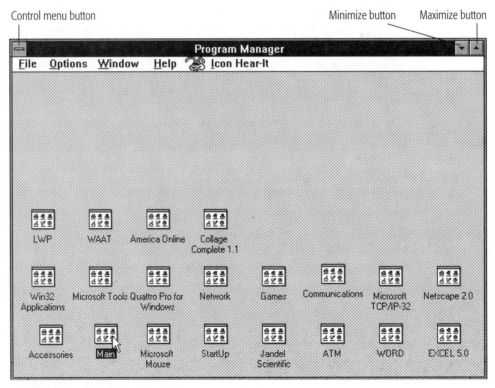

FIGURE B.1: When you start Windows, you'll probably see your Program Manager.

menu, in Windows 3.x, programs are found in *application groups*—icons that look like tiny windows within the Program Manager window.

This gives me a chance to quickly point out the difference between the title bar in a Windows 3.x program and one in a Windows 95 program. As labeled in the figure, in a Windows 3.x program, the title bar includes the control menu, minimize, and maximize buttons. You can close a window by double-clicking on the control menu button.

In the Program Manager window, you double-click on an icon to open it up into its own window. Since we want to use the File Manager, double-click on the Main group icon.

This will open up the Main window, as shown in Figure B.2. You should have most of these programs in your Main group, give or take a few applications for specialized needs.

You will certainly have a File Manager icon in your Main group, as shown at left. Double-click on this icon.

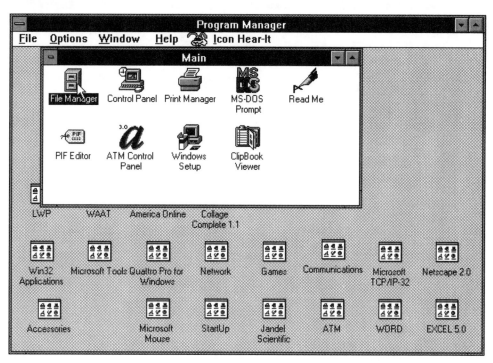

FIGURE B.2: When you double-click on the Main group icon, you open up the Main applications window.

The File Manager window will open up, as shown in Figure B.3. Here is where you manipulate (copy, delete, move, rename) files. You can also start the AOL Setup program here, which is what we'll do in the next section. For now, just browse around by clicking on the folders in the left-hand window to see lists of files within those folders in the right-hand window.

NOTE The Personal Filing Cabinet, discussed in Chapter 5, will remind you very much of the File Manager, which was replaced by Explorer in Windows 95.

Once you feel comfortable with the Program Manager and the File Manager, you're ready to install AOL. Read on…

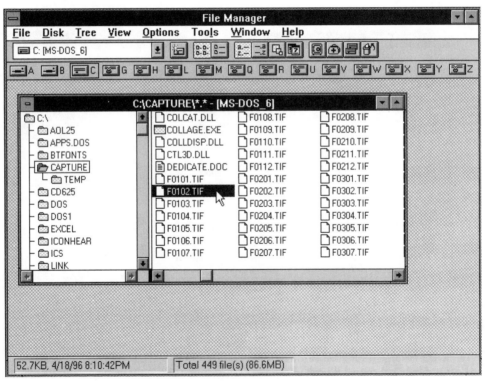

FIGURE B.3: You manipulate files and folders in the File Manager.

Installing AOL under Windows 3.x

Installing AOL under Windows 3.x is slightly different from doing so in Windows 95, because the former lacks the Start menu, a handy way to run things like setup programs. Never fear, though. It's not much more involved in Windows 3.x.

> **NOTE** Since AOL is continually updating both their software and the Setup program, what you see will almost certainly differ from what is shown here. Just follow the general steps, and don't let yourself get sidetracked by minor differences in the look of the Setup program.

In the Program Manager, open the Main applications window, as shown back in Figure B.2. Then open the File Manager, as shown in Figure B.3. (You may already be here if you've been following along.) Now, choose File ➤ Run to open the Run dialog box. Type in **a:\setup**, as shown below, and click on the OK button.

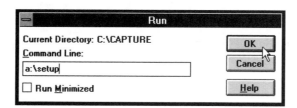

This will get the ball rolling. After a moment or two, you will see the AOL Setup screen (shown in Chapter 1). If you are running in 16 colors, AOL will advise you to use at least 256 colors. If you can do so, cancel out by clicking on Exit and increase the colors setting. If not, just click on Continue.

Next, AOL will attempt to figure out what kind of modem you have. If you do not have a modem, AOL will inform you of this, and you can either click on Try Again, click on Exit to check your modem, or click on Skip This Step to deal with it later. It is best to get your modem configured right from the start, so follow the instructions in this window to resolve the problem before moving on. If AOL finds your modem to be okay, you'll see the AOL Setup Welcome window, shown in Figure B.4.

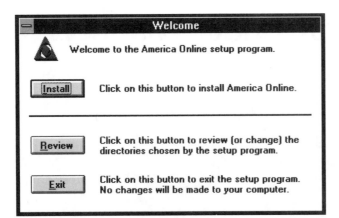

FIGURE B.4:
The AOL Setup
Welcome
window.

Click on Install to install the software. You will see a "thermometer window" which keeps you apprised of the Setup program's progress in installing AOL on your computer. If all goes well, you will then see the following congratulatory window—you're ready to use AOL!

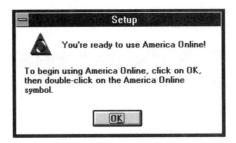

AOL will then return you to the Program Manager, where you'll see a nice new window open. Double-click on the AOL icon to start AOL, and then turn back to Chapter 1 to continue your exploration of the software.

TIP

Users of Windows 3.x can also add AOL to the StartUp folder, just like a Windows 95 user. Follow the steps outlined in Chapter 1, but do so in the Windows File Manager instead of in Windows Explorer.

Task Switching under Windows 3.x

Task switching is the somewhat grand term given to the action of going from one active program to another. The only real difference between Windows 3.x and Windows 95 is that in the latter, you see a window containing *all* active applications, and a "floating" outline surrounding the program that is to be activated, as shown below.

In Windows 3.x, you see only a *single* icon, that of the next program to be activated.

Apart from this difference, task switching is the same in Windows 3.x; you just hold down the Alt key and press Tab to cycle through all open programs.

Glossary

This glossary is included to help you quickly look up buzzwords that you might not know. Looking up words here can be faster than looking them up in the index; the latter, though, is a much more complete list of terms you'll find in this book. So if you can't find what you're looking for here, please turn to the index.

acronym A word made up of the first letters of other words. *FYI* is an acronym that stands for *for your information*. Acronyms are frequently used in e-mail and chatting as shorthand.

address A unique string of numbers and letters that identifies a person, place, or thing on the Internet.

Address Book A feature of AOL that allows you to store e-mail and Internet addresses that you use often.

AOL (America Online) An online service that lets you do e-mail, browse the World Wide Web, find interesting stuff to buy, write the President, and catch up on the ball scores, among a few hundred thousand other things. See this book for further details.

AOL guide An AOL staff member who acts as a combination traffic cop and good citizen in chat rooms. If you are having problems in a chat room, summon a guide.

AOL Live! An area of AOL where live events such as celebrity interviews take place. Often you can participate in these events in some way.

applets Small applications that people add to their Web sites to allow those who visit the sites to tailor them to their own needs.

archiving Systematic storage of files that you don't use or access frequently.

art Any nontext images that you see in AOL or in Web sites.

attached file A file (attached to an e-mail message) that contains formatting or an image or a program. Distinguished from *text,* which is just the words.

bouncing sounds Instructing another AOL member's computer to play a sound file (this only works if the other member has the sound file). You can bounce sounds from a chat room.

bps An abbreviation for *bits per second,* the speed at which your modem can send or receive information over the phone line.

browser A program that lets you navigate the Web in search of interesting sites.

buddy lists Lists you create of people you know or chat with regularly. The feature can automatically tell you if any of your buddies are online at a given time.

Center Stage A place in AOL where AOL Live! events take place.

Channels A place in AOL where you can click on any of several buttons to visit general AOL areas such as the Marketplace, the Newsstand, or Sports.

chatting Real-time interaction with other AOL members. When you type a response and press Enter, everyone else with whom you are chatting sees the message on their screens immediately.

Close All A command on the Window menu that closes all open windows.

community updates Periodic letters from AOL President Steve Case. A good way to catch up on what's going on in the AOL community.

Compose A command on the Mail menu that allows you to generate a new e-mail message.

daemon An automatic program that runs without your even knowing. AOL and Windows 95 use daemons, for example, to filter and send messages.

Delete A button found in many windows in AOL; clicking on this button gets rid of any highlighted items. Sometimes you will see a warning message before you delete something; other times you won't.

Digital Cities An area in AOL where you can learn various facts about any city that has a digital site.

downloading Copying files you find on remote computers to your own hard disk.

e-mail (electronic mail) A form of communication whereby messages are sent from one Internet address to another. Although the destination of the message is specified, the route it takes to get there can vary.

Edit A button included in some mail windows, which opens any selected messages for you to edit.

emoticons Small images you can create with just a few keystrokes in order to convey emotions in e-mail messages or chat rooms. For example, the happy face: :^)

Entertainment An area of AOL that connects you to the world of music, books, films, and art.

Excite A Web browser.

Exit A command on the File menu. You use Exit to close down the AOL program.

Favorite Places A list of places you visit frequently. Items can be easily added to or deleted from your Favorite Places area. You can visit any Favorite Place by double-clicking on it in the Favorite Places list.

fax A copy, or *facsimile,* of a document that you send over the phone line. Your recipient's fax machine prints out a copy of the document you've passed through your own fax machine. You can send faxes from AOL.

FAXLink A service that will fax you information on AOL.

flashbar The horizontal bar near the top of the AOL window that contains icons you can click on to perform certain tasks or go to specific areas in AOL.

FlashSessions The most economical way to send and receive mail. FlashSessions automate most of the business of sending and receiving messages.

formatting Any adornment of the text in your e-mail messages. This can include boldface, italic, a larger or smaller font, or even a different color text or background.

free areas Places in AOL where you don't have to pay for being online. The largest of these is the Member Services area.

FTP (file transfer protocol) A program that lets you upload or download files that would be cumbersome to send via e-mail.

Go To A menu that contains numerous areas in AOL that you can visit by using the Go To command. You can customize this menu to your liking by choosing Go To ➤ Edit Go To Menu.

Gopher A collection of sites (quite a lot of them) that are entirely text-based. You can search Gopher sites quickly using the search engine Veronica.

guest Someone who signs on to AOL from a computer other than their own, using their own screen name.

home location The location from which you usually sign on to AOL using a specified local access number.

home page A site on the Internet where a person, company, or institution can place information about themselves. This information can include both text and images.

HTML (hypertext markup language) A documentation language that tells Web browsers how to read a Web page. In other words, Web pages are written in HTML so that browsers can read them.

HTTP (hypertext transfer protocol) A set of rules for how sites are named.

hypertext Text that contains electronic links to other text. Usually, just clicking on a hypertext item will take you to the site that contains the linked item.

icons Small buttons with pictures designed to let you get to places with a single mouse-click.

Incoming FlashMail A window that shows you new e-mail that you've received.

instant messages A feature of AOL that allows members to communicate privately and instantly.

interface The configuration of the screens you see on your computer. The more intuitive the interface, the easier it is to find your way around the screens.

Internet A huge number of computers, both large and small, public and private, which are hooked together via telephone lines, over which enormous amounts of information (of every imaginable sort) are constantly flowing.

intranet An Internet site specifically designed to be used frequently by somewhat limited groups of people.

Java A programming language that allows Web page designers to include applets in their Web pages.

Keyword A command in AOL that lets you search for things by typing their names (or part of their names) into a dialog box. Basically, this feature serves as a search engine for AOL.

LAN (local area network) A small network, usually confined to a single outlet of a business or company.

lobby A place in AOL from which you enter chat rooms. Other members will probably be in the lobby, where you can chat with them before actually entering a room.

locations Files you set up for the physical locations you find yourself using AOL. A location generally includes local access numbers needed to call to connect to AOL.

Log Manager A feature of AOL that lets you keep a transcript of all that is said during a chat session.

log on To connect your computer to AOL.

Lycos A search engine.

Magellan A search engine.

mailing list An Internet site that has a (usually) automated program that sends messages delivered to it out to everyone on the mailing list.

marquee The part of a chatting box in which you can view scrolling text.

member profiles Brief personal descriptions of AOL members which you can access online. Watch out, though—these might not be completely truthful!

member rooms Chat rooms created by AOL members.

Member Services A free area of AOL where you can get help, post messages to bulletin boards, and find out more about the AOL service and its features.

modem An electronic device that lets your computer communicate with other computers over phone lines. The word *modem* is short for **mod**ulator/**dem**odulator.

Mosaic A search engine.

MS Internet Explorer A Web browser.

netiquette An unofficial code of conduct for conversing online.

Netscape Navigator A Web browser.

network A group of computers connected to each other for the purpose of exchanging files and messages.

News An area of AOL where you can get the latest news and weather.

newsgroup A Usenet site on the Internet where folks interested in specific topics can "meet" to exchange information, ideas, opinions, etc.

Open A command on the File menu that allows you to open a file.

Outgoing FlashMail A window that shows you all e-mail messages you have scheduled to be sent out.

paper mail U.S. Mail that you can compose and send directly from AOL.

Parental Controls A group of options that allow you to control which areas your different screen names can access in AOL and on the Internet. Parents often use this feature to limit what their children can do online.

password A secret word that you must type in when requested in order to sign on to AOL.

Personal File Manager A utility in AOL that helps you organize your files.

Personal Finance An area in AOL where you can get financial advice and read information about investing.

Print A command on the File menu, Print tells your computer to print out whatever message or document you've got open.

private rooms Chat rooms that are created by members but that don't appear on lists anywhere. Usually you will create a private room in order to chat with someone without others seeing your conversation.

public rooms Chat rooms created by AOL for discussions on a wide variety of topics.

right-clicking When you right-click in AOL, you bring up a set of very useful commands, such as Cut, Copy, and Paste. If you right-click in a message window, you can add formatting and even specify text strings as hypertext links.

rooms Places in AOL where you go to chat with other members. Often a room is created with a specific purpose (e.g., to discuss *Star Trek* or parenting).

Save A command on the File menu that saves the text of whatever document you are reading to your hard disk.

screen name A unique name that identifies you in AOL. You can have up to five different screen names.

search engine A program that helps you find stuff on the Internet.

Send A button in the Compose Message window that, when clicked, sends your message to the intended recipient(s).

Send Later A button in the Compose Message window that, when clicked, stores your message to the Outgoing FlashMail dialog box, from which it will be sent out the next time you run a FlashSession.

server A computer dedicated to processing the traffic of information over a network.

shortcut files "Shadow files" that you create in Windows 95. You can place a shortcut anywhere without moving or damaging the file of which it is a shadow. Then you can double-click on the shortcut to open the original file.

sign off To disconnect from AOL.

Sports An area in AOL where you can check out the latest happenings in just about any sport you can think of.

Stock Quotes An area in AOL that lets you get immediate updates on the value of any stock or commodity.

stored password A password that has been typed and stored in your computer to be used during automatic sign-on during FlashSessions. Storing your password saves you from having to type it in every time you sign on.

uploading Copying files, images, or programs from your computer to someone else's computer.

URL (uniform resource locator) A World Wide Web address that uniquely defines a site.

Usenet Another network service (similar to the Internet) that is essentially "the biggest bulletin board in the world."

Veronica A search engine for Gopher.

viruses Programs written by ne'er-do-wells to deliberately cause damage to files on your computer. It is a good idea to check your computer regularly for viruses.

WAN (wide area network) A network that connects several different sites; usually these sites are at an appreciable distance from one another.

Weather An area in AOL where you can turn to see if it's gonna rain on your parade.

Web site A place on the Internet that more or less conforms to certain rules about how it is set up and how it is browsed.

WebCrawler A search engine.

What's Hot? An area of AOL that tells you what is all the rage in AOL and elsewhere. This is how you can stay *au courant*.

What's New? An area in AOL that tells you about services that have recently been added.

Windows Microsoft's graphical user interface for PC-compatible computers.

World Wide Web An organization imposed upon some parts of the Internet that uses files linked by hypertext.

Yahoo! A search engine.

Index

Note to the Reader: Main level entries are in **bold**. **Boldfaced** page numbers indicate primary discussions of a topic. *Italicized* page numbers indicate illustrations.

Symbols

<< >> (angle brackets), 101
* (asterisks)
    in chatting, 190
    for highlighting e-mail, 90
    with passwords, 69
@ (at signs), 85
: (colons)
    in chatting, 195–196
    in URLs, 275
, (commas) in addresses
    CompuServe, 95–96
    e-mail, 88
    fax, 134
$ (dollar signs), 133
/ (foreslashes), 275, 286
- (minus signs), 13
() (parentheses), 88
. (periods)
    in CompuServe addresses, 96
    in URLs, 275
+ (plus signs), 13–14

A

A-List, 244, *245*
ABC Sports, 256
ABCs of the Internet, 306
About AOL Live! option, 187
About FTP option, 317
access lines, speed of, 35
Accessing America Online folder, 328
accommodations, travel, 232–233
Account Management & Billing option, 75, 77

Account Name/Address Information dialog box, 78
accounts
    cancelling, **341**
    checking balance of, 76
    setting up, **14–20**, *16–18*
Accounts & Billing dialog box, 75, 77, *77*
Ackerman, William, 257
acronyms
    in chatting, **191–194**
    description of, 351
    in e-mail, **90–91**
action buttons, *86*
Activate FlashSession Now dialog box, 160, *160*
Activate FlashSession Now option, 159
activating FlashSessions, **159–161**, *160*, *162*
active windows, 26–27
ad hominem arguments, 191
Add A Message window, 230, *231*
Add All newsgroup option, 158
Add Buddy option, 169
Add Favorite Place button, 50
Add Favorite Place dialog box, 50, *50*
Add Folder option, 50, 142
Add Newsgroups option, 314
Add option, 158
Add to Custom Colors option, 114
Address Book dialog box, 103–105, *103*
Address Book icon, 105
Address Book option, 118
address books, **102–103**
    adding names to, **103–104**
    copying screen names to, 176
    description of, 351
    editing, 105
    guest access to, 63
    in upgrading, 6
    using, **105–106**

N

Y

Z

About the CD

The America Online (AOL) Starter Software on this CD includes a one-month trial membership and 15 hours of online time. After the trial, you are charged based on the pricing option you choose. This fee is billed at the beginning of each month.

Pricing Options

- $9.95 per month. This rate includes five free hours per month. If you use more than five hours, you are charged $2.95 for each additional hour.
- $19.95 per month. This rate includes 20 free hours per month. If you use more than twenty hours, you are charged $2.95 for each additional hour.

Notes

- Members outside the 48 contiguous United States may pay an additional surcharge. Please check with your local AOL office for exact billing information.
- Both options include unlimited free use of the Member Services area of AOL.
- Under either option, unused time does not carry over to your next billing month.
- Both options support 2400bps (bits per second) or faster modem baud rates.

Billing

You select the billing option you want during the registration process. You may charge your VISA, MasterCard, American Express, or Discover Card, or deduct the bill from your checking account. Checking account customers are charged $3 per month to cover processing fees for this service.

Canceling

You may cancel your membership at any time by calling your AOL office. You must do so within 30 days of your initial connection to avoid being charged your first monthly fee. Your membership continues on a month-to-month basis until you cancel.

Terms of Service

Your use of the America Online disk constitutes your acceptance of the AOL Terms of Service. Those Terms of Service are available online in the free Member Services area. Please read them to get important information and conditions of your membership. America Online, Inc., reserves the right to change the Terms of Service, membership fees, and online charges at any time after giving notice to members.

Customer Service and Support
For AOL Billing, call (800) 827-6364
For AOL Technical Support, call (800) 827-3338